LIVINGSTONE THE LIBERATOR

LIVINGSTONE AND ANNA MARY

LIVINGSTONE THE LIBERATOR

A Study of a Dynamic Personality

JAMES I. MACNAIR

COLLINS
LONDON AND GLASGOW

FIRST PUBLISHED 1940
Reprinted 1942, 1945, 1946, 1949
New Library Edition 1958
Reprinted 1961, 1968

To My Wife

A TRIBUTE

THIS BOOK IS SET IN FONTANA, A TYPE FACE DESIGNED FOR
THE EXCLUSIVE USE OF THE HOUSE OF COLLINS, AND PRINTED
BY THEM IN GREAT BRITAIN

INTRODUCTION

An African from Northern Rhodesia whom I met recently, remarked how strange his people found David Livingstone to be when he first travelled there. This was not unnatural since they had never come into contact with a White Man before. They still tell each other stories of him as they first saw him. "Why," they said, "he actually had two pairs of feet! He used a black pair, not unlike our own, to walk with but when he came to the Zambezi River he took them off and used a white pair to wade through the water. We saw the black feet left sitting on a rock for one of his people to carry over after him." They must have been frankly puzzled, but later amazement gave place to admiration, for other Africans said of him, "We liked and trusted him because he did not come to the gates of our village stockades demanding admission—he always asked if he might enter and then he sat down among us and talked to us as if he was one of ourselves."

That is how my grandfather is talked about still. He is not forgotten. Nor in our own country is he forgotten judging by the number of books about him that are still appearing. Perhaps his reputation has grown with the passing of years, instead of diminishing?

Of the recent lives that have been published some appeal to the well-informed ; others are of the more popular type but none are more worthy to appear in a handy form than MacNair's *Livingstone the Liberator*. It is neither too short nor too long. It has the merit that the reader quickly gets into the swim of the story, interest in which never slackens until the tale is told. The selection of incidents is well made. It is accurate in detail and the writer does not overstress his admiration for his hero. He called it " A Study of a Dynamic Personality " and that is just what it is.

HUBERT F. WILSON

FOREWORD

THE justification for adding one more to the many "Lives" of David Livingstone is two-fold.

First. The year 1940 is the centenary of his departure for Africa. He sailed from London on the 8th December, 1840, disembarked at Simon's Bay on March 15th and reached Cape Town the same evening. Arrangements are being made in Africa and elsewhere, in spite of war conditions, to celebrate the event, and there is need of a book of moderate size and cost that contains the results of up-to-date investigation.

Second. Of recent years a considerable amount of new matter, especially of a personal kind, has come to light. Much of this, along with other material of great value, has been collected in the Scottish National Memorial at Blantyre, Lanark-shire, which was opened in 1929.

This biography begins with a somewhat detailed account of the boyhood, based mainly on floating tradition that still lingers round Blantyre. Some of the stories may be judged trivial, but the author believes that nothing that concerns the youth of so great a man is unimportant. Records left by the late Revs. John A. Lees and J. Brand Crombie have been drawn upon. Especially is the author

7

indebted to the late Rev. W. H. Macdiarmid, M.A., B.D., who, when minister of the parish, applied to Livingstone research so much energy and enthusiasm.

Thanks are tendered to members of the Livingstone family, Major A. Bruce and Dr. Hubert Wilson, for the loan of the original diaries.

Gratitude is due especially to the Governors of the Livingstone Memorial Trust for permission to use freely of their wealth of pictorial and other material, and hardly less to the Rhodes-Livingstone Memorial at Livingstone, N. Rhodesia, for permission to quote from their valuable manuscripts. Most of the stories, till now unpublished, of Catherine Ridley and of the visit to Brazil come from that source.

Thanks are also rendered to Professor Coupland, of Oxford, for permission to quote somewhat liberally from his works. These contain the most valuable contribution to Livingstone research of recent times. Also, to Professor Wallis, of Pretoria, for most kindly enabling the author to consult the manuscript of his *Life of Thomas Baines*, and to Mr. David Chamberlin, of the London Missionary Society, for a similar privilege in regard to his collection of Livingstone letters now in the press.

To personal friends much gratitude is owed: to Dr. Harold Wareham for help in the preparation of maps and in other ways; to Dr. J. T. Hornsby for his assistance in the correction of proofs, and to my wife and the Rev. J. M. Calder for advice and help in many forms.

8

Lastly and most particularly, deep gratitude must be expressed to Mr. James Paterson, Dalkeith, for careful examination of the matter of this book and for putting unreservedly at the writer's disposal his unique knowledge of all the things that concern David Livingstone.

The titles of the African parts of the book—"Missionary," "Explorer," etc.—follow the plan of the Blantyre Memorial. They are chosen for emphasis rather than for accuracy. Livingstone was Consul in the last as well as in the second journey, and he was Missionary and Explorer all through his life in Africa.

CONTENTS

11

CONTENTS

MAPS

ILLUSTRATIONS

All the following illustrations are from the groups of statuary by C. d'O. Pilkington Jackson in the Livingstone Memorial at Blantyre.

13

INTRODUCTORY CHAPTER

Africa in Livingstone's Day

SO great have been the changes in the century
that has followed Dr. Livingstone's landing
there, that some sketch, however slight, of the
Africa he first knew is necessary for a just
appreciation of his story.

Till then, as has been well said, Africa proper,
the land of the Negro, had had no history.[1] The
northern fringe—the countries of the Mediter-
ranean basin and of the Nile—have, it is true, a
civilisation second to none in antiquity, but its
contacts had been with Europe. The deserts of the
Sahara and the vast swamps of the Upper Nile
divided it effectively from the teeming multitudes
that inhabited the central parts of the Continent.
These had remained from untold centuries, completely unprogressive, asleep in barbarism.

From very early times Arabs had settled in
Mombasa and other eastern ports and had, for
purposes of trade, penetrated considerable distances
inland.   The Portuguese, from the fifteenth
century, had established themselves on both coasts,
and later the French and the British had founded
trading stations, also on the seaboard.   But
commerce, not conquest, had been the purpose of

[1] Professor R. Coupland. *Kirk on the Zambesi*, page 81.

15

all these early settlements, and there had been little exploration. Almost nothing was known of the hinterland, and the chief interest of all nations had been the trade in slaves.

Of this traffic little need now be said. Its horrible effects will become increasingly clear as this story develops. Suffice it to explain here, that it had had its origin with the Arabs in the early centuries of the Christian era. Many nations took part. Later, in Livingstone's day, it was growing with such rapidity and virulence, its evils becoming so widely spread, that it fully merited the striking name he gave it—"The Open Sore of the World." It is unfortunately no exaggeration to say that, till the beginning of the nineteenth century, the contacts of primitive Africa with European and other outside influences had been almost entirely hurtful.

Exception must be made, however, in regard to the gallant work of the Jesuit Fathers, who, in the seventeenth century, under the protection of the Portuguese flag, had pushed their way up the Zambezi on the east and the Congo on the west. Their hold, unfortunately, was not for long. Malaria overcame them, and when Livingstone passed down the Zambezi valley two hundred years later there was nothing but some ruined buildings left as evidence of their sacrificial labours.

The European thrust, however, that affected Africa most deeply and with which Livingstone had direct concern, came from the South. Here

16

the temperate climate and comparative freedom from malaria made the country suitable for white colonisation.

The Dutch founded the settlement of Cape Town in the sixteenth century. Later, Huguenot emigrants joined them and they established themselves firmly in the extreme south of the peninsula. A freedom-loving people, living simple patriarchal lives ; with a religion founded mainly on the Old Testament, they were intensely conservative in all their ways. The Africans were to them the Children of Ham, and this fact made it seem no wrong, in their eyes, that the Native should be used as a "hewer of wood and a drawer of water." Slave-owning was part of their traditional life and almost a necessity of their methods of farming. The slaves were, in general, not badly used, but they were regarded as a lower order of being and treated as such.

About the period of the French Revolution, when Britain became interested in India, she took over Cape Town as a place of call for her ships. The change was most unwelcome to the Colonists, and the Governors on their part were not infrequently tactless and unsympathetic. It was, however, not till the passing in 1833 by the British Parliament of the Slavery Emancipation Bill, that disaffection grew rife. This Act made slave-owning, in the Empire, illegal and voted £20,000,000 in compensation to owners.

The application of this Bill in South Africa aroused bitter resentment. It seemed to the

Colonists a flagrant interference with their liberty. There were 35,000 slaves in their service, and for their release £1,247,000 was granted. This amount appeared to the Boers—as the Colonists were called (the name means "farmer")—totally inadequate. When, in addition, it was discovered that through being paid in London the grant lost seriously in value, indignation became intense and a critical situation arose. There were other complicating circumstances but it is sufficient to mention these two.

The result was the remarkable movement known as the "Great Trek." Beginning from 1835, many hundreds of families, "Voortrekkers," as they are called, left their old homes and moved across the veld into the territories now known as the Orange Free State and the Transvaal. There they hoped to be allowed to live in freedom beyond British laws and interference.

It was a great adventure. The new country was occupied by virile tribes who, though armed with assagais only, were highly trained fighters, wily and ruthless. Gradually, by means of superior arms and tactics, the Boers penetrated and pushed their way irresistibly north.

We shall see Livingstone, early in his career, in the midst of this conflict. His sympathies were entirely with the African and he was never a man who feared to speak his mind.

In the country where Livingstone began his work there lived two distinct races of Africans—

Hottentot and Bantu. The former were probably the original inhabitants of Central and South Africa who had been gradually pushed south by the more vigorous and adaptable Bantu. The Hottentots were peaceable folk, good herdsmen and accomplished hunters.

It was, however, with various sections of the great Bantu race that Livingstone had lifelong connection. These are of higher type than the Hottentot, a people, when chance of development is given them, of considerable mental powers; a child race, naturally superstitious and capable at times of acts of great cruelty, but in general happy and attractive—a race with a future.

In Livingstone's day there was much unsettlement among these Bantu tribes. Long years before, a great racial storm had arisen in the tropical belt. Wave after wave of hardy warriors had poured southward, had crossed the Limpopo river, till, near the Vaal, they had met the new European civilisation and had been halted. These tribes, of whom the Zulu was the most important, were in a state of constant movement and change. Ever and anon some man of exceptional force or ruthlessness would rise, gather to himself a following and subjugate all the weaker groups he could reach. Mosilikatse and Sebituane, names that will appear in our narrative, and in more modern days, Cetewayo, were of this type.

The Bakwain, with whom in his early days Livingstone had most to do, were also Bantu, but of a less warlike strain.

19

It is important to remember that amongst all these peoples the primitive tribal system still held sway. Under it the tribe was as one family having most things in common. The spirits of the ancestors were part of the tribe and were indeed more potent than the living. They punished with fearful illnesses any breach of tribal custom. The chief represented these spirits and was sometimes regarded almost as a god, and had on that account often undisputed authority. Mixed up with their life were magic and witchcraft that kept the people in thrall. The system held much that was cruel, but none the less not a little that was fine. Its binding power was great.

Though before Livingstone's day much exploration had been carried out, Africa was still an unknown continent. Of the interior little had been learned. It abounded marvellously in animal life—" the finest collection of mammals in any district in the world. The lion and the cheetah, the spotted and the brown hyenas, the rhinoceros, the zebra, and other asses, the buffalo, the oryxes, hartebeests, gnus, pallahs and gazelles,"[1] besides the elephant, the hippopotamus and many more. It was without rival the ground for the big-game hunter.

Except near Cape Town and a few other centres there were no made roads. Travel was done on horseback or—in open country—by bullock wagon. In the interior the tsetse fly made life precarious

---

[1] Sir Harry Johnston's *Livingstone*, page 17.

for all cattle, hence there journeys were in the main done on foot.

There was, and still is, all over Africa a wonderful system of footpaths, that are shadier and more pleasant for travel than the modern roadway. These run from village to village, and it can, with some exaggeration, be said that on them a traveller may walk from end to end of the continent. They are about fifteen inches wide, beaten smooth by innumerable feet. They are never straight, for when a tree falls, or an ant-hill rises, the African prefers to walk round and let things lie. Besides what might be called the main pathways, there are near every village many others that lead to the streams and gardens. These explain Livingstone's dependence upon guides. It was easy to lose the way in a strange country.

Malaria was prevalent except in the extreme South and in the higher lands, and the toll of life amongst Europeans was terrible.

In order to realise even faintly the prodigious physical labour involved in Livingstone's journeys, it is necessary to expand our insular imagination and realise something of the vastness of the African continent. Let it be remembered that Africa is equal in extent to all Europe, India, China and the United States put together.

It may be said, in concluding this brief sketch, that Livingstone arrived at the beginning of a new era in African history. The old isolation was passing, slowly at first but with increasing rapidity. The slave-trader was pushing in from East and West. The Whites in the South were, year by year, absorbing more and more of the lands of the Native peoples. It was surely providential that just at this juncture there should have arrived in Africa a man of such dynamic personality, so equipped in mind and body, so understanding of spirit, so completely self-disregarding, so filled with a passion for justice and right.

Without question, David Livingstone's example has done much in the days since he lived, more indeed than during his lifetime, to temper to the Native peoples the effects of the clash of interests that has led to the partition of their country amongst races of a higher culture.

PART ONE

BOY AND STUDENT

A Hardy Training
1813 to 1840

Blantyre, Glasgow, London

"*Looking back on that life of toil I cannot but feel thankful that it formed such a material part of my early education and were it possible, I should like to begin life over again in the same lowly style and pass through the same hardy training.*"
Missionary Travels, Page 6.

1. Ancestry

DR. LIVINGSTONE was descended on both sides from humble, deeply religious people. His proud phrase describes them aptly: "my own order, the godly poor." The father was of immigrant Celtic stock. The mother came of Mid-Lanark folk, of Saxon origin and long resident in the district.

For a proper understanding of Livingstone's character this fusion of races must be remembered. He thought of himself as a Highlander and made frequent references to his "highland blood." Indeed in the short sketch he gives of his ancestry in his first book, he makes no reference to his mother's origin. To his Celtic forebears he owed much of his impulsive generosity, his imagination and fire: perhaps also his instinctive understanding of African tribal ways that have not a little in common with the Clan system. From his Lowland ancestry he inherited traits not less valuable: determination and tenacity, hatred of oppression, a self-reliant practical temper, and a sense of humour, and from both sides, his marvellous powers of endurance.

2. The Highland Strain

Much has been written about Livingstone's ancestry on the father's side. When honours fell to him he became the hero of all good Highlanders, and clan records were hunted and many romantic connections unearthed; but for few of these can any degree of authenticity be claimed, beyond the account he himself gives in the short auto-biography with which his first book, *Missionary Travels,* opens.[1]

He tells us that his grandfather tilled a small farm on the Island of Ulva—not far from Oban—and that his great-great-grandfather fell at Culloden "fighting for the old line of kings." Characteristically, however, it was the moral rather than the romantic that interested him, for he stressed the saying of one of his people "that he could never discover that there was a dishonest man amongst our forefathers" (cattle-rieving presumably did not count!), and that the precept he had left to his children was, "Be honest."

It may be mentioned that these Livingstones have no connection with the historic house so prominent in Scots history. Theirs was a Gaelic name anglicised—"Maclay" or "Mac-an-Leigh" was its original form. A tradition of considerable definiteness connects them with the Barons of Bachuill, a family who were custodians of an ancient stone crozier said to have belonged to Saint Moluag, the first Bishop of Argyle. This relic is now in Inveraray Castle.

The oldest document that concerns the family is to be seen in the Blantyre Memorial, in the

[1] For a detailed account of these traditions see R. J. Campbell's *Livingstone,* chap. II.

Ancestry Room. It runs: "The bearer Neil Livingstone, a married man in Ulva, part of the parish of Kilninian, has always maintained an unblemished moral character and is known for a man of piety and religion. He has a family of four sons, the youngest of which is three years, and three daughters of which the youngest is six years of age. As he proposes to offer his services to some cotton spinning manufacturers, he and his wife, Mary Morrison, and their family of children are hereby recommended for suitable encouragement. Given at Ulva this eighth day of January 1792 by

> Arch. McArthur   Minister.
> Lach. McLean   Elder.
> R. S. Stewart, J.P. Elder."

The ruins of the little "but and ben" that they occupied may still be seen in a pleasant bay on the island.

It was the Duke of Argyle who, in 1858, at a farewell banquet to his famous countryman, drew attention to the coincidence that the outlook from the cottage was towards the nearby Isle of Iona, the home of St. Columba.

The Livingstone family exodus was part of the tragic tale of the depopulation in the West Highlands. Sheep were gradually pushing the crofters from the glens. The fickle climate made crops and rents uncertain. Sheep paid better and gave a surer return, so the people had to go. Most found homes in Canada, and many, work at the great factories that were then being established on Clydeside—forerunners in the Industrial Revolution.

And this is how, according to a credible story, they came to Blantyre. A shipload of bewildered emigrants was storm-stayed at Greenock. David Dale, founder of the mill where afterwards young Livingstone worked, hearing of their distress, rode post haste and made them an offer of employment. This invitation was gratefully accepted, and thus there began a stream that carried Highlanders innumerable into the industrial districts of Scotland.

Among those thus attracted were honest Neil Livingstone and his numerous progeny. A position of responsibility was given him, and that he justified the trust is proved by the fact that for many years it was his duty to carry, week by week, from Glasgow to Blantyre, large sums of money for wages. Of his many sons, however, the Missionary's father was the only one who was content to remain beside him. The roving, fighting instinct was strong in the others. All took part in the wars with the French, and one or more fought at Waterloo.

3. The Lowland Strain

Of the Hunters, David's mother's people, much less is known. It is a curious illustration of the

lure of Highland romance, that while investi-
gators into the father's ancestry have been legion,
no one has thought it worth while to pry into
that of the mother's—less colourful probably, but
not less honourable.

Her people hailed from Shotts, a parish in the
bleak uplands of East Lanarkshire. It is in the
midst of "Covenanting country," and the moors
around were hiding-places well hunted in the
"Killing Time." No tradition, it is true, links
the Hunter family directly with those grim days
of struggle for freedom of conscience, but Agnes
Hunter's grandfather, Gavin, was remembered for
his strong Covenanting sympathies.

David Hunter, the father, from whom the
Explorer got his name, had also been a small
farmer and had been caught in the same economic
net. His croft could not be made to pay, so he
moved to the kindlier climate of Clyde Valley and
tried again. Here he added tailoring to farming,
but with no better success. Too easy with his
debtors, he failed, and had to begin life afresh
at Blantyre.

In these early days the big factories had great
difficulty in attracting labour. The country people,
pinchingly poor though they were, disliked long
hours and close confinement, and so the companies
took over charge of the city orphans and made
themselves responsible for maintenance and training, in return for their service. It was a system
that, in Blantyre at any rate, worked—except for
the very long hours—apparently satisfactorily.

The orphans were well cared for. It was as tailor to these youngsters—the "Barrack" children as they were locally called—that David Hunter settled in Blantyre. A family tradition tells how one of the Erskine brothers, on a revival mission —the church having probably been closed to him —held a meeting on a wintry day in a cemetery. At this Hunter, then a lad of seventeen, was present, and so entrancing was the preacher's eloquence that though snow fell heavily, the fact was not noticed till it reached the ankles of the hearers. This experience moulded the young man's character. He remained through life deeply religious.

Neil Livingstone, the younger, became apprenticed to this good man, and though he disliked the trade and soon left it, he stayed long enough to wed his employer's daughter. The marriage took place in 1810. They lived for a time in Anderston, Glasgow, but their first child having died there, they returned to Blantyre, where on March 19th, 1813, in the grandfather's house, David was born.

4. The Livingstone Home

The house, now the Scottish National Memorial, stands abruptly on a high bank above a beautiful curve of the River Clyde. In those days, and indeed still in spite of mines and mills, the situation was one of unusual attractiveness. Across the

LIVINGSTONE'S BIRTHPLACE, BLANTYRE

from a sketch by E. Eadie, R.S.W.

THE BIRTH ROOM

Here Livingstone was born on March 19th, 1813

broad stream lie the woods of Bothwell, through which in Spring there shimmers the blue of thick carpets of wild hyacinth. Below, between steep banks of magnificent oaks and beeches, the river winds. On the right it passes the grey walls of Bothwell Castle,[1] so prominent in Scots history; and on the left, the ruins of the Priory whither, in the days of the raids from the South, the Monks of Melrose often fled for refuge.

The house, the "Shuttle Row" as it was called, was built about 1780 to lodge the workers of the great factory that covered the nearer bank. The building is a three-storied tenement, made of harled brick. It contains twenty-four "single kitchens," in each of which a family lived. Two outside spiral stairways give to the block a certain dignity. So close did it stand to the mill that in only ten out of the twenty-four hours were the occupants free—save on Sundays—from the sounds of machinery and the splash of water-wheels.

David's father was a man of marked individuality—a Sunday School teacher and a total abstainer at a time when to be so meant ridicule. He was a keen student of theology and an omniverous reader of missionary books and reports. His famous son revered his memory deeply. "My father," he wrote, "by his kindliness of manner and winning ways made the heart-strings of his children twine around him . . . and deserved my

---

[1] A widespread tradition tells how Livingstone carved his initials high above all others on the wall of this Castle. Facts unfortunately do not bear out the story.

lasting gratitude and homage for presenting me from infancy with a continuously consistent pious example, such as that, the ideal of which, is so beautifully portrayed in Burns's Cottar's Saturday Night." Both parents were remarkably gifted story-tellers and loved to recount the family reminiscences, in which both sides were rich.

After the return to Blantyre, Neil became a tea merchant in a small way—peddling his wares from farm to farm. He liked this work because it gave him the chance to exercise his special hobby—personal evangelism.

The following local memory is worth recording. It was his custom to carry his tea in a tin box and to weigh out the ounces with meticulous care. One day a customer protested, "Come, come! Neil, dinna' be sae scrimpit." "Ma guid woman," was the stern answer, "I'll gie ye naether a plack mair nor a plack less than the weicht. I'm honest."

The mother, known according to Scots custom to her friends as "Nannie Hunter," was of sweet gentle nature. Small and delicate, her chief physical characteristic was markedly bright eyes, a trait that her son inherited. Her passion for cleanliness is recalled. This, too, she passed on to him. Even in his roughest times in Africa Livingstone never slackened his scrupulous care for his personal appearance. There were five children—John, David, Janet, Charles and Agnes. Two others died in infancy. Discipline in the home was strict. The rod was not spared and David received, we know, his share.

In spite of poverty it was a most happy home.
In early married life the Livingstones had belonged
to the local Parish church, but during David's
boyhood, under the influence of an itinerant
preacher from America, the father joined a small
Congregational church, at Blackswell Lane, Hamilton—three miles distant. Neil became an elder
and David, in due time, a member. The services
were held morning and afternoon, and the interval
was spent in the house of a fellow member, and
one of that family, William Naismith, of the
Hamilton Advertiser, used to recall how the visitors,
in their sturdy way, would accept nothing from
their hosts save only hot water for tea, and how
Mrs. Livingstone, following the old Scots custom,
would take the opportunity of solacing herself
with a few whiffs from her clay "cutty" pipe.
Mr. Naismith used also to tell how he, a small
boy, would look with something like awe on the
solemn young man, until one day David, catching
his eye, suddenly winked at him and "birled" a
penny across the floor. After that awe evaporated.

Low Blantyre in those days was an attractive
place. It was indeed counted a model village and
famed locally for its display of garden flowers.
The founder, "douce Davie Dale," was a kindly
man and very generous. Of him it was said "Dale
gives his money away but God shovels it back
again." Profits in these early days were high.
Robert Owen, the famous social reformer, one of
the inaugurators of the Co-operative Movement,
became Dale's son-in-law. He had no connection

with the Blantyre factory, but New Lanark is only a few miles away, and Owen's social experiments, which attained a European reputation about that time, had their influence in Blantyre, and James Monteith, when he took over the factory in 1792, continued all the kindly traditions. The management was paternal. The village was well planned and had an excellent water supply and though, by modern standards, the house accommodation was most meagre, it was well in advance of its day. The community had its own sick and benefit societies and its public wash-house. There was a church of which the company bore half the expense; a good school and a considerable library from which David, no doubt, obtained most of the books he says he "devoured." The village was surrounded by a wall. A bell was rung at ten o'clock and the gates closed till morning.

Of the village the author of the Statistical Account of 1835 wrote as follows: "Living in one of the faery neuks of creation, religious and moral, well fed and clothed, and not overwrought, they seem peculiarly happy as they ought to be." This eulogy may sound high-pitched when the smallness of the pay and the length of the hours of work are remembered. None the less, Livingstone's own recollections are hardly less warm.

5. *The Boy David*

It is surely more than a little surprising that a man who in his prime towered above his fellows, should have been so little noticed in youth. Sir Harry Johnston quotes a Blantyre man as saying: "Dr. Livingstone was no thocht to be a by-ordinar' (unusual) laddie; just a sulky, quiet, feckless[1] sort o' boy." "Sulky" here must mean "obstinate" and probably shy. "A' the Livingstones were dour," is a local verdict. "Feckless," too, can be understood in the light of another remark, probably the oldest story that remains.

A farmer who employed him on occasion as a small boy to herd his cattle, used to say in after years: "I did'na think muckle o' that David Livingstone when he worked wi' me. He was aye lyin' on his belly readin' a book."

It is easy to understand how those hard-worked, practical-minded folk would have little use for a boy who wandered about by himself, had no interest in games and girls as the other lads had; who was always reading and would spend his spare time scouring the country collecting "bits o' flo'ers and bits o' stanes and sic like trash."

Livingstone's story is not the usual "Kail-Yaird School" romance of the "dux," the protégé of the village dominie who clears all before him. On the contrary he seems to have developed slowly; to have received little encouragement from others and to have climbed step by step simply by that power of dogged persistence that was always his outstanding characteristic.

Apparently, two people alone, at this time,

---

[1] A word for which there is no adequate English equivalent. It means awkward, unpractical, and much else.

35

recognised the possibilities that were hidden in the boy. One was Mr. McSkimming, the teacher of the evening school. To him Livingstone always expressed the warmest gratitude. The other was an Irish lad, Gallacher by name, afterwards a well-known Roman Catholic priest in Partick. This boy was better educated than David, and helped him with Latin.

But Livingstone's "three R's" were acquired not under Mr. McSkimming, but in a small school "kept" in one of the lower rooms of the Shuttle Row (now part of the Memorial) held for the benefit of the "Barrack" children already mentioned.

6. The Mill Hand

The family income was scanty. Times were hard. Those were the days of the slump after the Napoleonic wars. David had very early to take his share in the upkeep of the home, so at the age of ten he had to enter the factory.

The working conditions he had to endure seem to us incredibly hard. Summer and winter he was wakened at half-past five by the mill bell—or more probably by being pulled out of bed by his mother. He would tumble into his scanty clothes, sup a plate of scalding porridge, or, if late, seize a "piece" that his mother had ready and rush down the short path to the gate of the grim building with high gables and windows innumerable. There in a humid atmosphere he would

36

work, except for meal-time intervals, till eight at night.

There was some mitigation in the fact that, as the best-known story of his boyhood shows, his work was not done under "speeding-up" conditions. He was a "piecer": that is, his job was to tend the spinning jenny and tie up broken threads. It was light work and there were short periods of leisure. He made use of these by placing his Latin grammar on some part of the machine and studying "between whiles." It is added, locally, that the mill girls got great fun out of pitching bobbins at the book and trying to knock it off the frame.

The toil of the day did not finish when the mill closed. Along with the other lads he had to attend night school for two hours. At the age of thirteen he joined a special Latin class and would, he tells us, continue the "dictionary part" of his study till midnight or till his mother snatched the book from his hand.

It would be a most interesting psychological study to trace the effects for good or evil of the confinement of those thirteen formative years upon a mind so sensitive and powerful. Livingstone himself claims that the conditions of his early toil greatly strengthened his power of concentration, and enabled him later to abstract his mind completely "amidst the dancing and singing savages" in an African village. The very closeness of confinement too, he says, increased his joy in the open air. Every free day found him, sometimes accompanied by a brother, more often alone, searching the fields and hills for rare flowers and geological specimens. He gained thus a discipline of sight and memory which later made him one of the keenest eyed and most reliable observers of Nature that the world has ever seen.

The life, too, trained the lad in self-reliance and the power to act fearlessly in emergency—a characteristic that stands out so clearly in after days. Here is an illustration.

Below Blantyre and on the farther side of the Clyde there stood the "Old Mill" and above it, a weir. In the Mill House lived two children— Eglinton by name. There was a boat on the pool above the dam and one day, when the river was running high, the girl, who was the elder, put her brother on board and, against orders, took to the river. All went well till an oar was slipped. Then the boat drifted rapidly towards the weir. Realising the danger and thoroughly frightened, the child shrieked for help. A youth who was sitting reading by the waterside heard the call and, taking in the situation, at some danger to himself, swam out, retrieved the oar, climbed aboard and brought the children home. The lad was only Dave Livingstone, son of old Neil who called once a month to sell tea, so little was said. But when David had become famous the story was recalled and treasured.

His inquiring mind probed into many things. He studied *Culpeper's Herbal* and scoured the country for "simples." Astrology even at one time attracted him, fascinating and frightening. It seemed perilous ground, he wrote, to tread on farther, "for the dark hint seemed to my youthful mind to loom towards ' selling my soul and body to the devil ' at the price of an unfathomable knowledge of the stars." And so he desisted.

A strange lad he must have appeared to the plain folk amongst whom he lived. Small wonder they thought him "feckless" and "sulky."

7. *The Missionary Call*

Livingstone's study of Latin under McSkimming did not last long. The other students in time lost interest and "the master not wishing to be troubled teaching one person only, advised him to give it up unless he had a prospect of needing it, which he knew he had not.[1] So David kept his ambitions to himself, continuing to study in private and reading eagerly every book he could reach. Since, as he used to say, "I knew Virgil and Horace at sixteen better than I do now," he must have read to some purpose.

It was a time of unrest and political agitation, and in Blantyre, he tells us, there was much intelligent interest in the progress of the Reform Bill. And since the Scottish weaver was always a man of radical leanings and at times an accomplished "heckler," no doubt argumentation was

[1] Letter from Neil Livingstone to London Missionary Society quoted in R. J. Campbell's *Livingstone*, page 59.

general. Further, Owen's experiments in New Lanark and the unsuccessful attempt to establish at Orbiston, which lies nearby, a communistic settlement, gave the politically minded much food for discussion.[1] But the only evidence we have that, in his youth, David took any interest in politics is found in the story that he carved on a tree the slogan "No State Church," but that seems to have been only a boyish prank. The interests of the home were religious rather than political.

There might perhaps be a hint of politics of the radical colour in the story that Dr. Blaikie has preserved, of how David once bagged a salmon and, no other means of concealment being available, pushed it down the leg of brother Charlie's trousers. It is told that as they passed through the village, much sympathy was evoked by the laddie's swollen limb! Neil, for all his rigid honesty, would eat his share of the poached salmon without a qualm. The Scots peasant has no scruples as to infringing riparian rights, as long as the fish is destined for the family pot.

The books most easily accessible were those on theology, such as Boston's *Fourfold State* and *Marrow of Modern Divinity*, the favourite reading of the serious-minded peasantry of his time. These stood on the household bookshelf. The youth, however, turned from them and preferred travel and science, and he records that the last time his father used the rod to him was on his refusal to read Wilberforce's *Practical Christianity*,

[1] See *Adventures in Socialism*. Alex. Cullen.

a book of apologetics and a best-seller in its day.

This unwise severity caused a revulsion against all doctrinal reading, and as the father was suspicious of scientific books there was, it would appear, for a time, estrangement.

About the age of twenty, however, David found in the writings of Dr. Thomas Dick a solution of the doubt that had long troubled him and which his father's anxiety had increased. The author argued that science and religion were not hostile to each other but rather complementary. Livingstone found in this congenial teaching confirmation of his own opinions, and the discovery brought to him intense relief and in considerable measure accounted for the religious crisis through which he passed at that time. He found the peace he sought and to quote the phrase which became the constant undertone of his life, "In the glow of love that Christianity inspired I resolved to devote my life to the alleviation of human misery."

About this time there came to his hand a copy of a pamphlet recently issued by Karl Gutzlaff, of the Netherland Missionary Society, who pled for medical missionaries to be sent to China, urging that they could enter where no others could penetrate. Thereafter, to be a medical missionary in China, in spite of apparently insurmountable difficulty, became the consuming ambition of his life.

Poverty was, naturally, the main obstacle. Unemployment in his trade had been severe, and in consequence promotion in the mill very slow.

It was not till he was nineteen that, having become a spinner, he could save any money worth considering. This was heavy work for a youth of his build—"a slim, loose-jointed lad," he called himself—but abundant consolation was found in watching the little pile of savings grow. At the end of the fourth year sufficient had been garnered, with some small help from the family, to pay for the first part of his medical training.

It was apparently about this time that Livingstone applied for membership in the little church with which he had been connected. The Deacons' Court, grave serious men, examined him and "dooted David was no soun'," and appointed two of their numbers to instruct and guide. Of these, one—Arthur Anderson, weaver and later coachman, was a remarkable man, much beloved and admired by his pupil. It took five months to complete the training and secure acceptance.

In the Blantyre of those days there were not a few men of this fine calibre. One especially, Livingstone mentions, whose dying words he cherished and quoted. "Now lad, make religion the every-day business of your life—not a thing of fits and starts, for if you do not, temptation, and other things, will get the better of you."

8. The Student of Medicine

In the autumn of 1836 then, the young missionary aspirant entered Anderson's College, at that time a prominent medical school in Glasgow. It was the first great adventure of his life and may well have been one of the most trying. Twelve pounds of his hard-earned savings were swallowed up in fees! With his father's advice, rooms were found that cost two shillings and sixpence a week.

The "Andersonian" was then situated at the north-east corner of George Square, and the half-crown lodgings were in Rotten Row—a mean locality—on the hill just above, a sad contrast to its aristocratic London namesake. Livingstone admits that at first he felt very lonely, but he was determined either to "mak' a spune or spoil the horn." This sudden transition from the narrow circle in Blantyre to the wide, free life of a college, must have been a most exciting experience. Humiliating at times too, for, having been almost entirely self-taught, his preliminary education was very imperfect. But his modesty was disarming and he soon made good friends.

The course he had mapped out for himself was a curious one. Theology, under Dr. Ralph Wardlow, Principal of the Congregational Seminary; Greek, probably at the University; and medical classes at the "Andersonian." His Sundays were spent at home, and so great was his keenness to miss no opportunity, that he resolutely refused a "lift" back to town, a distance of eight miles, in a friend's gig, on Monday mornings, because to have accepted would have meant cutting a class.

Livingstone speaks affectionately of three of his professors. Of these, Dr. Wardlaw, whose church

43

he joined, was one. Wardlaw was an outstanding figure in his day, a theologian whose books are even now in request. He was a Calvinist of liberal sympathies. Livingstone was never a systematic theologian, but he continued to hold to the end the general positions he learnt from his tutor. Darwinism, when it arrived, disturbed but did not convince him, and he was made somewhat uncomfortable at one time by being associated with Bishop Colenso, of heretical reputation.

Dr. Thomas Graham, who lectured on chemistry, was another very distinguished man whom his pupil revered, and Dr. Andrew Buchanan, professor of medicine, became a lifelong and most attached friend.

A distinguished writer in a recent book has spoken of Livingstone as a "lonely" man. This is a misunderstanding. Towards the end of his life, it is true, circumstances compelled him to draw in upon himself, but he had, without question, a genius for friendship. All through his life he attached to himself men of the highest type and never lost them. Even when there was occasional temporary estrangement, they came back to him again. And Livingstone paid the price of friendship in full measure in voluminous letters. His correspondence might not unfairly be called prodigious.

Dr. Graham's assistant at this time was a man called Young—son of a joiner, afterwards well known as Young of Kelly, the inventor of the process of distilling oil from shale and the founder

of a great industry in Midlothian—"Sir Paraffin,"
as Livingstone used in after life to call him. The
two were much of an age. Young was quick to
recognise the Blantyre lad's grit and helped him,
in study and other ways, and continued through
life Livingstone's best friend. Out of his wealth
he supported the Explorer's expeditions with
princely generosity.

9. The Next Step

By the end of his second year young Livingstone
felt himself sufficiently established to make a
formal offer of his service to the London Missionary Society. He chose this body chiefly because,
as he says, of its Catholicity, since it aimed "not
to send Presbyterianism, Independency, Episcopacy
or any other form of church order, but the glorious
gospel of the blessed God, to the heathen."

The letter containing his application is the
earliest specimen of his correspondence that sur-
vives and is particularly interesting as showing
how imperfect, at this time, his education still
was. It is stilted in style, singularly different from
the freedom of his later writing. It is composed
largely of the religious clichés in use in the evangelical circles of his day, and though obviously carefully penned there are mistakes in spelling, and
the words "God" and "Jesus" are written without
capitals. It may be mentioned in passing that
the great man was habitually shaky as to spelling

45

—surely a curious fact psychologically, when his marvellous powers of observation and his photographic memory are considered.

The application was favourably received and he was called to London to meet the directors. Friends in Hamilton helped him with travel expense, and he arrived in the Metropolis in September, 1838. He lodged at the missionary hostel in Aldersgate Street. He found there another youth on the same quest—Joseph Moore—a happy meeting since they quickly became, what they remained, bosom friends. It is from Moore that we learn most of what has been recorded of Livingstone's life during this period.

Both passed a test examination and were sent, as was the custom, for three months' provisional training under the charge of the Rev. Richard Cecil, to Chipping Ongar, Essex. Here Livingstone's experiences were by no means happy. The students lived in lodgings and went for meals and for instruction in classics and theology to the tutor's house. It was a most uncomfortable time, for David failed to impress favourably the teacher on whom his fate seemed so completely to depend, and moreover, he knew he was failing.

At this age Livingstone was not attractive, except to intimate friends. Mr. Cecil reported that "he had heaviness of manner united with rusticity not likely to be removed." On the other hand he gives him credit for "sense and quiet vigour, good temper and strength of character." At this age other observers, too, speak of him as "ungainly in movement, slow and indistinct of speech"—a fact due no doubt to an enlarged uvula that troubled him in Africa. Probably, also, he spoke with a marked West of Scotland accent. For his intimates, however, it should be added, he had an extraordinary charm—"a kind of spell," Moore calls it—which, in after years, when shyness had been in good degree mastered, was felt and spoken of by many.

To his tutor he was a disappointment. Part of his duty was to take his turn in family worship. Extempore prayer was no new exercise to Livingstone, and in mature life he showed a gift in this way that was frequently commented upon, but the same exercise in the presence of a critical tutor, and probably of still more critical fellow students, was somewhat overwhelming. Hence petitions were laboured and pauses painfully long. But the most damning experience must be given in his friend Moore's words:

"One part of our duty was to prepare sermons which were submitted to Mr. Cecil and when corrected were committed to memory and then repeated to our village congregations. Livingstone prepared one and one Sunday the minister of Stanford Rivers having fallen sick . . . he was sent to preach. He took his text, read it out very deliberately and then—then—his sermon fled. Midnight darkness came upon him and he abruptly said, ' Friends, I have forgotten all I had to say,' and hurrying out of the pulpit he left the chapel."

"Midnight darkness" indeed, but with no "joy

47

coming in the morning." A crushing experience when so much depended upon it. The immediate result was an unfavourable report, and for the time Livingstone's fate swayed in the balance. In the Board a decision was all but given against him. What a test for fitness for Africa! "Sense and quiet vigour, good temper and strength of character" all to go for nothing, and an uncouth manner and a stuttering tongue to outweigh all! Happily one grey-beard, wiser than the rest, pled for another chance. Several months' grace was given him. This time he was accepted and directed to continue his medical course in London.

10. A Student in London

The two years that followed were among the happiest of his life. To a man of Livingstone's versatility and keenness to learn something of everything, the Metropolis surged with interests and opportunities. He had money enough and plenty of congenial friends.

In the course of his study he met physicians and scientists who were in the front rank of their professions. He became attached to the church of Dr. Bennett, a Congregational minister, and thus came to know his son, Dr. J. Risdon Bennett, afterwards President of the Royal College of Physicians, whose friendship he gained and held. Through him he was given entry into Charing Cross and Moorfield Hospitals. Dr. Bennett was drawn to the plain young Scot by his "simple loving christian spirit and the combined modest, unassuming and self reliant character of the man."

He got to know intimately, Professor Owen (afterwards Sir Richard), the famous Zoologist, and became a few years later Owen's most valued correspondent and sent him, whenever opportunity offered, reports and specimens of the then largely unknown fauna of Africa. These men, in their turn, kept the scientific societies in touch with his discoveries and had thus much to do with the amazing reception that was to greet him on his first return home.

About this time Livingstone was sharply and all but fatally ill. "Congestion of the liver with lung affection" was the diagnosis. On recovery Moore saw him off to Scotland, where he rapidly regained strength.

Up to this date his mind was still on China as the sphere of his effort "to relieve human misery." But the events which led up to the Opium War were making entry into China impossible. An appointment in the West Indies was offered him, but life in a settled country had no appeal and for some months his destination remained in doubt. Moore informs us that in the spring of 1840 he met his friend at a meeting held in Exeter Hall, called to support an ambitious scheme for the "Amelioration of Conditions of the Races of Africa." The Bill of 1833 had liberated all slaves in the Empire but it had not stopped the slave traffic, and the conscience of the British people

49

was troubled. They felt that they still owed to Africa a debt for their share in the havoc the old slave trade had wrought. A plea that every effort should be made to place at the service of Africans the best that the West could give in agriculture, science and religion, had just been made in a book, entitled *The African Slave Trade*, by T. F. Buxton.

The great meeting acclaimed Mr. Buxton's contention and supported it generously. The following year a strong expedition was despatched to the River Niger. It was a noble conception but it failed tragically. The preliminary scouting had been badly done. The conditions of the country had not been studied. Malaria prevailed, and of the large company of Europeans who went up the river, a fourth did not return. Livingstone makes no reference to this meeting, but from the similarity of its ideals to those which he himself advocated later, we may presume that what he had heard he had digested. In any case, he was to follow the same general aim and to succeed in the end, where the Niger Expedition failed.

About this time he met the man who, more than any other, was to affect his life—Dr. Robert Moffat, afterwards his father-in-law. This missionary had worked with the London Missionary Society in South Africa since 1816. A Scot, by training a gardener, he had changed the wilderness of Kuruman into a fruitful field. A striking figure, a popular speaker, he had a great gift of vivid description. One picture that he was fond of painting captured Livingstone's imagination.

Moffat used to tell how often of a morning he had stood upon a height and had seen clearly to the North "the smoke of a thousand villages where the gospel had not been proclaimed." Moffat happened to visit the hostel, and Livingstone, with shy diffidence, approached him and asked if he thought he "would do for Africa." "Yes," was the momentous reply, "if you are prepared to leave occupied ground and push on to the North."

No words could have appealed to the young student more powerfully. To "build on another man's foundations" was the last thing he desired. The matter was quickly settled. Livingstone was appointed to Kuruman with instructions to wait there the return of Dr. Moffat. What other arrangement could have suited him so well? That night he must have thanked God with an overflowing heart. It was surely "A moment to which Heaven had joined great issues."

11. The Last Days at Home

No time was lost. Livingstone hurried to Glasgow, and there sat an examination and qualified as Licentiate of the Faculty of Physicians and Surgeons.

Tact—at least in dealing with Europeans—was never his strong suit, and in this case he tells us that he jeopardised his chances by the extreme imprudence of arguing with his examiners! The

51

use of the stethoscope was the point in debate. The final hurdle passed, he hurried to Blantyre to say farewell.

Livingstone's last night at home is one of the best remembered of Scottish scenes. The family gathered in the dimly-lit but cosy room. The little mother, her eyes alight with pride and tears; the old father, whose lined but kindly face is masked by a grimness that hides deep emotion; a brother, a sister or two, and in the middle David speaking excitedly of the glorious life ahead of him. The wish is to talk the night through, but to this the mother will not agree.

And so they sing, and David prays and reads from the big family Bible the 121st psalm.

I will lift up mine eyes unto the hills
From whence cometh my help . . .
The Lord is thy keeper.
The Lord is thy shade upon thy right hand . . .
The Lord shall preserve thy going out and thy
    coming in
From this time forth and even for evermore.

And then to rest.

In the morning, the 17th of November, long before the sun is up—it is a bleak November day —they rise. Coffee is made and drunk, and then farewell is said not without tears.

Father and son tramped the eight-mile road to Glasgow, to the Broomielaw Pier. It was the day when small paddle steamers were coming into use for coastal service. And so they parted not to meet again—two men so much alike—the old Scots Puritan type at its best. Neil died a few months before his son, now become a world-famous explorer, returned from Africa.

On November 20th, 1840, Dr. Livingstone was ordained as missionary in Albion Chapel, London, and his tutor, Mr. Cecil, took part in the service. A fortnight later—on December 8th—he sailed for Africa on the ship *George*, commanded by Captain Donaldson.

12. A Broken Romance

This pause in the young Missionary's history is a suitable place to tell a little human story that has recently come to light.

It is noticeable that among the many traditions that continue to be remembered round Blantyre there is none that ascribe to him any interest in the other sex. The extreme, absorption in study no doubt accounts for this. His application to the Missionary Society was amusingly dogmatic on the subject. In reply to a routine question as to marriage arrangements, he answered: "Under no obligation as to marriage; never made proposals of marriage; nor so conducted myself to any woman to cause her to suspect that I intended anything related to marriage." So much for Blantyre! But there are hints that in London he did not quite escape the universal malady. Thereby hangs a little story.

53

Some years ago there was gifted to the Blantyre
Memorial a faded little book made valuable by
this inscription in Livingstone's characteristic
handwriting:

"To Cathrine (*sic*) Ridley
with the best wishes and Christian regards of D.L.
London 25th June 1840."

The book is Sigourney's *Lays of the West*. The
authoress is described in the preface as the "Mrs.
Hemans of America." It consists of moral and
religious musings with a strong missionary bias.
No clue to Miss Ridley's identity appeared at the
time, but two years later certain letters, that had
lain in private keeping for a century, came into
the hands of the Committee, and from these it is
easy to put together the facts of a romance that
failed to blossom.

During his months of training at Chipping
Ongar Livingstone joined a group of ardent
young people who were looking forward to
missionary service in Africa. Among them were
two brothers called Prentice, and a girl, Catherine
Ridley. They belonged to families of some standing. The letters referred to, show without question
that David was attracted to Catherine. This is
not to be wondered at since she was probably the
only girl of education whom, up till then, he had
known at all intimately.

In a letter to her from the *George* these words
occur: "You know I am not very well acquainted
with those who have been ladies all their lives"—

a curious phrase from one so completely free of snobbery, but an obvious indication of a certain ingenuousness, perhaps over-modesty, that he showed at this stage.

Catherine remains a shadowy figure. Livingstone had a successful rival in Thomas Prentice, and it seems hardly likely that this girl had for her diffident admirer anything more than a friendly feeling. But that she held his imagination for some years is placed beyond doubt by the inevitable way in which her name appears in letters to this group of friends right up to the time of Mary Moffat's arrival.

He was concerned about her health. She had the right spirit but could she face the life? "I believe the difference between the elegant little carriage they used to drive and the bullock wagon of South Africa will be very great." To this Prentice replied with spirit: "Ever since she thought of becoming a missionary, she wrought like a servant and did a great part of the work of the house."

When the young people parted they expected to meet again as colleagues in Africa and the little book was his parting gift. The lady in return gave him a keepsake, a watch guard made by herself and an "elegantly bound" copy of *Bridges on the 119th Psalm*.[1] He read this on the voyage and it warmed his "heart with heavenly-minded reflections."

[1] Exposition on Ps. 119 by Rev. Chas. Bridges, M.A., Vicar of Newton.

In Africa Livingstone was often lonely. He craved for news from his friends as a thirsty man does for water, and he was anxious about the girl. She had been ill when he sailed; but Prentice did not write. "Wee Tom," David grumbled to a mutual friend, "the shabby thing, has no time to write to any one but Catherine."

In the end, for health reasons, the missionary ambition was abandoned. The girl married Thomas Prentice and settled at home. There is no indication that they met again in later life. Probably the wound had not been deep.

13. Livingstone in 1840

When the young pioneer climbed the gangway of the little ship, about to sail on what proved a somewhat dangerous voyage, he was twenty-seven years of age.

In figure he was slight and wiry, somewhat above middle height—five feet eight and a half inches to be exact. His shoulders were well set and he held himself erect. His friend Vardon spoke of him later as "a little fellow"; probably the somewhat unusually large size of his well-proportioned head gave that effect. In complexion he was sallow. The features were strong and rugged, the chin and mouth heavy and broad, and eyebrows shaggy and thick.

There is a curious difference of evidence as to the colour of his hair and eyes. The former was

56

probably brown with a hint of auburn. The latter
have been described as black and brown; H. M.
Stanley said they were hazel and the owner himself called them blue! All agree on one point.
Under bushy eyebrows they shone with a brilliance
quite unusual. By middle age they had grown
strong and commanding, and account largely for
the impression of almost daemonic strength that
his later photographs give.

Though self-reliant he was unusually shy.
Modesty is indeed his most frequently mentioned
trait. At the same time he was determined—
"dour" would probably not be an unfair description. He loved argument; held his opinions
dogmatically and expressed them with bluntness.
He was keenly interested in people, and his familiar
letters of the time show a delightfully human
absorption in their affairs and are full of a somewhat rollicking humour.

He was essentially a simple character—sincere
and free from subtleties. His was what the
Scriptures call the "single eye." His outlook was
Puritan. He had their rigid sense of duty. It was
said of him "Fire, water, stone walls would not
stop Livingstone in the fulfilment of any duty."
None the less he was a genial, indeed a charming
companion, and had a full share of the joy of life.

Although every opportunity had been heroically
used, his schooling had been spasmodic and he was
therefore, in that sense, imperfectly educated. (The
London Missionary Society had not thought him
cultured enough for the standard of their Indian

Missions). But in fitting him, in the wider sense, of equipping him for the life he had to lead, his training had been unique. Few men have lived who could do so many things well and so much supremely well.

On the aesthetic side he was, in a sense, not strong. He shows no interest in pictures. True, he did sketch a little in water colours, but what specimens of his work remain have a value that is geographical, certainly not artistic. As regards music the impression left is that he was what the Scots call "timmer"—toneless. "I, poor mortal," he wrote to Kuruman, "am as mute as a fish as regards singing." Kirk tells us of the trying habit he had on tense occasions of humming tunes. Perhaps some of the exasperation this trick caused to his colleagues may have been due to their being sung out of tune.

Livingstone's aesthetic sense found its expression in his almost rapturous joy in the beauty of Nature. Not infrequently his sober prose becomes lyrical as he describes scenes around him. He had, further, a wide acquaintance with the best verse of his period. Thirty years after, H. M. Stanley was amazed by his being able to recite whole poems—"Byron, Burns, Tennyson, Longfellow, Whittier and Lowell." His diaries, further, show acquaintance with a wide range of prose writing; with Pepys, Sir Thomas Browne, Burton of the *Anatomy of Melancholy* and much else. As far as evidence shows, he did not outgrow the prejudice of the Blantyre home against novels.

His personal habits were of the simplest. He hated all softness or extravagance. He was a non-smoker always and a total abstainer most of his life, though in later years he modified his practice somewhat for medical reasons.

To understand Livingstone aright, the depth and power of his religious convictions must be recognised. His Christian faith permeated and illumined his life. Its foundation was his unfaltering belief in the sovereignty of God and in himself, in all humility, as God's instrument. This it was that, as a steel framework, sustained him through incredible hardships and gave him patience and endurance that nothing could divert.

To the student of his life it is a continual surprise that, up to this stage, the tremendous powers that lay in him were so little recognised. No doubt they were screened by shyness. Doubtless, too, they were still only in the bud. It was in Africa that they blossomed.

While it may be said, in a limited sense, that Livingstone made Africa, it may be asserted without qualification that Africa made Livingstone.

FIRST INTERLUDE

A BRAVE NEW WORLD

THE VOYAGE TO AFRICA AND A VISIT TO BRAZIL 1840–1841

"You cannot imagine with what a light heart I visit these foreign shores. Everything is different from the idea I had formed of them when reading. The actual sight and the imagination are two very different things. This is really a fine world we live in after all. Were it not for that hateful rebellion against God, it would be quite a Paradise."
From a letter to T. L. PRENTICE,
dated 5th March, 1841.

1. *"Where every Prospect Pleases"*

Young Livingstone counted it a piece of great good fortune when the *George*, because of a split foremast, had to put into Rio de Janeiro.

The voyage had been for him, as first voyages are for most people, a liberal education. He had learned many things. The ship was small, and for ten days in "The Bay" and beyond, the weather had been wild, and though he had proved to his own considerable satisfaction a good sailor, conditions had been most uncomfortable. Hence, after eight weeks cooped up on shipboard, the prospect of a run ashore was alluring. Nor was he disappointed. It was his first sight of tropical vegetation and of a land other than his own. Hence the adventure was to him of intense interest.

He wrote about it thus to Catherine Ridley:

"I could not cease gazing at the beautiful mountains that meet the eye in every direction and there was so much in the people that called for observa tion. I wished to see a little of the interior and as nobody else was inclined to stand the heat and fatigue of the walk beneath an almost vertical sun, I set off alone and having walked six or seven miles got into the Brazilian forest.

"Really it was a fine sight. Orange and cocoa-nut were the only trees I could claim acquaintance with. Butterflies and grasshoppers of gigantic size in great numbers. Lizards and scorpions, with vegetation on a most luxuriant scale. Parasitic plants of immense variety. I saw many vallies (*sic*) lovely beyond description. Little shed-like cottages of the natives were scattered here and there, peeping out beneath orange trees and the spreading leaves of the banana."

Wishing to buy some fruit, he approached one of these houses but was quickly "surrounded by three half-starved dogs, who seemed inclined to make an end of me, but having a good stick in my hand, I soon convinced them that I was not a member of the Peace Society! That brought out the inmates. By means of a few words in latin, I made them understand that I wanted to purchase some fruit, but they had none ripe. They however beckoned me into the cottage and the good lady pressed me to partake of their dinner, being fish, rice, bananas, bread and cheese, and tapioca. Her husband brought out a stone bottle and filled up a glass of some sort of liquor. I could not tell him that I was a teetotaller but kept asking for ' aqua.' The kind people would take no payment."

Though the style of the letter shows still the "prentice pen," the little adventure has the authentic Livingstone stamp. The going alone in scorn of heat; the delight in beauty and power of observation; the unique gift of establishing friendly contact with strange people, and the religious concern. For he adds: "I wish I had had some Portuguese tracts with me."

There was a touch of the recklessness, too, that always characterised him. Quite unknowingly he had caused his friends considerable anxiety. The forest was made dangerous by the presence of runaway slaves who "frequently committed depredations." The main object of the jaunt had been to get a bath "under a natural shower." He was told that he was most fortunate not to have returned unclothed.

2. " And only Man is Vile"

One effect of the varied contacts that this first experience of the "Brave New World" gave Livingstone, was a glimpse of the difficulty of the task to which in the fire of youthful enthusiasm he had dedicated himself—the task, as he would have phrased it, of "winning the world for Christ."

On the voyage out he had read some theology, and among other books, with keen appreciation, Finney's *Revivals of Religion*, a classic of the school of evangelical teaching in which he had been trained. In this book great stress is laid on "witness"—concern for the souls of others—and on personal appeal, and Livingstone felt this delicate task heavy on his conscience and he was never one to shirk a duty. But the results were not encouarging, as with the honesty natural to him he reports to his Society. True, the "Captain rigged out a church on Sunday and we had a service, but I being a poor preacher, and the Chaplain addressing them all as Christians already, no moral influence was exerted and even had there been on Sabbath, it would have been neutralised by week-day conduct. In fact no good was done." It was a test to his faith.

His experience in Rio must have upset him even more. The reports he heard of the drunken rowdyism of British and American sailors when in that port disturbed him deeply, and he took upon himself a duty that was not without danger. "I went," he tells Prentice, "into two public houses where a great many seamen lodge (and gave) tracts to one to take on board to his ship-mates whom he said were all drunkards. An American seaman who stood by requested one or two but added 'Remember we are not all drunkards.' I said, 'It did not matter what we were if we were Christians.' He got into a rage and asked if I thought he was a robber or thief or a murderer. 'Am I not as good a Christian as you are?' . . .

"As I did not wish to argue with him and about twenty around, some of them drunk and swearing, I gave him some tracts and told him they would inform him. . . . I confess I was afraid of my countrymen although they treated me with the greatest respect, and those who were sober listened to what I said."

He also visited the Misericordia Hospital, where a British lad, stabbed in a debauch, lay mortally wounded.

After four days the *George* put to sea again and the Cape was reached without further mishap. The trip had lasted over three months.

Captain Donaldson, a Scot, had taken a fancy to Livingstone, who characteristically used the opportunity for learning, with his help, something of the principles of navigation. He thus laid the foundation of that skill in making geographical observations which added so greatly to the value of his explorations. Sir Harry Johnston, than whom no one was better able to judge, gives it as his opinion that Livingstone became "perhaps the most exact computer of astronomical observations who has yet appeared amongst African explorers."

PART TWO

THE MISSIONARY

1841 to 1852

BECHUANALAND

"*Building, gardening, cobbling, doctoring, tinkering, carpentering, gun-mending, farriering, wagon-mending, preaching, schooling, lecturing in physics according to my means, besides a chair of divinity to a class of three; filled up my time.*

"*My wife made candles, soap and clothes and thus we nearly attained the indispensable accomplishment of a missionary family in Central Africa, the husband a jack of all trades without doors and the wife a maid of all work within.*"

LETTER TO REV. D. G. WATT. 1845.

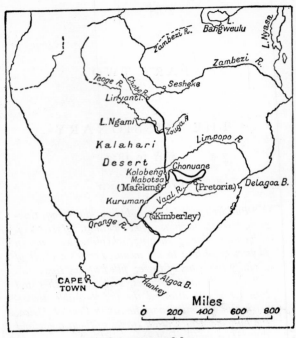

SIMPLIFIED MAP

showing Livingstone's journeys as described in

PART TWO

1. Cape to Kuruman

MARCH 15th, 1841. Africa at last!

Deeply as Livingstone was moved when he stepped ashore at Simon's Bay on that memorable day, how profoundly more deeply would he have been stirred could he but have realised that his landing was, a hundred years later, to be celebrated as one of the great events of African history.

Dr. John Philip, his host in Cape Town during a visit of about four weeks, was, at the time, one of the most outstanding men in South Africa. An Aberdonian, he had left an important pastorate to superintend, in a period of emergency, the London Mission Stations there. He remained to champion the black races—especially the Hottentot. His book, *South African Researches*, had done much to secure their emancipation. A strong man of this type, fighting in such a cause, was bound to have many opponents, and Philip was unpopular.

Livingstone had come to him prejudiced; prepared to resist stoutly the "despotism" with which certain of his colleagues had charged him. But he found no desire to dictate and conceived for his host and hostess sincere admiration and affection. He soon drew the conclusion that the accusations arose from a lack of harmony in the local mission, and he suffered the disillusionment that at times falls to the lot of the young enthusiast when it dawns upon him that his colleagues are after all but human, and not always free from man's besetting sins.

Especially did it pain him to notice that many members of the church had scant sympathy with Dr. Philip's fight for black, as against white, interests, and with an impulsiveness that was probably embarrassing to his host, he used the pulpit to give blunt expression to his feelings on the subject. The action was plucky, no doubt, but somewhat tactless. Dictation from one so inexperienced was resented and a legacy of dislike remained from which he was later to suffer.

Though we know that Philip was attracted by the newcomer, his comment on Livingstone, and his colleague Ross, was a model of Scots caution. "They seem to be worthy men," he reports, adding perhaps significantly, "I have endeavoured to impress upon their minds that the first and most important thing they have to do in this country, will be to make peace and live at peace with their brethren."

Bent on reaching Kuruman without loss of time, Livingstone took ship to Algoa Bay. The distance from there was 530 miles and the only means of transport, ox wagon. These great lumbering vehicles were admirable for their purpose. They were houses on wheels, dragged by anything up to eight yoke of oxen. They were driven by natives armed with whips with thongs of great length, made of giraffe skin. Progress was slow, ten to twenty miles a day.

The journey took six weeks and was not an hour too long. Livingstone learned to shoot on the way. Everything teemed with interest, trees, flowers, animals, birds, and above all, people. The pace was slow enough to give ample time for investigation as he went. Day by day, as they climbed, the aspect of the country changed—at last the plateau was reached. Here the air was crisp. It grew cold at dusk and there was frost at night.

It was his first taste of the romance of the camp-fire: of the strange thrill that the innumerable noises of the bush can give. He learned the glorious sense of freedom that wide spaces hold. To one whose life had thus far been cribbed by factory and classroom, and who had recently been cooped up for months in a small ship, it was an intoxicating experience.

On his way he stopped at Hankey, and was much encouraged by what he saw of the Hottentot Christian community there.

His first impressions of Kuruman when he reached it were, however, not so favourable. Indeed, he was disappointed. The station, which lies to the west of Vryburg, was in itself attractive, a long established, and well-equipped mission settlement that the skill and loving care of Dr. Moffat had made beautiful with flowers and fruit trees. But the district around was sterile and un-interesting—wide monotonous expanses, long undulating slopes, a few straggling mimosa trees and thorns innumerable.

Nor did the mission work itself impress him. The number of converts was less than he had expected, and it depressed him to learn that the neighbouring tribes, because of their attachment to polygamy, were still hostile, even after so many years of work.

Although hardly yet three months old in Africa, he had already formed very definite views on certain important aspects of mission policy, and what he saw in Kuruman did not conform to these. It seemed to him wrong that so many missionaries should continue to live in safe and comfortable localities in the South—treading on each other's heels, and sometimes on each other's corns, while innumerable villages in the North remained unvisited. There should be, also, he urged—and this was his second great point—much more use made than there had been, of the help of African workers. These views, which have long become accepted mission policy were, at the time, somewhat premature. Moreover, expressing as they of necessity did, criticism of established practice, they did not sound too well on the lips of a youth of a few months' experience. They were received with coldness, and in these early days personal relations with colleagues were somewhat strained. Had the wise Moffats been at Kuruman the position would have been easier.

2. Days of Waiting and Working

Livingstone's instructions were to wait at Kuruman till the Moffats arrived. The understanding was that he should open a new station farther north as soon as practicable. But the Moffats' return was delayed, and Livingstone's energy had to find a congenial outlet. So, in a very few months we find him, accompanied by a senior colleague, Roger Edwards, on a journey of exploration, the purpose of which was to discover a suitable place for the new settlement. It may well have been that the somewhat uncongenial atmosphere of the Head Station had not a little to do with this early shaping of his destiny.

It should be emphasised that though Livingstone was, by his very nature, a pioneer and explorer, he had not come to Africa with that intent. His was the customary missionary motive. His ambition was to proclaim the Gospel of Christ, and his expectation was to settle somewhere and live there permanently doing the ordinary work of a missionary. For the next eleven years that was what, in general, he actually did. During that time, it is true, he accomplished much "exploration," and he would have disliked, in the ordinary meaning of the term, such a description of his labours. All his effort had a definite missionary purpose. That was to discover localities where white people, but particularly missionaries, could live in health. Nothing hurt him more to the

71

end of his days than to have his missionary vocation called in question. None the less, the passion for exploration, pure and simple, grew in him, probably more quickly and more strongly, than he realised.

It was never his habit of mind, however, to plan ahead. He did the duty that lay before him as he saw it, trusting in God to guide, but he had his own notion as to what was involved in "waiting for guidance." He wrote to his brother Charles a few years later from Kolobeng. "I think you are not clear on the indications of Providence. I don't think we ought to wait for them. Our duty is to go forward and look for the indications as to where Satan hinders. But, in general, I have observed that people who have sat waiting, have sat long enough before they saw any indication to go."

It was, therefore, in search of some place suited for his own residence that, along with Edwards, he travelled northward. In the first year they covered seven hundred miles. It was a pleasant experience. The country was fruitful and thickly-populated and the chiefs were jealously eager to have a missionary live amongst them. The reason of this was not far to seek. Mosilikatse, the dreaded Matebele marauder, by his sudden forays, was keeping the Bechuana tribes in constant turmoil. A white man settled in their midst would, they believed, give them "sleep"—security.

This opportunity of breaking new ground seemed to Livingstone providential, but the senior missionaries doubted and were discouraging.

They advised him to be careful about building on a volcano. Mosilikatse, they told him, had threatened to pounce on any white man and "spill his blood." Threats, however, never frightened Livingstone. Indeed, his unconsciousness of danger was at times his best protection as the following incident will show.

One of the Bechuana tribes which he visited—this time alone—was the Bakaa. This people had a bad name, and had deserved it. A few years before they had killed by poison a white trader and two of his men, and had strangled a third.

There is no trace of boasting in Livingstone's story as he tells it. He was apparently quite unconscious of the risk he ran. He writes:

"As I happened to be the first European who had visited them since this deed of darkness, their consciences loudly accused them, and when I came into their town, except for the chief and two attendants the whole tribe had fled my presence. On their faces they had evidence of perturbation such as I never saw on black faces before. Nothing I could do in the way of appearing perfectly at ease, and squatting down beside them, could remove the almost ludicrous expression of fear; until they got a dish of porridge cooked and when they saw me partake of this without distrust, the act seemed to excite their confidence, but lying down to sleep, in consequence of the fatigue of the long walk, seemed to have the full effect I desired, and they soon came round in considerable numbers."[1]

[1] Letter dated 3rd July, 1842, to Rev. J. Freeman, L.M.S.

Thereafter he adds that he had—and surely deserved—the "more than ordinary pleasure" of delivering his message. It was the first time he had attempted to use the Sechuana language extempore, and it is hardly to be expected that much of meaning went home, but there was little need. The sermon had already been preached.

The first place selected by Edwards and Livingstone was Lepelole in the territory of the Bakwain. The Chief Bubi had given them a most hearty welcome and Livingstone for that reason chose to live here for some months entirely alone. He wished to master thoroughly their language, and study, without distraction, the customs of tribal life.

In both these objects he was markedly successful. He wrote at this time to one of his friends. "I found no difficulty with the language and I am no genius on languages." This remark is typical of his modesty. The truth is, as he was to prove later, that he gained such a complete grasp of this tongue that it made the acquiring of other related languages comparatively simple. But it was a more difficult task than he admitted. "I must," he wrote to Drummond, his friend in Samoa, "form my own vocabulary and nearly construct my own grammar and must mingle with the natives so as to learn their mode of thinking or I shall never be much of a preacher."

The chief Bubi, unfortunately, came to an untimely end. He had quarrelled with his Paramount Chief, Sechele, of whom we shall hear much. On receiving from this man a gift of gun-powder, a substance that was new to him, he thought it suspicious as coming from an un-friendly quarter. He feared it might contain some hidden evil and so to test it he burnt near it a "powerful magic." The explosion that resulted amply justified his suspicions!

It was while on a journey at this time that there occurred the well-known incident which reveals the attitude that he was to adopt later towards slavery.

"When we were on the way a little girl, about eleven years of age, came up and sat under my wagon, having run away with the purpose of com-ing with us to Kuruman. She had lived with a sister, whom she had lately lost by death. Another family took possession of her for the purpose of selling her, when she was old enough for a wife, but not liking this she had run away.

"I was pleased with the determination of the little creature and gave her some food but before long I heard her sobbing as if her heart would break. In looking round I observed the cause. A man with a gun had been sent after her. I did not know well what to do, but Pomare, a native convert, started up and defended her cause. He, being the son of a chief, possessed some little authority and managed the matter nicely. She had been loaded with beads to render her more attract-ive and fetch a higher price. These she slipped off and gave to the man and desired him to go away. I afterwards took measures for hiding her and though fifty men had come for her they would not have got her."[1]

3. Two Years of Apprenticeship

In one of his tours Livingstone traversed part of the Kalahari Desert and there received a very friendly reception from Sekomi, the chief of the Bamangwato. This man was the father of the celebrated Christian Chief Khama, whose visit to England in 1895 to petition, among other things, for the prohibition of the sale of alcoholic liquors in his territory, is still remembered. He was also the grandfather of Tshekedi, now the Chief of the tribe.

These journeys, the work of his first year, laid the foundation of his remarkable knowledge of African customs. He had an instinctive appreciation of and sympathy with, primitive intelligence. "It is clear," says Professor Coupland, "that he had a peculiar gift of seeing what lay at the back of the native mind. Irrational suspicions, mysterious motives, ridiculous arguments, he could understand and deal with them all."[2]

Especially he delighted in and learned much from, chats innumerable with his men round the camp-fire. Many yarns that he heard reminded him of the clan stories his father used to tell. "The uncertain flickering light, catching the dim

[1] *Blaikie*, chap. III.
[2] *Kirk on the Zambezi*, page 40.

outline of dark faces and showing up, in sharp relief, the whites of the eyes and the sheen of the smiling teeth." He loved it all. He enjoyed their merry laughter and his hearty response mingled with theirs.

He was not, in spite of his many other activities, allowed to forget that he was a doctor. Indeed his reputation in Kuruman grew so embarrassingly that, before long, he had to restrict his practice. His attitude towards his profession was curious. In writing to his tutor, Mr. Cecil, about this time, he speaks of the kind of "mania" that seized him when he first studied medicine and feared that, if he practised much in Africa, it might seize him again. That would make him, perhaps, a good doctor, but it would turn him into "a useless drone of a missionary." "I feel," he added, "this self denial very much." Though "Nyaka" (doctor) was one of his best-known native names, he was always more the preacher than the doctor. He never built a hospital and on furlough he did not "rub up" his medical knowledge. His scientific training was useful to him mainly in that it educated his naturally powerful mind in keen observation and accurate recording. Throughout life he devoted himself with amazing success to the study of botany, zoology, geology and anthropology. In none of these subjects had systematic training been possible for him. He used such books as came his way, but it was sheer force of genius alone that soon enabled him to become the highly-appreciated correspondent of some of the first specialists of his day. The information he sent them was of priceless value. It was a wonderful achievement for one whose life was always full of manifold other duties.

These first two years were exacting but fruitful. The young missionary had developed rapidly. The greatness of the man was becoming evident, and Africa had been his instructor. Physically he had changed. He was still spare, but the filling out of his chest and the tightening of his muscles was making appropriate the adjective "stocky" afterwards generally applied to him.

He was fond of chuckling over a prank he played on his porters about this time:

"Some of my companions," he wrote, "who had recently joined us and did not know that I understood a little of their speech were overheard by me discussing my appearance and powers. ' He is not strong. He is quite thin. He only appears stout because he puts himself into these bags (trousers). He will soon knock up.' This caused my Highland blood to rise and made me disguise fatigue by keeping them all at top speed for days together until I heard them expressing proper opinions of my pedestrian powers."

It is worth recording here that on this tour the caravan came within ten days' journey of Ngami, the lake, to the discovery of which he was, a few years later, to devote so much energy. Yet, though he knew, he did not turn aside to investigate. This would seem to prove that the passion for exploration that grew so strong later was then hardly born.

4. Settled at Last

In June, 1843, permission to begin the new station arrived. The word "go forward" brought Livingstone "inexpressible delight." He added, "I am willing to go anywhere, provided it be forward."

The same post brought further good news. An old friend, Mrs. MacRobert, the wife of the minister of the Congregational Church at Cambuslang, had promised, in the name of the congregation, £12 annually to support a native teacher. This encouraged him greatly as it enabled him to begin his plan of using African helpers, and in his enthusiasm, with that generosity that ran so close to prodigality, of which his life gives so many examples, he promised, out of his salary of £100, a similar amount for the same purpose. His faith thus reinforced, he looked forward with all the eagerness of his intense nature to the splendid prospect he saw ahead of him.

Troubles he had, however, in plenty. Shortly before he had met with one of those crippling little accidents of which he had his full share, so many indeed as to suggest more than occasional absent-mindedness. One day, while coming down a steep pass, accompanied by some Natives, to whom he was talking, his mind absorbed in the difficulty of their speech, he slipped and struck his hand between a rock and the bible he was carrying. A finger suffered a compound fracture. The wound healed quickly but before the bones were completely united there came in the middle of the night a sudden visit from a lion. In the confusion that followed Livingstone seized and fired a heavy pistol. The recoil was so sharp that it reopened the wound and the second state was much worse than the first. He found comfort, however, in the sympathy and helpfulness of his Bakwain.

The original intention had been to make Lepelolo the new headquarters, but the death of Bubi and a sudden movement of the tribe due to enemy pressure made the site unsuitable. Mabotsa, in the territory of the Bakhatla, a tribe related to the Bakwain, was chosen. It was situated 220 miles north east of Kuruman and not far from where Mafeking now stands. It was a most desirable situation, in many ways a happy contrast to Kuruman. It lay at the foot of picturesque hills and was surrounded by fine wooded country in which game abounded. There was water in plenty. The district was thickly populated and the people were industrious. They excelled in iron work. The drawback to Livingstone's mind was that though the tribe was friendly it showed no religious interest, no inclination to give heed to his message.

The first task, and a laborious one, was to build a house. It had to be large since it had to serve not only as dwelling house but as school and church. He and his colleagues received no help in the work. The industrious Bakhatla lent no hand.

The main comfort at this time came from the

Chief Sechele, who had at first shown a jealous and unfriendly front. He had resented their early association with Bubi. It was Livingstone's medicine that opened that door. The Chief's only child, and a child also of one of his headmen, happened to be seriously ill when Livingstone visited his town. He treated both successfully and a friendship was sealed which lasted through life.

Sechele was in many ways a remarkable man. He was baptised after five years of training and probation, and was the young Missionary's first convert. Not an entirely satisfactory one, as it proved, but in the end a stalwart and upright Christian, who had to suffer many things for his faith. A typical Bantu in features, somewhat corpulent, very dark but with fine large eyes—"Black Sechele" he was called. He was a man of considerable mental gifts—a fluent speaker and, as so many Africans are, an effective orator. He learnt to read quickly, mastering the alphabet in one day. He came to have a real appreciation of the beauties of the bible. "He was a fine man that Isaiah. He knew how to speak," he remarked after reading one of the great chapters of that book. He proved himself one of the Doctor's most loyal friends—and suffered, too, for the friendship.

5. *The Lion and Livingstone*

Mabotsa was infested by lions. Since game was abundant, they did not in general molest the cattle. The Bakhatla did not greatly fear them and, when needs must, attacked them boldly, armed only with spears.

Livingstone was rather fond of "debunking" the lion. "Nothing I have ever heard of the lion, would lead me to attribute to it, either the noble or the ferocious character ascribed to it." But there were exceptions, and one occurred while Edwards and he were busy with their house-building. The adventure nearly cost Livingstone his life, but at the same time gave him a great standing with the tribe.

In this case a troop of lions was taking heavy toll of the herds. They leaped into the cattle-kraals and killed the cows. They even attacked the watchers in daylight. This was so unusual that the people came to believe themselves bewitched, "given over to the lions" of another tribe. The troop was led by an animal of unusual size.

Livingstone was no lion hunter. He never shot merely for sport but on this occasion he went because the people needed encouragement. He was working at his house when the summons came. He seized his gun, threw on his tartan coat, and ordering Mebalwe, his teacher, to follow, hurried out to where the hunt was in progress. One beast had been located on a small bush-covered hill and the hunters had drawn a circle round it and were closing in slowly. From the lower level on which they stood they could see the lion seated on a rock and Mebalwe fired over the head of the hunters. The bullet struck the rock on which the animal sat. He snarled and bit at the spot where the bullet had hit, as a dog does at a stick thrown at him. Then he leaped up, broke through the circle, and escaped.

Two more lions were spotted. Another circle was formed but once again the animals burst through. The men seemed afraid to face them. It looked as if all had escaped, and Livingstone and the teacher were moving back to the village when, passing round the bend of a hill, they saw plainly, thirty yards away, a lion of huge size seated on a knoll above them. Except that a little bush came between, the sighting was good and Livingstone gave him both barrels.

"He is shot, he is shot!" shouted the people. "I saw," wrote Livingstone, "the lion's tail erect in anger and turning to the people said, ' Stop a little, till I load.' When in the act of ramming down the bullets I heard a shout, and looking half round saw the lion in the act of springing on me. He caught me by the shoulder and we both came to the ground together. Growling horribly he shook me as a terrier dog does a rat. It caused a sort of dreaminess in which there was no sense of pain or feeling of terror, though I was conscious of all that happened. As he had one paw on the back of my head I turned round to relieve myself and saw his eyes directed to Mebalwe." The teacher fired twice. The flints missed but the noise was enough to distract the beast which sprang on the African and bit him in the thigh. A second man who tried to help was also wounded. The bullets then began to take effect and the spear of a third African finished the work.

When he was, in later days, asked as to what he was thinking of during these exciting moments, he used to answer with a twinkle in his eye: "I was wondering which part of me he would eat first!"

The consequences were very serious. For three months he suffered terribly though, with the taciturnity he invariably shows in all personal matters, he says nothing. Skilled nursing was, of course, not available. Edwards did his best and under the patient's directions set the splintered bone. A false joint in the "upper third of the humerus" resulted. That the eleven ugly gashes the brute's teeth had made caused comparatively little trouble, Livingstone ascribed to the fact that he was wearing a woollen tartan jacket, which kept the poison from the wound. He used to say that he had a "joint too many in his arm." To make matters worse, not long afterwards he slipped while on a scaffold and, to save himself, caught hold of a beam with the damaged arm. This severed the false joint and caused excruciating pain.

He never again had full use of the limb. The bone might at times have been seen sticking up under his coat. A man who met him fifteen years later spoke of the mauled arm as hanging idle, and as being "usually much indulged." It was painful for him to raise the left arm to any position above the elbow.

What a handicap! How much it must have added to his discomfort in his 20,000 miles of travel and how very rarely he refers to it. It spoiled his shooting. He could not depend on his aim unless he could rest the barrel on a branch or some other object. This, for a man on whose hunting the caravan had frequently to depend, was a very serious disadvantage.

6. Marriage

In his private correspondence up to about the date that our story had now reached—i.e., 1843— Livingstone makes frequent reference to his bachelor state. He claimed half ruefully, half humorously, that celibacy was better for a man of his kind of life and prospects. How far this was pose, how far genuine, it is impossible to judge, but news that the Moffat family was on the High Seas was no doubt to him all the more interesting when he learned that Mary, their eldest daughter, was with them. He had heard much of her, for she had been born and brought up in Kuruman.

The lion may well have caused a change of outlook on this subject. In his long weary days of illness and convalescence, he must often have craved for some softening of the roughness of pioneer life, for something of the comfort and refinement that a woman can bring. Edwards—not a congenial companion at best—had done all he could, but was an incompetent nurse. As soon as he was able to move with safety, therefore, the patient went to Kuruman for better treatment and there waited.

January brought word of the Moffat party's approach and Livingstone—his arm still probably in a sling—a romantic invalid, rode a hundred and fifty miles—as far that is as to the river Vaal, to meet the party. Edwards had set out with him but, unable to secure a horse, had returned.

This is, as far as we know, the first meeting with Mary. There is no record of her first impressions, but Dr. Moffat doubtless spoke for all when he wrote of the pleasant surprise. "Such a visitant as Mr. Livingstone in the wild wilderness was to us a most refreshing circumstance. Few can conceive the hallowed feeling his presence gave."

Young Livingstone's own account of the important events that followed is most meagre. All he says is, "After nearly four years of African life as a bachelor I screwed up my courage to put a question beneath one of the fruit trees (at Kuruman) the result of which was that in 1844 I became united in marriage to Dr. Moffat's eldest daughter, Mary." Local tradition still points to a particular almond tree as the spot. Like many other men, Livingstone could not remember the correct date of his own wedding! Actually just a year after their first meeting, on the second of January, 1845, the two were united by Dr. Moffat in the old church that still stands in Kuruman. No formal register was kept and the record may be seen in Moffat's handwriting in the minute book of the church.

The marriage was an ideal one. They were excellently suited. Mrs. Livingstone's training in Africa equipped her admirably to be the bride of a pioneer. As befitted the daughter of a remarkable mother, Mary was an excellent housewife and a woman of cultured instincts.

In spite of his scorn of anything like luxury, Livingstone speaks enthusiastically of the comfort and refinement that his wife brought into his life. But even his most devoted admirers cannot claim for him adroitness in conveying to others the sense of his wife's charm. In a private letter sent soon after the marriage, the bridegroom describes her as a "not romantic but a matter-of-fact lady, a little, thick, black haired girl, sturdy and all I want." Was Mary shown that letter it may be wondered? Well, "all I want" was the main matter and a very adequate description. Still, the pictures that exist of the lady in middle age—there are none of an earlier date—show a face that merits more praise. Well-shaped features, somewhat heavy it is true, but good eyes and a fine placid brow. She had more claim to good looks than her husband ever had. One observer records of her that she was scrupulously tidy in dress even in the trying conditions of African travel and even in a wagon was able to create some semblance of a comfortable home.

Mary Moffat's share in the great story should not be overlooked. Her disregard of hardship was almost equal to his. One of Livingstone's biographers, who spoke from experience, writes, "The settler's life in an outpost is always hard, but for a young wife and mother it is hard beyond words."[1] The Livingstones' mutual affection was profound, if not demonstrative. The enforced separation that his long journeys entailed was the great sacrifice of their life and of this she, because of her marked dependance on him, had to bear the heavier share. Her death, in 1862, was a shattering blow from which Livingstone never fully recovered.

It may be noted, in passing, how little—apart from his wife—female influence counted in the Explorer's life. The mother's care sweetened the Blantyre home, but it was the father who dominated. The Catherine Ridley romance was a fleeting phase. In a life so unusually rich in male friendships there, was no woman except his sisters and his mother-in-law, with whom he corresponded. Mary's devotion was, therefore, all the more deeply valued and it was given without stint.

7. Mabotsa—the First Home

The young couple entered upon their new life with enthusiasm. He was now able to put to the test some of the many plans with which his brain

[1] *Nyaka.* W. Elliot. Page 16.

seethed. He knew already and was to learn in Mabotsa ever more clearly, the stiffness of their task. The people were unusually superstitious and unresponsive, but the difficulties only braced him. His favourite Scots proverb—"A stout hairt to a stey brae"—was often on his lips. The life was full of interests for both. Mary had her infant school; he, his preaching and labour of a hundred kinds. "I have now," he writes, "the happy prospect before me of real missionary work. All that has preceded has been preparatory." In another letter he puts in a nutshell one great secret of his powers. "I have a great objection to school keeping, but I find in that, as in everything else I set myself to as a matter of duty, I become enamoured of it."

This year, however, full of happiness as it was had also some very painful incidents. Keener than ever on his plan for the use of trained Africans as evangelists, he drafted and submitted to his colleagues a scheme for a seminary. He met with no support. Some thought the times too unsettled, but some others were uncharitable enough to impute to him personal motives; the wish to win favour with the Directors and the desire to become a professor! This hurt him grievously and the sting of it remained long. He abandoned the plan. Later it was carried through by other hands.

Soon, too, a painful difference arose with his colleague that made harmonious working impossible. Edwards was an artisan missionary, a worthy man, no doubt, but prone to take offence and

magnify trifles. He was eighteen years the senior
and apt to insist upon his greater experience. It
was a delicate situation in which petty grievances
tended to grow and be remembered. In African
eyes the younger was so obviously the abler that
the older would inevitably be passed over and
Edwards could hardly be expected to accept the
position without some protest. But he took the
wrong way of objecting. He wrote a long letter
to the Home Directors, the gist of which was that
he, Edwards, was not prepared to play second
fiddle to a junior.

While impartial opinion would clear Livingstone of any fault in this most unfortunate dispute,
it would still have a good deal of sympathy left
over for Edwards. The truth is that Livingstone
was of a personality so powerful that he could not
but lead in whatever company he found himself.
Born to dominate, he was apt, on occasion, quite
unwittingly, to domineer. Oswell the hunter,
one of his best and most appreciative friends, who
comes so delightfully into the story a few years
later, puts the position neatly thus. "One trait in
his character was to do exactly whatever he set his
mind on. . . . It was not the *sic volo sic jubeo*
style of imperiousness but a quiet determination
to carry out his views in his own way without
feeling himself bound to give any reason or
explanation further than that he intended doing so
and so. It was an immense help to him, for it
made him supremely self-reliant and if it had not
been, he never could have done half that he did."

Livingstone's work was a marvel and he himself a miracle of grace, but the greatness of his achievement is best understood if it be realised that he had his share of human limitations, and the weaknesses of his strength; that his struggle was not merely against "principalities and powers" but often, like the rest of mankind, against himself; against unregenerate patches here and there and the outcrop, now and again, of Highland pride and Covenanting dourness.

As was to be expected, the Directors of the L.M.S. had not, up till then, got the true measure of this outsize missionary. They thought him unbalanced and impulsive and were slow to support his plans.

All these things greatly puzzled and distressed him. His only wish was to live at peace and get on with the great work, and this he could not do in an atmosphere of criticism and irritation. He solved the difficulty in his own heroic way. He surrendered to his partner the station that he had laboured so hard to build and the rough house that Mary had made a home, and trekked once more farther north. It was no light parting. Following his father-in-law's example he had made a garden, and he grudged to leave it. Further, the financial difficulty was severe. One hundred pounds a year left little margin and as the Society did not relish frequent changes, he had himself to bear a good deal of the cost.

It is at least satisfactory that Edwards was so much impressed by his colleague's generosity, that he let it be understood that if he had known their purpose of moving he would not have spoken against them as he had done. Obviously, however, in the end it was for the best; for the full scope of the work he was to do, it was necessary that he should be untrammelled by partners of restricted outlook. From now on, except for the short period of the Zambezi Expedition, he was to work alone.

8. Still on the Move

The place selected for the next halt was Chonuane, a village in Bakwain country, some forty miles farther north. It was a hurried and unfortunate choice.

Sechele was the Paramount Chief here also, and a good friend, but water was soon found to be scarce and the aggression of the Boers was raising an ever-increasingly acute problem. They had by this time extended their influence to the western border of the district now called the Transvaal, and were claiming jurisdiction over the native population.

Accompanied by his wife, Livingstone made occasional short trips from Chonuane eastward in the direction of Magaliesberg. She was somewhat ailing at the time and the change did her good. His purpose in these short journeys was to discover what opportunity existed for the settlement of African teachers among the people in the wide plains beyond. As Africa counts, the population was dense. He had a chance "to preach at least once every day." The people were industrious and their Chief Mokhatla friendly. He could, however, give no promise without permission of the Dutch commandant. This man received favourably the suggestion that Mebalwe should be stationed there, but unfortunately, a neighbouring farmer was of different temper and announced his opinion that the only proper way to treat a native missionary was to shoot him! Wisely deciding that it would be unfair to expose his African helper to hostility so unreasoning, Livingstone postponed the matter. It was about this time and apparently on Mabotsa that their first child, Robert, was born.

It is necessary, at this point, to say something of the antagonism that had grown up between many of the Dutch farmers and the missionaries, especially as Livingstone took a prominent part in the controversy. It is a subject on which there is even now difference of opinion. In South Africa, in certain circles, there is still the belief that Livingstone's criticisms were unduly severe and that he prejudiced British opinion against the Boer community.

What is said in *Missionary Travels*—Livingstone's first book—of the treatment of the Bechuana people by the farmers is expressed, it is true, with characteristic forthrightness. But Livingstone is careful to state that his complaint is not against the Cape Dutch, but against the hotter spirits who had "fled from English law," and had been joined by "bad characters." The conflict was, however, not personal but on a fundamental issue—on the proper treatment of Black by White, and in speaking and acting as he did, Livingstone was simply sustaining the historic rôle, in South Africa, of the London Missionary Society, of Philip, Moffat, and later of John MacKenzie. As a curious illustration of the way in which the L.M.S. had come to be regarded by the Boers, the fact may be mentioned that in a provisional constitution adopted by a section of them in 1837 at Winburg, it was decreed that "all should join in a solemn oath to have no connection with the London Missionary Society."[1]

The original immigrants, though narrow-minded and often illiterate, were, according to their lights, God-fearing men, capable of genuine heroism, but their success attracted many others of a lower type. It was not long before they began to subject the Black to a system of compulsory service, that was often hard to distinguish from slavery, and which could be carried out only by force.

To the Natives they said, "We have driven out your enemy the Zulu. You live here in safety because of us. In return you must give us so many days a year of free labour. You must weed, manure and reap our fields." These demands were sometimes backed up by the seizure of the water holes, and there was nothing left for the Blacks to do but to submit or emigrate. Livingstone gives instances of worse things: of raids when cattle were appropriated: when women and children were captured and retained as household slaves.

[1] Theal. *Progress of South Africa in the Century*, page 228.

In all these controversies the missionaries had naturally been on the side of the African and frequent protests had been made by their Societies to the Home Authorities. Since, however, at that time the power of the Cape Government did not extend so far north, the Boers regarded such appeals merely as impertinent interferences and many of them put every possible obstacle in the way of mission work among the tribes.

Livingstone was a fighter by nature and when, as in this instance, his feelings were deeply involved, he said many hard things, as he did later against the Portuguese. It is only fair to remember, however, that the Boers were at that time a self-contained community who had lived in isolation and unchanged since they left Europe. As has been well said, it was an instance of seventeenth-century standards coming suddenly into contact with nineteenth-century ideals. The views which the farmers held were those that had been entertained by Dr. Samuel Johnson, by John Newton and men of their day. To all these the Negro was a lower type of man, if indeed fully human.

It need hardly be added that this attitude to mission work has long since become a thing of the past. The Dutch Reformed Church, to which most of the Voortrekkers belonged, has for the last forty years been in the forefront of missionary activities in some of the districts that Livingstone explored.

Thus far the Doctor had had but small satisfaction in his work as a missionary. The Bakhatla had showed little response. In one of his moments of depression he wrote of them, "You cannot expect wolves to be turned into sheep dogs in a generation." Nor were the Bakwain as a tribe much more susceptible.

The main obstacle was, undoubtedly, the deeply-entrenched social system of polygamy. To cleave to one wife and put away all others, involving as it did much disturbance of the tribal life, seemed to the ordinary African not only impossible but unjust. Livingstone was himself not quite clear in his own mind on the subject. He wrote thus to his friend Watt in regard to Sechele's difficulties in this matter. "On the subject of admitting (to church membership) a man who has more than one wife . . . though not clear that I ought to refuse, I am glad that I have not been asked to baptise a polygamist." He followed, however, the usual missionary custom, to which when he was baptised, the Chief conformed.

9. The Rain Maker

One great trouble in Chonuane was the continued shortage of rain. It was a trial also to Livingstone's faith, for the rain passed over the Bakwain and fell plentifully on the land of the tribes who had no missionary! And, in the way natural to them, the people put these two uncomfortable facts together. "We like you," said one, "as well as if you had been born among us but we wish you would give up your everlasting praying and preaching. We can't get used to that. You see, we never get rain, and the tribes that never pray as we do, get plenty."

With the frankness and sense of humour that he so often shows, Livingstone gives an account of an argument he once had with a medicine man on that subject.

He begins:

"You have plenty of medicines with you this morning."

"Very true," answers the Rain Doctor. "For the whole country needs the rain I am making."

"So you really believe you can command the clouds. I think that can be done by God alone."

"We both believe the same thing," comes the reply. "It is God who makes the rain. I pray to Him by means of medicines and when the rain comes it is mine. I have made rain for the Bakwain for many years. By my wisdom, too, the women are fat and shining."

"But," says Livingstone, "we are told in the parting words of our Saviour, that we can pray acceptably only in His name, and not by means of medicines."

"True, but God told *us* differently. He made the Black man first and did not love us as He did the White man. He made you beautiful and gave you guns and things we know nothing about. He gave us knowledge of certain medicines by which we make rain. You should not despise our little knowledge though you are ignorant of it."

Livingstone had to admit that his own arguments not only were ineffective, but were even likely to produce the impression that he himself was not anxious that rain should fall. So he turns to a practical method of rain-making that they could not but feel convincing. The following description of his tactfulness in dealing with his people refers to an incident that happened two years later, but is appropriate here.

"I wished water to irrigate a garden and explained my way of making rain. They were delighted and the Chief sent as many men as I needed. We raised a huge dam of earth and stones and dug a canal. The whole labour was performed by themselves. I was unable after the first day to stimulate them as I had wished, on account of having got both legs and arms severely sunburnt and that too although most of the time immersed in the water.

"The digging was performed by sharpened sticks. When they came to a large stone, they just dug round it. So it is quite of a zigzag form. The earth was lifted out in handfuls and carried in their karosses, a wooden bowl and a tortoise shell.

"I have been astonished at the industry of these wild ignorant heathen, as the early missionaries could never get them to work. At Kuruman the missionaries were obliged to perform most of the manual labour themselves. I am quite ignorant of the scientific way of irrigation. It was almost all guess work and with trembling heart I watched till I saw the water assume its new course.

"You can with ingenuity lead this people to work, but you can never drive them. They are mere children, as easily pleased as babies. But if you are habitually kind to anyone in particular you will spoil him and get the envy of the rest."

There was, however, one difficulty that no ingenuity could counter—the rapid desiccation of the country; the drying up of familiar streams and water holes. This was a matter that engaged his attention deeply at this time. It was particularly marked in Chonuane district. In consequence, Livingstone soon decided that another move had become necessary, and this water difficulty combined with the dread of Boer aggressiveness, enabled him with little opposition to persuade Sechele to countenance yet another change. The tribe was transferred to a site on the bank of the Kolobeng, at that time a free-flowing river. The situation chosen was forty miles north-west of Chonuane.

Livingstone habitually made light of hardship and despised the "whiner," but there can be no question that these frequent changes must have been a heavy trial, especially to the young wife. For him the drudgery of so much building, with the handicaps of a damaged arm and little native help, must also have been very severe. Three new settlements in five years! Three groups of buildings put up largely by his own labour! Three wilderness gardens to be civilised! Three rough houses to be made homelike!

It is somewhat pathetic to learn that none of

these halting places on which so much loving labour had been lavished became places of permanent residence. Mabotsa did not thrive after the Livingstones left. Edwards moved elsewhere. The stations were forsaken and soon became heaps of rubble and mud, overgrown with thorns. Comparatively recently, however, at the instigation of General Smuts, Mabotsa and Chonuane have been taken under the care of the Union Government, and Kolobeng, which lies in the Bechuanaland Protectorate, is being looked after by that Administration.

10. A Home at Last : Kolobeng

The five years that followed were the happiest in the experience of the Livingstone family; were indeed, except for a few feverish months during the first furlough, the only time of real home life that they ever enjoyed.

Kolobeng was built on the eastern edge of the Kalahari Desert. The native town—newly erected —stood as Oswell put it, "in naked deformity on the side of and under a ridge of red iron sandstone, the mission house on a rocky eminence over the river."

The settling in was uncomfortable. The move had been sudden. No house was, of course, ready, and the young family suffered the inconvenience of life in a draughty hut "through which the wind blew our candles into glorious icicles (as the poet would say) and the flies settled on the eyes of the poor little brats by day." Mabotsa was often regretted, so "beautiful for situation, so full of happy memories." Of all the hurts that Livingstone suffered, nothing cut him so deeply as being forced to leave that much-loved spot. The wound continued to throb throughout life. It was recalled in letters to friends written twenty years later.

It seems strange that one who met unfairness with such magnanimity should have found it so difficult to forget. This "hardness of heart," as no doubt he would have called it, troubled him. On one of the rare occasions when he revealed the inner workings of his mind, he wrote to his intimate friend, Dr. Risdon Bennett, thus, "I often think I have forgiven, as I hope to be forgiven, but the remembrance of the slander often comes boiling up, although I hate to think of it. You must remember me in your prayers that more of the spirit of Christ may be imparted to me."

These years in Kolobeng, were, except when he was on journeys, absorbed by the ordinary duties of a missionary, save that, because of his great versatility and overflowing energy, his tasks were much more varied than usual. In a letter dated 1848 he gives this account of his daily routine. "We get up generally with the sun: then have family worship, breakfast and school, and as soon as these are over we begin the manual operations needed, sawing, ploughing, smithy work and any other sort of work by turns as required. My better half is employed all morning in culinary and other work and feels pretty well tired by dinner time. We take about an hour of rest then, but, more frequently without the respite I try to secure for myself, she goes off to hold infant school and this, I am happy to say, is very popular with the youngsters. My manual labour continues till five o'clock. I then go into the town to give lessons and talk to any who may be disposed for it. As soon as the cows are milked we have a meeting—this is followed by a prayer meeting in Sechele's house, which brings me home about half past eight and generally tired enough—too fatigued to think of any mental exertion."[1]

His religious work had now grown much more satisfactory. There seemed more understanding and response. But he was willing to wait and feared superficial results. "Nothing will induce me," he declared, "to form an impure church." It was with Sechele that he found most satisfaction and also, sad to say, all too soon, keenest disappointment. The Chief had become, his teacher believed, a devout Christian. He had accepted the consequences of discipleship and had—an exceedingly hard thing for an African chief to do—renounced polygamy.

It was a great day for the Livingstones when Sechele was baptised. It seemed the crown of all their efforts, the full recompense for all their troubles. He wrote home to the Directors in a tone of triumphant thanksgiving, but the tribe resented the defection of their Chief hotly. To them it

[1] *Blaikie*, chap. V.

seemed that he had broken faith with the tribal spirits and they treated him publicly with contumely. Though before his baptism he would have destroyed any man who spoke one disrespectful word against him, he bore the humiliation with a patience that did Livingstone's heart good to watch. And then, within nine months, the Chief was convicted of having broken his vows; of having cohabited with one of his former wives, whom, being without parents, he had not been able to send home.

It was a staggering blow, made not the less hard by the fact that the Missionary was, as we have seen, not clear in his own mind as to how he should deal with such a case. No one knew better than he, how disturbing to tribal life a rigid application of this New Testament principle might become.

But the problem having arisen in this acute form, for a man of Livingstone's moral integrity, there could be no shirking of consequences. Although sincere penitence was shown and mitigating circumstances recognised, Sechele was "cut off from the fellowship" and put under church discipline. For a chief, accustomed to the reverence of his people, the punishment was terribly severe, but so great was Livingstone's influence over him that he accepted the decision with loyal humility. (It may be added that he was, in due course, restored to church membership and continued, into old age, a consistent Christian).

A few months later further embarrassments

arose. Serious moral irregularities amongst members of the families of some of his teachers came to light. They, too, were expelled; but grievous harm had been done. So, when the Missionary wrote that nothing would induce him to form an impure church, he was using no empty phrase.

The work of these five years was exactly of the type that in his student days Livingstone had looked forward to, and in which he believed he would find complete satisfaction. But contentment did not come. His eyes were already on wider horizons. The "Unknown North" had begun to draw him like a magnet. Phrases like "Providence seems to call me to regions beyond," and "I will go whoever opposes," begin to appear with increasing frequency in his letters. The restlessness of the pioneer was growing. It was becoming obvious, too, that the change of station had given only a temporary respite from Boer hostility. Indeed, Sechele had become a special object of their enmity.

The reason for this was that the Farmers were anxious to prevent the tribes from acquiring firearms and for this reason had ordered Sechele to close the road from the South along which the traders passed. This ran through his territory. They threatened drastic consequences if he refused, and when he ignored their orders, the Boers, not unnaturally, attributed his recalcitration to Livingstone's presence in Kolobeng. It was rumoured among them that the Chief possessed many guns and it was alleged, quite unjustly, that the Missionary had sold these to him. Livingstone had been complained about to the Cape Government as a dangerous person, and his deportation had been demanded.

All this distressed him because it made the prospects of mission work in those districts more than doubtful. He saw that in the long run the Bantu could not continue to resist the White Man's pressure. Hence his gaze turned north to the country beyond the fearsome Kalahari Desert. Stories of thickly-peopled lands, of great rivers and lakes, had reached him. There, if only healthy sites could be found, he would establish work that the Boers could not spoil, since their cattle dare not face the waterless desert. So more and more the ambition grew to become a missionary pioneer and explorer; to open up the mysterious North and find healthy places for missionary homes.

Then, providentially, there occurred a circumstance, or a set of circumstances, that helped him greatly towards the realisation of his dream.

11. The Coming of the Hunters

The visits of his friends the big game hunters may fairly be claimed as a major influence in Livingstone's life, not only from the point of view of exploration, but also of his personal development.

As has already been said he had a genius for friendship, and few men have been so fortunate in their friends. Africa then provided the best hunting opportunities in the world and it was customary for men of means to spend their holidays there, partly with a view to exploration but mainly for the shooting. Not a few such hunters passed through Chonuane and Kolobeng. They were, without doubt, happy to enjoy Mrs. Livingstone's delightful hospitality, and the help and advice that her husband was so competent to give.

It was in this way that Livingstone acquired some of his best friends—Steele, Oswell, Murray, Webb—all men of a fine type, of social standing and university education and, at the same time, religious and sympathetic to his work. One and all they were attracted to him and, long before he became famous, valued his friendship and set themselves to promote his interests. They spoke of him among themselves affectionately as the "little man," respected him profoundly, and deferred to his knowledge of African ways. This is all the more remarkable since Livingstone strongly disapproved of their methods as hunters. Splendid men as they were, and most kindly in all human relationships, they, on occasions, indulged in an indiscriminate slaughter of wild life that filled him, as it fills the modern reader, with something like disgust.

Livingstone in his downright way called it "butchery," and that he did not hold his opinions unexpressed we gather from a sentence by Oswell. "I am afraid he despised the rôle of sportsman but would fain believe that his grand work was occasionally made a little smoother by the guns." Livingstone often speaks with admiration of the daring and skill of these Nimrods, but he asserted frequently that, except for food, it was wrong needlessly to destroy animal life.

In this, as in so much else, he was a man before his time. In his instructions to the members of the Zambesi Expedition, he wrote, "The wanton waste of animal life I have witnessed from night hunting, and the ferocious but childlike abuse of instruments of destruction . . . make me anxious that none of my companions should be guilty of similar abominations." None the less, he enjoyed these men's company as much as they did his. The arrival of the hunters became probably the great event of his year. They were almost his sole contact with civilisation. Easy social intercourse with men of cultured minds must have been like nectar to one starved intellectually as he necessarily was.

Of Captain (later General Sir) Thomas Steele he wrote, "He is the politest of the whole—Well versed in the classics and possessed of much general knowledge." This man helped him to fame by becoming his intermediary with the Royal Geographical Society. Of Mungo Murray, companion in the Lake Ngami discovery, and of Captain Vardon, of the Madras Infantry, less is known. But they were men of the same type.

Acquaintance with Mr. W. F. Webb, his host for many months at Newstead Abbey, in 1865, was also made at this time in a dramatic way. Word

reached Kolobeng that a white man was very ill
with fever in camp some distance away. Livingstone hurried to his aid and reached him in time.
This benefit was never forgotten.

But probably the most valuable friendship of
these years was that of W. Cotton Oswell, an
Indian Civilian, one of Dr. Arnold's old boys; a
man of fine gifts and magnificent physique. A
hunter of complete fearlessness, he valued his
friendship with Livingstone as perhaps the outstanding good fortune of his life. "I love him,"
wrote the Doctor, "and I think he loves me though
we never show it." Rich and generous, he financed
their joint expeditions. Magnanimous to a degree,
he refused to claim his proper share in the honour
of the discoveries that brought Livingstone renown. In the months that they travelled together
Oswell came to know his companion perhaps more
intimately than did any other friend, and his
admiration was unbounded.

It was not a little significant that among the
pall-bearers at the funeral in Westminster Abbey
a quarter of a century later, three were friends
from this company—Oswell, Webb and Steele.

12. Problems New and Old

Association with these travellers would not tend
to lessen the restlessness that was growing yearly
more marked. The longer he stayed in Kolobeng
the clearer it became that it could not be his

permanent home. The increasing desiccation of the country was becoming evident here also. The river was drying up.

This made Livingstone think hard. The whole population of South Bechuanaland could not be more than twelve thousand. Why should he not cross the Kalahari and open up work in the country beyond, amongst the people of Sebituane, the chief of wide repute who was reported to be anxious to meet him?

He would discuss these problems with his friends and always into the conversations would come the name of this Lake Ngami, then the lodestar of African explorers. Livingstone had had thoughts of visiting it since he landed in Africa. He had been within ten days' travel of it in his first year. Now the way was opening up and if only his friends would join him and share the cost it should not be an over difficult task.

Expense was increasingly one of his hardest problems. One hundred pounds a year might perhaps keep in moderate comfort a family that lived a stationary life, but for one that moved about constantly, as the Livingstones did, it meant much hardship. He was never one to "cut his coat to his cloth." His schemes were generally much beyond his means. So he had to pay the balance of the bill in privations. Each of his changes of location had cost him heavily. All the journeys had to be paid out of his own pocket. Hence his salary was generally overdrawn, and sometimes the family even on the verge of actual want.

In a letter to the Rev. A. Tidman, in 1848, he wrote, "I can bear what other Europeans would count hunger and thirst without any inconvenience, but when we arrived (at Kuruman) to hear old women, who had seen my wife depart, two years before, exclaiming, 'Bless me how lean she is—— Has he starved her? Is there no food in the country in which he has been? This was more than I could bear." If it had not been for Mrs. Moffat, the Lady Bountiful of Kuruman, they would often have been hard pressed. It is true that when appealed to, the London Missionary Society authorised him to draw £30 above the usual salary but still his financial margin was always narrow.

The hunter friends had added to his expenses in a rather amusing way, by making him self-conscious about his clothes!

In a letter to his tailor, Henry Drummond, of Glasgow, these instructions appear.

"For jackets, I should like something that my good lady calls *respectable* and which though I can catch the idea, I cannot describe. We have gentlemen from India, occasionally as visitors, and others, as officers of the Army, coming up, on hunting expeditions. Now it sounds rather discordant when we hear the title 'Doctor' applied to a poor fellow in a fustian[1] jacket. You must have seen the sort of fustian, which after a shower, assumes a peculiar crumpled appearance." Trousers

[1] Fustian—"a kind of coarse twilled cotton fabric including moleskin and corduroy."

were to be selected for severely practical reasons. "The country is one of the most thorny in the world," he states. Sailcloth had proved excellent but it washed white and soon looked soiled. Moleskin he inclined to "no matter what the shade. It might be scarlet,—colour is nothing, strength everything." But he "inclined to drab. The strongest you can furnish no matter how thick and tradesmanlike looking."[1]

Money being so important, the chance of sharing costs was too good to be missed, so we find him about this time—probably in 1847—making the suggestion of a trip towards Lake Ngami to Captain Steele, then in England, and through him to Murray and Oswell. They accepted gladly and offered to bear the whole expense.

It must not be thought, however, in spite of these exciting prospects, that Livingstone allowed what he later called his "vagabond nature" to interfere with his work. Whatever he did, he did with his might.

Never was there a more indefatigable evangelist. He preached wherever he could gather an audience. His methods, in the judgment of Dr. Moffat, were very effective, and his knowledge of the dialects was intimate. He was master of those little turns of phrase and inflection that make speech sound homely. His topics, too, were simple—his illustrations apt. His style, as in English, was conversational and his favourite subjects were the love of Christ, the fatherhood of God, the resurrection

[1] *Letters of Livingstone.* D. Chamberlin. Letter 30.

and the last judgment. He could paint a beautiful picture and appreciate one. He quoted the following reply of an African to the question, "What is holiness?" "When copious showers have descended during the night, and all the earth and the leaves and the cattle are washed clean and the sun rising shows a drop of dew on every blade of grass and the air breathes fresh—that is holiness."

Often he was depressed at the apparent fruitlessness of his evangelical efforts, but certainly, if they did nothing else they had added much to the marvellous influence he had gained among the people. Africans are naturally religious, they incline to, and are influenced by, those whom they realise to be servants of God, and Livingstone's frequent preachings, and still more frequent times of private devotions, classed him for them among such.

His study of several related Bantu languages was now advanced enough for him to propose to his friend Watt a project for which he had long been making notes. "I have been hatching," he wrote, "a grammar of the Sechuana language." Previous attempts had been made on the model of the classical tongues but, he explains, "mine is on the principle of an analysis of the language, without reference to any other." He asked his friend to inquire the cost of the publication of a small edition.

Nothing is heard, however, of the plan till 1859, when he had thirty copies printed for the use of the members of the Zambesi Expedition. The book was lost sight of till recently, and now only three copies are known to exist.

The *Analysis* constituted a contribution of much importance to the study of Bantu languages, but it failed to do its proper work, because the author, in his modesty, did not appreciate its importance. Livingstone claimed to be "no genius in languages." If that be true, it makes this little book all the more a great achievement. His was that rare type of mind that by sheer intellectual force, without apparent effort, pushes aside conventional methods and reaches fundamental truths.[1]

All the while he kept steadily to his lifelong practice of making careful note of everything of scientific interest that he saw. His energy seems to have been unending, and yet on looking back on these happy busy days Livingstone found their memory tinged with one pathetic regret: this, that he had worked so hard and had been by evening so tired that he had had no inclination to play with his children. After his wife's death this note of something near to remorse ran through all his remaining years and appeared frequently in his letters.

[1] Dr. A. N. Tucker, Professor of Bantu in the School of Oriental Languages, London, says, "It is a great pity that the *Analysis* had not a wider circulation at the time of publication, as Livingstone's method of presenting his material would have been a great inspiration to all grammarians in all parts of Africa. It is possible that, had the work been well known at the time, it would have given a great impetus to a movement away from the conventional classical grammar that is only now making serious progress in the realm of African linguistics." (December, 1936)

The work he did could not have been accomplished except by unrelenting concentration. But it was not he alone, it was also his family that had to bear the sacrifice.

13. *The Discovery of the Lake Ngami*

Nothing could have delighted Livingstone more than the prospect that lay before him when in June, 1849, he set out with Murray and Oswell and a trader called Wilson on the journey that was to be the first rung of his ladder to fame.

What Mrs. Livingstone thought of being left alone with three young children many days' journey away from all white friends, is not recorded. She was not the kind of woman to "record." Whatever David did was right.

Steele had not been able to come; but it was a large company, far better equipped than anything Livingstone had known. It was a luxury to be mounted once more on horseback. The weather was perfect and the rains were over and the long grass was tinged with brown and the going was at first not too difficult. They reached a flat sandy country that had patches of bush and open forest. Soon, however, the party turned northward facing the dreaded Kalahari desert, desolate stretches relieved only by low bush and clumps of mimosa— a land abounding in poisonous snakes, scorpions, and other unpleasant creatures.

Farther on conditions grew much harder. They

came on wide expanses of soft sand in which, for miles together, the wagons sank above the felloes. It needed constant shouting and the cracking of long whips to keep the oxen on the move. For four days the cattle had no water and only a few sips could be spared for the horses. At last water was found, but progress continued slow and the sun was very hot. They could not help recalling a prophecy by the Chief Sekomi—made years before —that cross the desert they never would, for it would kill them on the way.

Adventures were mainly concerned with lack of water. The staggering oxen are outspanned and, in desperation the drivers disperse through the scrub in a forlorn hunt for the precious fluid. A harsh croak! A frog![1] A patch of marsh and once more the poor beasts are refreshed.

Oswell sees what he thinks to be a lion in the scrub. He gallops after it. It is a bushwoman running away in a bent position. She grovels and offers the hunter all she possesses—a few traps made of cord. "Water," they explain, and she guides them eight long miles to plenty. In reward she is given a bundle of beads and a piece of meat, and in surprise she burst out into merry laughter.

At last after six weeks of intolerable hardship they struck a river valley of wonderful beauty— that of the Zouga, that flows out of the Lake. The rest of their journey—two hundred miles up stream, was laborious but no longer dangerous.

[1] "The pleasantest music in Africa is that made by merry frogs." (D.L.)

At last Lake Ngami was reached and viewed for the first time, by Europeans. It was then a sheet of water so wide that the farther shore could not be seen. Now it is only grass land.

Though the journey had thus far been a great feat of courage and endurance, it was to fail in one of its main objects. They had hoped to reach the country of the Paramount Chief Sebituane, whose territory was still two hundred miles farther on. In between, however, there ruled a troublesome young chief called Lechulathebe whose ambition it was to keep to himself a monopoly of firearms. So he refused guides and, still more important, the canoes needed to cross the river. Not to be beaten Livingstone moved upstream hoping to get over by some other means. "I tried hard to make a raft but the wood was worm-eaten and would not bear the weight of a single person. I worked many hours in the water for I was not aware of the number of alligators in the Zouga, I never think of my labours now without being thankful I escaped their jaws."[1]

It was near Lake Ngami that there first dawned upon him the conception that was to mean so much to him in later life—the thought of a great navigable waterway running through Africa. "The prospect of a highway traversed by boats grew stronger and stronger in my mind. So much so that when we actually came to the Lake the discovery seemed of little importance."

The season was now far advanced, return had

[1] *Missionary Travels*, chap. III.

become necessary. Oswell volunteered to go to the Cape and come back the following year with a boat. So they turned south.

Kolobeng reached, Livingstone lost no time in writing up his accounts of the expedition and in sending them home. These documents were brought to the notice of the Royal Geographical Society by Captain Steele, and by the London Missionary Society. The result was almost sensational. Frank Vardon wrote of "immense renown." This was the harbinger of Livingstone's popularity.

But there was another side to this success. The unexpected fame brought a full harvest of criticism —as most things that Livingstone accomplished did. He was charged, and even to this day the statement is occasionally made, with appropriating to himself kudos that was rightly due to his companions and especially to Oswell, who expended £600 on the expedition.

This censure was unjust. The plan was originally his. The others came in as companions. It is quite true that Oswell did not, at the time, receive the recognition that he deserved, but that was due to his own reticence, probably to his own magnanimity. His family, as his biography shows, felt aggrieved but their irritation was not against Livingstone but against Oswell himself, for having kept in the background.

Livingstone made no exclusive claims. Under the picture of Lake Ngami that appears in his book, is this inscription, "Discovered by Oswell, Murray and Livingstone." While in the Journal of the

Royal Geographical Society which contains his
original report stands this entry. "Two English
Gentlemen, Mr. Cotton Oswell and Mr. Mungo
Murray, to whom I communicated my plan of
penetrating to the great lake, reported to be
beyond the Desert, came from England expressly
to take part in the discovery and to their liberal
and zealous co-operation, we are specially indebted
for the success of the Expedition".[1]

Livingstone was much gratified soon after to
receive, as from Queen Victoria, from the Royal
Geographical Society a gift of £25. Characteristically, he spent this on his special work. He asked
Steele to buy him a watch "for observing the
occultation of the stars by the moon, in order
thereby to find the longitude."

14. I will go no matter who opposes

For some reason that is not explained, Livingstone did not wait for Oswell's return but in April
of the following year began on another attempt
to reach Sebituane's country. This time he took
Mrs. Livingstone and the children. The Chief
Sechele and Mebalwe accompanied them.

It seems that he was already contemplating yet
another change of station and this time to the

---

[1] R.G.S. *Journal*, vol. XX., 1850, page 138. The Acting-
Secretary to the R.G.S. adds, "From this and other references
in our *Journal* I think there can be no doubt that Mr. Oswell's
share in the journey was fully recognised at the time."

plains beyond the Kalahari. Not unnaturally, the Moffats objected to a plan that would have put Mrs. Livingstone and the children beyond any help that they could give. But when Livingstone's mind was clear no opposition could shake his resolve. "Providence seems to call me to regions beyond," he wrote to London, and acted before permission could reach him. Obviously a man of such iron will could hardly be expected to be an easy colleague, still less a satisfactory agent, and it is little wonder that on the Society's Board in London there were critics who made themselves uncomfortably audible later.

The criticism has often been made that, in his absorption in his work, Livingstone did not sufficiently consider his wife and family. Aloysius Horn speaks of his "dragging that poor girl Mary Moffat, half over Africa." Whatever justice there may be in this charge it is certain that Mrs. Livingstone was the last to complain. Probably, indeed, she may have insisted on going with him. It was less trying to travel along with him, than to be left alone in an outstation with her husband in possible danger. Feeling, no doubt, that justification of exposing his family to danger was necessary, Livingstone explained that the presence of his wife and children was of the greatest value in securing confidence among strange tribes. In Africa celibacy is looked upon as unnatural, hence a married man's influence is greater than that of a bachelor. Further, it is only fair to remember that in suitable places and in good weather, travel by bullock wagon was like a camping holiday, a substitute for a trip to the Hills or the Coast, and greatly looked forward to and enjoyed.

On this journey the Kalahari Desert was less difficult than usual, except for high winds. The rains were just over and water was procured without much trouble. It was a heavy going, however, because of a detour made necessary by discovery of the tsetse fly, so deadly to cattle, on the route they had planned to follow. The Lake was reached at last and the children had their first sight of the "big water," and the father had a boisterous time "paidling" with his little ones in "his own lake."

Amity with the troublesome young chief, Lechulatebe, had to be purchased by a valuable gift. He took an insistent fancy to a favourite gun that had been given to the Doctor by his hunter friends, and as it was necessary to secure his friendship the gift could not be refused. Livingstone's scheme was to leave his wife and children in the Chief's charge and make a dash into Sebituane's territory to prepare the way for the family's coming later.

But once again there was to be bitter disappointment. A serious epidemic of fever broke out among the porters and two of the children caught the infection. Lake Ngami was revealed to be an extremely malarial neighbourhood. All too obviously, no settlement was possible here. Return had become urgent. The cattle were sickening from attacks by the tsetse fly, so a push was made and, happily, in the pure air of the desert the children recovered. Here, to their intense relief and pleasure, they were met by Oswell posting hard after them with his usual well-equipped caravan. In his courteous way, he accompanied them back to Kolobeng, which was reached in July, 1850. The consequences to Mrs. Livingstone were, however, to prove serious. Shortly after arrival home their fourth child was born but died a fortnight later of the prevailing fever. Mary herself became seriously ill and suffered temporarily partial paralysis.

It was one of the compensations of their life thus far, that they could always fall back upon Kuruman and on Mrs. Robert Moffat, as now, as soon as possible, they proceeded to do. That great-hearted lady had an intense admiration of her son-in-law. "The Wonder of the World," she called him at a later date, but for the moment, it is to be feared that other sentiments would be uppermost. Here they recruited.

Few are the men who would not have accepted this defeat as evidence that they had done enough and that a less exacting life was, for a time at least, advisable. Not so this man of steel. Every rebuff but heightened his resolve and widened his vision. Always there arose some challenging sentence such as "I shall open a path into the interior or perish," and soon new and greater plans were shaping themselves in his indomitable heart.

In Kuruman he had leisure to discuss the future with his sick wife. To him his duty was already clear. Many things had led up to it. He had heard on reliable authority of high and healthy country to the North, "a land of many lakes and big forests; of the River Teoge that falls into Lake Ngami from the North that ran so swiftly that canoes cannot paddle against it and have to be punted all the way; of the large trees, and the bodies of animals that are at times swept down it." That way lay the new path. The Bechuana Mission had been carried on in a "cul-de-sac" and the Boers had shut the door South and East. There remained only the North. "It appeared very plain that no mission could succeed unless we could get a well-watered country having a passage to the sea either to the East or the West Coast. This is a project I am almost afraid to meet but nothing else will do. I intend (D.V.) to go next year and remain a twelve-month. My wife, poor soul, I pity her, proposed to let me go for that time while she remained at Kolobeng." "Poor Soul," indeed! It needed a heroine to remain happily wed to a man of such tremendous courage and such an exacting sense of duty.

Meanwhile, they returned to their station, now become, for him, somewhat stifling.

15. Almost a Tragedy

The project stated in the last paragraph was not to remain the final form of Livingstone's purpose.

Next year—early that is, in 1851, Cotton Oswell again arrived. He was eager as Livingstone to meet the great Sebituane, and his coming seems to have caused a further development of plan. The new idea was even more open to objection than the last. It was apparently to find a healthy site in Sebituane's—that is the Makololo-country, establish the family there, and make this the starting point for his endeavour to open roads to the Coast.

When the Moffats heard of this decision they opposed vigorously. It was not the plan itself, but the risk to the family, that troubled them. Moffat proposed, as alternative, that if they would only wait till he had completed a translation of the New Testament on which he was then working, he would go with them. But to the younger man, with the sense of his mission heavy upon him, this seemed like trifling. "The King's business required haste."

Mrs. Moffat was outspoken in her opinion, and her son-in-law's reply was more vigorous than polite. "I have occasionally met with people who took upon themselves to act for me and have offered their thoughts with an emphatic ' I think ' but I generally excuse them on the score of being a little soft headed in believing that they could think both for me and themselves." Most people have written letters they regret and Livingstone must have repented of this one. He had the highest possible regard for the lady. It is one of the penalties of greatness that such peccadillos are not easily allowed the oblivion they deserve.

Cotton Oswell once more provided the finance.

To lessen the danger of the Kalahari crossing he sent men ahead to deepen the water holes and because of his thoughtfulness the party got through in comparative comfort and reached the Zouga river in good time. But the presence of the tsetse fly once more caused an alteration of the course and a prolongation of the desert journey.

They now faced the worst country they had ever seen. Not an insect, not a bird, broke the stillness. Lack of water soon became the acute problem. The guide—Shobo—a light-hearted, irresponsible Bushman, lost his way and then vanished. Through the carelessness of one of the servants, the water tank leaked and only a little remained. Two days, three, and then a fourth, and still no water. The poor children, their tongues parched, and their lips cracked, whimpered all day long. The possibility of their all perishing in this horrible place became near and terrible. Livingstone's comment is, "It would have been almost a relief to me to have been reproached with being the entire cause of the catastrophe, but not a syllable of upbraiding was uttered by their mother though the tearful eye told of the agony within. On the afternoon of the fifth day to our inexpressible relief some of the men returned with a supply, only a little, but it saved our lives."

The mosquitoes of these parts, too, were most ferocious, and their bites unusually painful. The children were covered with their marks so that not an inch of whole skin could be found on their tender little bodies. These experiences gave the

father plenty to think about, as well they might.
One misfortune of this journey was that on one
occasion the exhausted cattle had been allowed to
shelter in a thicket, where unnoticed the fatal fly
abounded. Though not all bitten, in the end all
were lost.

After these and many other hardships the Chobe
river was crossed and they were most heartily
received by the Chief Sebituane, the great dream of
whose latter years had been to make friendship
with a white man. All their needs were amply
supplied. The loss of oxen was made good. Nothing could exceed the Chief's pleasure in seeing the
lady and especially the children in the party. The
confidence in his goodwill thus shown, gratified
him intensely. Livingstone and Oswell were
equally delighted. They had never met an African
to whom they had felt so much drawn.

He was a Basuto by birth. A famous warrior, he
had made himself feared even by the terrible
Mosilikatse. Like other chiefs he had had to
struggle for his place. He had been the best
fighter and runner of his tribe: stern though
just. "A gentleman in thought and manner."
Widely popular for his kindness to all.

Oswell describes in vivid detail a secret visit the
Chief made to their tent.

"In the dead of night he paid us a visit alone and
sat down quietly and mournfully by our fire.
Livingstone and I sat up and greeted him, and then
he dreamily recounted the history of his life, his
wars, escapes, successes and conquests. By the

fire's glow and flicker among the reeds, with that tall dark earnest speaker and his keenly-attracted listeners, it always appears to me the weirdest scene I ever saw. With subdued manner and voice he went on the livelong night till dawn, only occasionally interrupted by an inquiry from Livingstone."[1]

The Missionary was delighted with all he saw, and elated as never before. This was the opportunity he had toiled for; here, the man to back his plans with an influence which stretched all along the upper Zambezi. But alas, tragedy was near. A few days later Sebituane contracted pneumonia from an old wound. The Doctor saw at once that the case was dangerous but hesitated to interfere lest, had he failed, he should be blamed. Had his treatment not succeeded all would most probably have been killed.

"I visited him," says Livingstone, "in company with my little Robert on the Sunday afternoon he died. "Come near," he said, "and see if I am any longer a man. I am done." "After sitting with him some time and commending him to the mercy of God, I rose to depart, when he raised himself a little, called a servant and said 'Take Robert to Maunku (one of his wives) and tell her to give him some milk.' These were the last words of Sebituane."

What hopes died with him! The previous Sunday he had attended service and had listened reverently to what the preacher had said. It was like the

[1] W. C. Oswell. Vol. I. p. 242.

126

shock of an earthquake to all, and might easily have led to disaster. It would have been natural, according to African thought, to have put the blame on the visitors. Happily their fears proved groundless. The successor, a daughter, Ma Mochisane, continued friendly and so far from being suspicious gave permission for further exploration. So the family was put in charge of a headman while the two friends travelled northward.

Very soon they made a discovery that sent Livingstone into transports of joy. Near the kraal of Sesheke they came upon the upper Zambezi River. Here was what he had sought—a magnificent stream, a great central water-course, and much farther inland than he had expected. It was a triumph far more important than the discovery of Lake Ngami. But, in the essential aspect of their investigation they were again disappointed. This was no country for European residence. The land was low lying and water-logged. So back the caravan must go, back through the long waterless miles and at the hottest time of the year.

A month later the "Lady of the Wagon," as Cotton delighted to call her, gave birth to her fifth child—a boy. He was called "Oswell," after the family friend, but his pet name, the one the father generally used, was "Zouga," from the river near which he saw the light.

16. A Shock, a New Vision and Some Consequences

This great discovery—the finding of the Upper Zambezi—filled Livingstone's mind with a vision of ever-widening possibilities and ever-increasing duties. He wrote thus to the Directors of his Society. "So powerfully am I convinced that it is the will of God that I should go that I will go, no matter who opposes, but from you I expect nothing but encouragement."

The truth is that on this journey he had received a shock that had opened his eyes to a matter that up till then he had not fully realised, and that gave to his project for exploring a path to the Coast a new and even more urgent reason. He had seen for the first time the slave trade in action and had realised its menace. He discovered with dismay that Sebituane's people, the Makololo, had begun, in a mild form, a trade in slaves. Arab and half-caste Portuguese merchants were penetrating into the interior and in exchange for slaves were offering guns, and here the people were already beginning the practice of raiding weaker neighbours, of taking prisoners and of selling them in exchange for muskets.

This was to Livingstone a new problem, and he saw at once its almost infinite possibilities for evil. Guns made capture easy and causes for quarrels were never hard to find. He realised that the craving for articles of European manufacture was bound to grow. It could not be stopped. He welcomed it as a civilising influence but saw its dangers. Honest commerce might do great good; corrupt methods like those he feared would inevitably do irreparable harm.

From now on he began to urge with growing fervour his conviction that only by Christianity and Commerce (business, that is, conducted under the guidance of Christian men) could the evil that was then eating into Africa like a canker be cured. The idea was not, of course, original, but he did more than any other to make it feasible.

To those who look back upon nearly a hundred years of experience it may occur to wonder at Livingstone's confidence in the benefit of the revolution that in the end Commerce brought about. None the less, there is no question that his influence did give to business in Africa, at least in certain districts, a philanthropic bias, the fruits of which still remain.

Kolobeng, on their return, added an additional argument—a sad one, to his new resolve. It was deserted. Sechele had removed his people to Limavi. The increasing dryness of the country and fear of the Boers had forced him to find safer headquarters.

The Makololo country had been proved impossible as a place for his family to live. So the immediate problem, and a very anxious one, was how to make suitable arrangements for their future. Where was he to leave them that he might begin his great journey with a quiet mind? There was nothing for it but to send them home to Britain, and the prospect appalled him. They were four in number, all young—Robert, the eldest, was only six. Mrs. Livingstone was full of nervous fears. She had had little experience of the home country and was very dependent on her strong-minded husband. There were, in those days, no schools for missionary's children. No wonder that Mary, in spite of her heroic assent, wept as she thought of the long months of separation, full for her husband of dangers unimaginable.

Livingstone very rarely revealed the depth of his feelings as he does at this time. "Orphanising (a home-made word) my children" becomes a usual phrase. "To orphanise my children will be like tearing out my bowels. For they will forget me." So they said farewells at Kolobeng and, after spending a short time with the Moffats at Kuruman, trekked to the Cape.

Kolobeng was for the Livingstone family a home of happy memories—and they left it with many regrets. He was to see it only once again and then to find it in ruins.

SECOND INTERLUDE

A CONFLICT OF LOYALTIES

CAPE TOWN, 1852

" How I miss you now, and the dear children. My heart yearns incessantly over you. How many thoughts of the past crowd into my mind.

" You have been a great blessing to me. I see no face that can be compared with the sunburnt one that has so often greeted me with kind looks. My dearest, I loved you when I married you and the longer I lived with you, I loved you the better.

" Let us do our duty to Christ and He will bring us through the world with honour and usefulness."

LETTER TO HIS WIFE. Cape Town, 5th May, 1852.

The first and most urgent problem for the Livingstone family on its return to civilisation was that of clothes. "The costume of the whole party was somewhat on the style of Robinson Crusoe." Finance was again a difficulty. His next year's salary was overdrawn by £57, a formidable sum for him.

Oswell, once more played god-father, at the cost to himself of £170. To make the gift more easy of acceptance he, with his customary delicacy, gave the sum with the remark that it was the profit on the sale of ivory from Livingstone's estate (all unexplored Africa—presumably!) to which he had as good a right as the donor. Richly did Oswell deserve his companion's praise. "The best friend we had in Africa."

The family sailed on the *Trafalgar* on April 23rd, 1852. The anxiety of the parting was somewhat lessened by the knowledge that they would find in Britain many helpful friends—Young and Oswell and others. The L.M.S., too, made financial provision for their needs on a scale that seemed to him, at the time, almost lavish.

The days that followed were amongst Livingstone's hardest. He was passionately attached to his wife and family and he knew that to a great extent he was losing his children; deliberately surrendering them to his duty. It was a conflict that was, from this time on, never to be absent from his life.

He was hospitably entertained by Dr. Philip's successor, William Thompson, and found in him a stalwart friend. He needed such comradeship, for the general atmosphere of Cape Town was, at this time, unfriendly.

Two years before the "Kaffir War" had happened. The tribes, resenting the confiscation of their lands by the Whites, had revolted. Similar things had occurred before, but this rebellion became serious when the trained and armed Native police mutinied in sympathy. Almost more disturbing was the fact that the Hottentot Christians of the London

Mission in Theopolis threw in their lot with the rebels. There followed the usual outrages and reprisals. So critical did the situation become that troops had to be sent out from England.

For reasons already given, the London Mission had long been unpopular with a large section of the Europeans and, naturally, their attitude was stiffened by the conduct of the Christian Hottentots, and Livingstone, on this visit, came in for his full share of dislike. He was well known as a champion of native rights and was regarded by many as a spreader of disaffection.

One consolation in this depressing time was the friendship of Sir Thomas Maclear, Astronomer Royal at the Cape. Livingstone had already used to great purpose the knowledge of the science of nautical observation which, it will be remembered, he had gained through the kindness of the captain of the *George*. He felt, however, that in the epoch-making journey that lay before him, for the accurate statement of positions and for the drawing of maps, more skill and better instruments were essential, and he applied to Maclear for help.

Assistance was enthusiastically given. The two became devoted friends, and in later days the Astronomer could never speak too highly of the value and the accuracy of the records that were systematically sent him. Livingstone's reports to Maclear are said to have filled a large tin box.

He took at this time the opportunity of skilled help and had his uvula cut. It had given him great trouble.

The most important work of these days, however, was the assembling of equipment for his journey. It was no easy matter. Funds were scarce and the Local Authorities far from helpful. So suspicious, indeed, were they that he had difficulty in securing even a moderate quantity of ammunition. Then, and this was the most tantalising thing of all, an officious country postmaster, to whom he had complained of an overcharge, threatened to bring an action for libel against him. To defend the case would have meant costly delay so, although already heavily in debt, and sorely against the grain, he compromised by paying the man a considerable sum.

Cape Town, 1852, was not a happy memory. How different was the visit that took place six years later.

PART THREE

THE EXPLORER

THE GREAT JOURNEY ACROSS AFRICA

The Campaign against Slavery begins—
1853 to 1856

LINYANTI, LOANDA, QUILIMANE

" *The mere animal pleasure of travelling in wild
unexplored country is very great. . . . Brisk exercise
imparts elasticity to the muscles, fresh and healthy
blood circulates through the brain, the mind works
well, the eye is clear, the step firm and the day's
exercise always makes the evening's repose thoroughly
enjoyable. We have usually the stimulus of remote
chances of danger either from beasts or men. Our
sympathies are drawn out towards our humble
and hardy companions by a community of interests
and it may be of perils, which make us all friends.*"
LAST JOURNALS. March 26th, 1866.

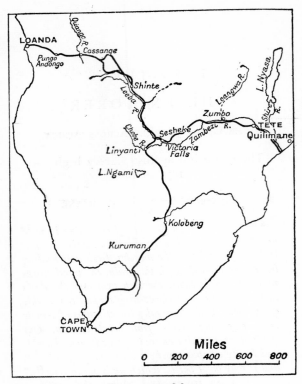

SIMPLIFIED MAP
showing Livingstone's Journeys as described in
PART THREE

1. *The Last of Kolobeng*

WHEN in June, 1852, Dr. Livingstone embarked upon the journey of exploration that was to make him famous and remain one of the most remarkable in the world's history, he was in his prime—forty years of age—and in perfect physical condition.

When driven to do so he could live without hurt, as few Europeans have ever attempted to do. He could say: "I have drunk water swarming with insects, thick with mud, putrid from rhinoceros' urine and buffalo's dung, and no stinted draught of it either, and yet felt no inconvenience from it." He could exist for months on native food. He had always a fearless confidence in his power to "win through."

He was in all ways supremely well equipped for his great adventure. His missionary apprenticeship had given him the knowledge of how to deal with the African. Politeness, consideration, and when needed, firmness, were his practice. "If one behaves as a gentleman he will be invariably treated as such," is one of his sayings, and for him that was true, equally for Black and White.

There was in him a power that for lack of a better word might be called "daemonic," a sense of an overwhelming personality, which remained with him till his physical strength became impaired.

137

Primitive people felt it at once and generally yielded to it, and since this power was backed by a patience that was imperturbable and a good humour that was infectious, there were few who could resist him. At this period, too, his spirit was invariably optimistic. "The world is rolling on to the golden age, our dreams must come true," he wrote, and phrases like "Try again," "All will come well in the end," were constantly on his lips and meant much. Like the Celt he claimed to be, he had fits of depression, it is true, but wonderful resilience, physical and mental, was an outstanding gift. The "dourness" of his youth had become sublimated into a fixed determination that nothing could divert. There was something revealing even in his walk, so much so that many observers remarked upon it. It was best described by a friend of his youth, Dr. Isaac Taylor. "After nearly forty years I remember his step—the characteristic forward tread, firm, simple, resolute, neither fast nor slow, no hurry, no dawdle, but which evidently meant getting there."

A story which hails from Blantyre underlines this description in a picturesque way. "Oh, aye," an old inhabitant was fond of saying, "I kent the Livingstane laddies—Dauvid and Chairlie—weel. And there was a queer differ atween them. If they was walkin' along a road and cam' tae a puddle, Chairlie wud walk roon, but David—he'd stamp stracht through." The same sense of the inevitable arrival.

Reference has already been made more than

once to his powers as an observer and conscien-
tiousness as a recorder. His eye had a keenness
that nothing escaped. His method was to make
rough jottings in a small note-book that he
carried in his pocket, and when camp was reached
to elaborate and copy these with great carefulness
into large diaries. Many of these note-books still
exist. They are at times refreshing reading. In
them he now and again allows himself the liberty
of caustic comments that do not appear in his
published works.

He arrived at Kuruman by the end of August.
It had been slow going. The climb before the
central plateau is reached is steep—an ascent of
3,000 feet in thirty miles—and his cattle, all that
his means could afford, were poor beasts compared with Oswell's. Then, in his good-natured
way, he had allowed his wagon to be overloaded
with "everybody's packages," the result of which
was a breakdown just before Kuruman came in
sight. This meant loss of time, but the delay
proved providential. Had he gone straight on
he would have arrived at Kolobeng just at the
moment when a Commando of Boers was engaged
in attacking Sechele and wrecking the station.
"Kind Providence," he wrote to his wife, "detained
me from falling into the thick of it." It is an
interesting speculation as to how Livingstone
would have dealt with the situation, or more
aptly perhaps, how the Commando would have
treated him. He believed that they would have
shot him, and considering their habit of "breathing

out slaughterings" against him, the fear had some justification.

The Boers, as we have seen, had a special grudge against Sechele, because almost alone among the chiefs he resisted them, and naturally they believed that Livingstone inspired this opposition. Rumours were current that he had acquired an arsenal and sold weapons freely to the Bakwain—"Two hundred guns and a cannon," was the gossip that swept the country. There was no truth, as is now admitted, in the yarn. Five guns were all that Sechele's people possessed. The arsenal was nothing more than a handyman's workshop.

The Missionary did not worry about these stories—indeed he let the gossip go uncontradicted. "This belief," he wrote to London, "tended to keep them from slaughtering the Bakwain. . . . Knowing this, though applied to for information, I have declined speaking on the subject." Considering the rough crowd he was dealing with, such tactics were, to say the least, imprudent. The result was that a strong force, under Andries Pretorius—six hundred Whites and seven hundred Natives, are the figures given—raided Sechele's town and set it on fire. The tribe defended itself bravely, and inflicted considerable casualties. Sixty Bakwain were killed, the cattle were confiscated, and many of the younger people carried away as slaves. The Chief himself escaped.

The Mission station was then sacked, the best of the furniture looted; the medicines destroyed: Livingstone's precious books were torn to pieces and all his invaluable notes scattered to the four winds. It was a piece of vandalism that all decent Boers regretted, as may be seen from the historian Theal's shamefaced defence. If the purpose was to revenge themselves on Livingstone, it failed. Apart from the loss of some £300 in property—which of course was hard to bear—it did him no permanent injury.[1]

He took the destruction with the philosophy of one who never cared much about possessions. In fact he came in the end even to rejoice in the loss, since it set him free for his great adventure. He applied for compensation to the Government but without result. The Governor of the time—Sir George Cathcart—was very unfriendly to missionaries. "It would be unspeakably pleasant to Sir George," remarks the sufferer, "to hang us all on one gibbet."

The final word on the matter is thoroughly in character. "The Boers," he exclaimed, "are determined to shut up the interior. I am determined to open up this country. We shall see who have been the more successful in resolution, they or I."

Burning under a sense of injustice, Sechele determined to go to London and lay his grievance

[1] In his address delivered in Edinburgh, November 21st, 1929, General Smuts said, "I once took the opportunity to discuss the matter with President Kruger, and his explanation of the differences which arose between the Boers and Livingstone was that Gordon Cumming—another of your errant countrymen—had supplied the border tribes with rifles and ammunition in exchange for ivory, and the Boers, finding the natives armed, concluded—erroneously—that Livingstone had done so, and treated him accordingly."

before the Queen. Livingstone knew full well that the Cape authorities would refuse him permission to sail and tried to dissuade him. But he would not be deterred. He made his way to the Cape, where he was stopped and had to return home. Later he recovered his position and gathered round him many tribesmen who had fled from the Dutch, put into action some lessons he had learned in the Colony, and ruled wisely.

So ended Livingstone's life as a Missionary in the ordinary sense. He had devoted to the work twelve of his best years. To many a hard-working colleague he must have appeared unstable, something indeed of a rolling stone. If the number of converts be made the criterion of success, there were scores of ordinary men who had left him far behind. But always it was the hard task that had attracted him, and the fruits of his labours in this and other spheres were to be abundantly evident in later days.

There was one pleasure awaiting him in Kolobeng that in the end outweighed for him all loss. He received news that the Missionary Society had given cordial approval to his opening work in the country of the Makololo. He accepted this long-expected permission as a providential confirmation of his plans and, in the end, put into the permission a much wider interpretation than had been intended.

2. *The Upper Zambesi Zalley*

Many precious months were thus wasted in vexatious delays, but at last the caravan started. It was familiar country and much of it beautiful, and till they reached the Chobé river, just south of Linyanti, travel had been pleasant and easy. Here the going changed rapidly for the worse. The land was waterlogged and the vegetation rank. The rains, just over, had been unusually heavy and every water-course was like a small river. Some of these contained great holes made by elephants' feet, and into one of these the wagon slid, the pole broke and the cumbrous vehicle nearly upset.

At last a large stream, the Sanshure, was reached which, in its flooded condition, proved unfordable. The situation looked serious. No further progress that way was possible, so Livingstone set out with one companion to find a path through. They took a collapsible boat they had brought—a "pontoon," he calls it—and had to carry it a good part of the way. All day they splashed on, ankle and knee-deep, but could find no way through. They were fortunate in being able to shoot a lechwe (a species of antelope discovered by Oswell and Livingstone four years before). They had to camp. A fire was lit on a hillock and a meal and a "good cup of tea" enjoyed. They dried themselves and passed a comfortable night.

The story goes on: "On climbing the highest trees next morning we beheld a large sheet of water surrounded by an impenetrable belt of trees. This was the Chobé river. Our first effort was to get to two tree-covered islands that seemed much nearer to the water than the point where we stood. The reeds were not the only obstacle. Mingled with them was a peculiar serrated grass which at certain angles cut the hands like a razor, and the entire mass was bound together by climbing convolvulus with its stalks as strong as whipcord. There was no ventilation and the sun's heat was stifling. After several hours of toil we reached one of the islands.

"Here we met an old friend the bramble bush. The legs of my companion were bleeding and his leather trousers torn. My own were worn through the knees. We were still forty yards from the clear water and now encountered another difficulty—a great mass of papyrus, eight or ten feet high and an inch and a half in diameter and so strongly lashed together by living convolvulus that the weight of both of us had no effect upon them. Eager to look along the vista to clear water I stepped in and found it took me, at once, up to the neck.

"Returning nearly worn out we proceeded up the bank of the Chobé but could see nothing from the highest trees except a vast expanse of reed. After a hard day's work we came to a deserted hut on an ant-hill. Not a bit of fuel could we get except the grass and sticks of the dwelling itself. But as we were tormented outside by the thousands of mosquitoes and the cold dew began to fall, we were fain to crawl beneath for shelter.

"After a damp cold night we, early in the morning, commenced our work of exploration. Some of the ant-hills here are thirty feet high. From one of these we discovered an inlet to the Chobé. We forthwith launched our boat upon a deep river. A hippopotamus came up at one side and went off with a desperate plunge. We had passed over him." [1]

The two companions paddled from midday till sunset and saw nothing but a wall of reeds on each bank, and were just reconciling themselves to a supperless night when they struck a Makololo village. "The inhabitants looked like people who had seen a ghost. 'He has,' they cried, 'dropped among us from the clouds. Yet came riding on the back of a hippopotamus (the pontoon). We thought no one could cross the Chobé without our knowledge but here he drops like a bird.'" This quotation is given at length because with variations it tells the kind of hardship the devoted company faced on most of the way to the West.

They received a hearty welcome when in May, 1853, they arrived at Linyanti. They had been on the journey over a year—one out of the two of his original arrangement with his wife.

There had been a change in the government of the tribe since his visit two years before. Sebituane's daughter had found it difficult to agree with the

[1] *Missionary Travels*, chap. VIII.

number of husbands whom by tribal custom she was required to entertain. She preferred her own children and had handed the authority to Sekeletu, her brother, a youth of eighteen. This man, though kindly disposed, was not his father's equal. He listened willingly to Livingstone's teaching, but the difficulty as regards polygamy intervened. He refused to learn to read, afraid that "it might change his heart."

The great welcome that the Explorer received was mainly due to the people's fear of the Matebele. The Makololo were nervous as to the future. The death of the great Sebituane had undermined their confidence. "We want sleep (peace). Give your son Sekeletu sleep," was their cry. If the missionary would but stay with them they would be safe.

Livingstone had brought with him, as representing a company in Cape Town, a half-caste trader called George Fleming. This was intended as a first step in the establishment of the honourable trade relationships about which he had grown so keen. The attempt was fairly successful, but for various reasons was not continued.

The Chief showed his gratitude by gifts of ivory. These were welcome, but at the same time embarrassing. Livingstone needed finance badly, but he was, as always, jealous of his reputation for disinterestedness. He did not accept valuable presents. So he gave trade goods in exchange for the ivory and a careful list of these was entered into his Diary. Such was his custom.

They found the country round Linyanti saturated with malaria, and cold east winds in May brought on an epidemic and Livingstone succumbed for the first time to the disease to which he was always afterwards subject. Indeed on this journey the attacks became so frequent that he ceased to record them lest he should weary his readers. It was part of his philosophy to pay a minimum of attention to bodily pains—and that, to the extent perhaps of somewhat justifying the complaint made against him later, that he lacked sympathy with those of less spartan habit. He describes his symptoms with characteristic objectivity, leaving to the imagination of those who have experienced them the splitting headaches, the back-breaking pains, the teeth-chattering rigors and profuse perspirations that leave the patient feeling like a rag. Livingstone had himself invented what he considered a specific for malaria. He had tried it with success on his infant son Thomas. It is a medicine still in wide use in tropical countries and is known by the name of the "Livingstone's Rouser." [1]

It may be noted here that his attitude towards native doctors was not the indiscriminate scorn often found amongst scientifically trained physicians. Freely admitting that their reliance on spells and charms was foolish, he recognised none the less that age-long practice, however unintelligent, must have discovered some remedies of

[1] Ingredients : Jalap, rhubarb, calomel, quinine sulphate and aloes.

147

value. Hence he treated the medicine men with habitual courtesy and did not interfere in a case unless it was obviously beyond them. In this instance, in order to find out if they had any methods for the curing of malaria of which he was ignorant, he let them experiment on him. He allowed himself to be "stewed in their vapour baths, smoked like a red herring over green twigs." But he concluded he could do better himself, and adds: "There is a good deal in not giving in to this disease. He who is low spirited will die sooner than the man who is not of a melancholic nature." He was much impressed, as he had only too good reason to be, with the terrible power of this illness as an obstacle to progress in Africa, and was ready, he said, to devote part of his life to discover a remedy. The connection of the anopheles mosquito with malaria did not suggest itself to him, though he does record the observation that it seemed to occur most where mosquitoes were most prevalent.

3. Among Barbarians

The friendly Makololo gave him abundant opportunity for preaching, and Livingstone let no chance pass unused. His Diary testifies repeatedly to his gratification at the attention with which they listened. But like many another in a similar position, he looks at the dark faces before him and wonders how much is being understood and how much of what is understood will bear fruit. He was no facile optimist, but in times of depression found comfort in the thought of himself as a layer of foundations. Others would build up on his work. If he could have read the future he would have found other reasons for encouragement. Fred Arnot, a Scots missionary, famous in his day, writing about 1884, says: "Although thirty years have elapsed since Livingstone first visited the Barotse valley and more than twenty years since he was last seen there, yet the remembrance of him; his ways, his words, his physique is fresh as yesterday. Many of the older men had whole sermons of his by heart. One old blind man, at my request, gave me one of Livingstone's sermons. He got up and went through it bravely, spoken in a high authoritative voice."

About this period Livingstone's plans seemed to have been subject to somewhat frequent change. Apparently at this time his intention was to solve successfully, as he hoped, the question of a trade route to the Coast and then return and settle with his family somewhere in the Makololo country. Nothing could have delighted the young Chief more than to have the Missionary live with him, not only for Livingstone's own sake but perhaps quite as much for Mrs. Livingstone's, and that for a special reason. The tribe lived in constant dread of Mosilikatse, the Matebele Paramount Chief. Now, it was well known that Dr. Moffat had acquired a wonderful influence over this formidable individual. If, therefore, his daughter and his grand-children would but settle amongst them, life would become secure.[1]

Sekeletu, for this and other reasons, was most friendly and helpful. He gave willing consent to further exploration and volunteered to go himself with him. The travel was very pleasant. Canoes were used and no less than thirty dugouts were needed to carry the large company. It was now the cold season. Game was plentiful and the country very beautiful.

Livingstone was troubled, however, to notice that everywhere there was evidence of inundation. The villages were built on mounds, probably artificial. The land was in general low-lying and marshy. The search was pushed to the farthest limits of the Barotse territory but the quest was unsuccessful. There could be no healthy sites in such a country. He returned to Linyanti disappointed.

In spite of his intimate knowledge of African customs, good and bad, Livingstone was distressed by the barbarism of the Makololo. Young Sekeletu had a rival claimant for the throne, a half-brother called Mpepe, and just about the time of the missionary's arrival this man had planned a revolt with the help of some Mambari—half caste slave-traders who had arrived from the West Coast. If the plot were successful these men were to be given many slaves. Mpepe asked for a conference with his brother, planning to kill him without warning. Livingstone attended and quite unin-

[1] *Isabella Price, Pioneer*, page 174. Livingstone Press.

tentionally saved Sekeletu's life by coming between
the brothers at a critical moment. The young
Chief soon learned of the plot and had his brother
seized and executed. This happening in itself did
not greatly upset Livingstone. Such murders
were common in African tribal quarrels. It was
the sequel, which took place in his presence, that
shocked him horribly.

In the course of their journey they came to the
village where Mpepe's father lived. This man
was questioned as to his knowledge of his son's
treachery and, in the course of the inquiry, Sekeletu
suddenly sprang up—all had been carefully
planned—seized the old man and handed him
over to his warriors. Livingstone could do nothing.
He had to watch helplessly while the captives
were hewn down by axes and the pieces of their
bodies flung into the river to the crocodiles. He
was so upset that he could stay in the place no
longer.

On this trip Livingstone had nine months of
close companionship with this barbarous people,
and respectful as they always were to him personally, it was one of the most trying times of
his career. He writes: "Though all were kind
and attentive to me as possible, yet to endure the
dancing, roaring and singing, the jesting, grumb-
ling and quarrelling and murdering of these
children of nature was the severest penance I had
yet undergone in the course of my missionary
duties. I thence derived a more intense disgust of
paganism than I had hitherto felt and formed a

greatly elevated opinion of the effect of missions in the South among tribes which are reported to have been as savage as the Makololo."

He goes on: "Missionaries ought to cultivate a taste for the beautiful. We are necessarily compelled to contemplate much moral impurity and degradation. We are so often doomed to disappointment. We are apt to become either callous or melancholy. On this account it seems necessary to cultivate that faculty for the gratification of which God has made such universal provision. See the green earth and the blue sky, the lofty mountain and the verdant valley, the glorious orbs of day and night, the graceful flowers so chaste in form and perfect in colouring."

It is a supreme testimony to the Christian grit of this man that he was prepared to spend his life among people whose ways seemed to him so horrible. But he had resources within himself and was in his own way content. He wrote to Thompson: "My thoughts never turn with any longing except to my family."

It is noticeable that in later life Livingstone judged the African more genially and came to see good that at this time was apparently hidden from him. What may be called his mature judgment appears in his *Last Journals*. "Devote yourselves heartily to the savages, as they are called, and you will find with some drawbacks and wickedness, a very great deal to admire and love."[1] "Everyone who lives long among them," he once wrote,

[1] *Last Journal*, Vol. II, page 190.

"forgets that they are black and remembers that they are fellow men." He got to be quite fond of those Makololo. The men who went west with him were the most loyal of his followers, and he looked back to their faithful service with longing many a time in later days.

It was at this point that he saw for the first time a picture that haunted him—a long line of slaves in chains. He realised once more how active the evil had become; how the slave trade was pushing its way into the heart of the Continent.

4. The Road to the West

Satisfied that he had done all that for the moment he could in his search for healthy sites, he set himself to decide which was the better route—east or west—for his purpose of bringing Central Africa into touch with civilisation. He chose the west. It was somewhat longer, but he had been informed that in Loanda—in Portuguese West Africa—there were many British people.

Sekeletu was eager to share in the adventure, partly because of his unbounded confidence in Livingstone; not less, however, because of the trading prospects it opened. A council of the tribe was held. Not all approved. One old diviner objected strongly. "Where is he taking you to?" he demanded. "This white man is throwing you away. Your garments already smell of blood." But the Chief only laughed. One difficulty was that Livingstone was in bad health, subject to fits of giddiness, and the Natives feared that should he die on the way they would be blamed for allowing him to go among unknown enemies. To meet this objection and absolve the tribe from possible blame Livingstone deposited with the Chief part of his Diary and with it a written explanation. The wagon also and other heavy articles were left in charge of two headmen. The trust was faithfully kept.

Twenty-seven porters were lent to him free of charge. His equipment, due to the meagreness of his funds, was totally inadequate for a journey so arduous. Three muskets for his carriers, a rifle and a double-barrelled smooth-bore gun, for himself, were all they had. His men carried the spears that Africans always take when on a journey, but to show that their purpose was peaceful, shields were left behind. Since the expedition would depend for food mainly on what could be shot, the ammunition was carefully packed, divided into small bundles to guard against any possible large loss. A few pounds of biscuits, tea, coffee and sugar were all the stores. There was a stock of medicine, and in a tin canister, fifteen inches square, were packed spare shirts, trousers and shoes to be used when they reached civilised life. He also carried a magic lantern to help him in preaching, and a few simple instruments for geographical observations. The only books that went with him were an almanac, some nautical tables and his indispensable bible. A small gipsy tent just sufficient to sleep in, a sheepskin mantle as a blanket and a horse-rug completed the equipment. He adds stoically: "I had always found that the art of successful travel consists in taking as few impedimenta as possible since much luggage excited the cupidity of the tribes." This last sentence is doubtless justified, but it remains true that the outfit was dangerously insufficient. Poverty alone could explain the risk he took. There can be no question at all that had he been more comfortably furnished he would not have suffered in health so lamentably. But then he would not have been Livingstone if he had counted the cost carefully and had ruled out risk and hardship.

In November, 1853, the canoes[1] moved down the Chobé and turned into the Zambezi. It was the hottest time of the year and fever racked him horribly. The rains were late. The thermometer ranged from 100° to 128°. The following extract from his Diary gives a graphic account of the daily routine of the company:

"We rose at a little before 5 a.m. and having taken a light breakfast of coffee, we loaded the canoes and embarked. The next two hours were the most pleasant part of the day's journey. The men paddled away vigorously and occasionally relieved the tedium of their work by loud altercations—about eleven we landed and had a light

---

[1] The African canoe or dugout is made from a single tree-trunk. It varies in length from twenty to sixty feet. In the longest two men sit abreast, and cattle can be carried.

meal. After an hour's rest, we again embarked and I sheltered myself with an umbrella from the intense heat. Sometimes we reached a sleeping place two hours before sunset."

Then followed arrangements for the night:

"Some of the men cut a little grass for my bed and planted the poles of my tent. The bed being made, boxes are arranged on each side of it. The tent is then pitched and the principal fire, or kotla, was lighted some four or five feet in front of it. Each person knows the station he is to occupy in reference to the post of honour at the kotla. The two Makololo[1] occupy my right and left, both in eating and sleeping as long as the journey lasted, but as soon as I retired, the head boatman made his bed at the door of my tent. The rest divide into small companies according to their tribes, make sheds all round the fire, leaving a horse shoe shaped space in front, sufficient for the cattle to stand in. The fire gives confidence to the oxen, the men are careful to keep them in sight. The sheds are formed by planting two stout forked poles in an inclined direction and placing another across them in a horizontal position. A number of branches are then stuck in the ground in the direction in which the poles are inclined and tied to the horizontal pole with strips of bark. Long grass is then laid over the branches in sufficient quantity to draw off the rain.

[1] Though the carriers are always called "Makololo," there were only two of that tribe among them. The company was mixed, but mainly Barotse.

In less than an hour we are usually all under cover."

This extract shows how closely Livingstone lived to his men. To one who, as was the case in this journey, was frequently in poor health, it must often have been very trying. Their noisy quarrelsome ways got at times on his nerves and he was glad of the little tent that gave him a certain amount of privacy. But for three years, except for one short interval, he had no other company. None the less, he never lost his affection for his Makololo, and only very rarely his patience.

During the journey, as he passed along, he continued day by day to describe, as if he had no other thought in his mind, the beauties of the country, the habits of bird and animals, and the customs of many peoples. In the exercise of these hobbies he found distraction and relief.

Not the least of his difficulties—especially as his physical strength deteriorated—was to live up to the ideal he had set himself of showing unvarying courtesy and maintaining civilised personal habits. This is a duty on which he constantly insists. "It is questionable," he says, "if a descent into barbarous ways ever elevates a man in the eyes of savages. I taught several of my men to wash my shirts, and they did it well, though their teacher had never been taught the work himself. Frequent changes of linen and sunning of my blanket kept me more comfortable than might have been anticipated, and I feel certain that the lessons of cleanliness rigidly instilled by my mother in

157

childhood, helped to maintain that respect which these people entertain for European ways." [1]

5. *Through Unknown Tracts*

At this period Sekeletu's authority stretched far to the North and travelling was easy. The people were friendly. Rains had begun, and the fresh greenness of Spring was over everything. Game swarmed to a degree that even Livingstone had never before seen. He soon found that his Africans could not be trusted with the business of hunting since they light-heartedly blazed away his precious ammunition. So providing for the larder became his special task, and at this stage it was not unduly heavy.

No sooner had he passed beyond into the Balonda country than he found himself involved in a local feud that might easily have put an end to the journey. It seemed that some of Sekeletu's warriors, acting without the Chief's permission, had raided the Balonda territory and had taken a score of prisoners. Hearing this, and in dread of serious consequences, Livingstone immediately summoned the culprits and, with the authority of the Chief behind him, ordered that the captives be restored. The headman unwillingly obeyed, and taking a large quantity of butter as compensation to the injured people, they advanced into the enemy country. They were met with a natural suspicion, which was aggravated when the man who had

[1] *Missionary Travels*, chap. XIV.

acted as guide to the marauders was recognised among his followers. When, however, the Balonda saw that all the prisoners had returned safely they accepted Livingstone's assurance that the raid had been contrary to Sekeletu's orders, and the trouble simmered down.

By the beginning of the New Year (1854) the rains had fully set in and movement grew increasingly difficult. They were drenched day and night, and dry resting-placcs were often not available. They turned west and followed the line of the Leeba river. In spite of its over-abundance, Livingstone records his pleasure in the rain. He could hardly persuade himself that he was getting too much, or rid himself of the feeling that the water was being "thrown away" and that they were being guilty of waste, an impression that only those who have lived as he had done, in rainless tracts, can appreciate.

As they journeyed westward the scenery changed rapidly. The vegetation grew heavy and close. The deep gloom of the forests was in sharp contrast to the well-remembered glare of the Kalahari. At first the contrast was delightful. Before long, however, it reacted on the spirits of the company as it was to do increasingly as the journey continued.

In the Balonda country the people were noted as being much darker than the Bantu, amongst whom he had thus far lived, and approximating more to the Negro type. Many other differences were recorded, and one thing that impressed him much was the position the women held among them. Frequently the chiefs were women, and their influence was remarkable. One Chieftainess, Nyamoana, whose territory lay about the point where the Leeba ceased to be navigable, insisted upon their leaving their canoes and paying a visit to her brother Shinte, the supreme chief of the district, at a town of that name. Partly for safety and partly because supplies had run out, Livingstone thought it wise to consent; whereupon a daughter of the lady, Manenko by name, took them vigorously in charge. A tall strapping woman of about twenty years of age, and an Amazon indeed, she appeared "in a state of frightful nudity not so much from want of clothing as from her peculiar ideas of elegance in dress." She mounted Livingstone on an ox and "herself started the march with her husband, her drummer and a suite of ladies and gentlemen and walked at the head of the caravan herself at such a pace that few men could keep up with her." Livingstone was relieved to be able to preserve his dignity by riding. But the pace was deceptive. There was much delay, and meanwhile it rained unendingly. Everything was soaked. The guns grew rusty and food was scarce, and all were hungry.

When at last the town was reached, it was brought home to Livingstone that he was now in West Central Africa. Shinte was regularly built, the houses, unlike those in the East, were square. There were fine banana groves and the place was well shaded by green trees. To his discomfort he noticed two mulatto Portuguese traders, and many

MRS. LIVINGSTONE AND OSWELL

VISION
THE CALL FROM THE NORTH
(*Gift of the London Missionary Society*)

Mambari, and the Makololo saw for the first time a slave gang in chains. "They are beasts who treat their children so," was their indignant exclamation.

The Chief received them with barbaric splendour, seated on a sort of throne that was covered with a leopard skin. About a thousand people were gathered and three hundred braves. The place of audience was about one hundred yards square. The Chief looked a dignified figure, dressed in a checked jacket and a kilt of scarlet baize, and loaded with beads and copper ornaments. On his head he wore a great bunch of goose feathers. Behind him sat a hundred of his wives.

During the stay an amusing incident happened. One night Livingstone fitted up his lantern and showed slides on Old Testament subjects. The first was of Abraham, arm uplifted, about to strike his son Isaac. The speaker explained the meaning. All listened awestruck until the slide being extracted, and the uplifted blade suddenly seemed to move towards the place where the women were seated. Pandemonium broke loose. The women shrieked "Mother, Mother," and tumbled over each other in their eagerness to escape, and could by no means be persuaded to return.

6. Still Westward

Shinte was gracious and a fortnight was spent in his town. He provided a guide who conducted them to the adjoining country of Lobale where Katema was Chief. Soon they reached the watershed between the Zambezi and the tributaries of the Congo. Though the country was rich and the people prosperous, they became less friendly as the Expedition advanced. Livingstone saw clearly that the reason for this change was that they were in frequent contact with the slave traders and had been demoralised thereby. Even here, however, the trade had not the brutality of the traffic that he was to see later. The slaves were bought or kidnapped but the fire and slaughter methods were in general not used.

The tribes grew increasingly grasping and obstructive as they moved west. Food could be bought only at high prices, and tricks were played upon them and fines levied. One day a knife was purposely left on the path. One of the porters lifted it and hid it in his load. Soon after they were stopped and a charge of theft preferred. Livingstone declared angrily that his men were not thieves, but when, the load being opened, the knife was discovered, there was nothing to be said. A fine had to be paid. Such annoyances became frequent. The trouble was not all with the tribes, however. The Makololo were great people in their own country and given, themselves, to plunder. Indeed the only journeys they were in the habit of making were for that purpose. Hence they were apt to hector. It took all the Leader's care and tact to avoid quarrels.

And all the time it rained and rained. "Never

did I endure such drenchings. I don't care much for fatigue but when compelled to stand still in pouring rain, then fever laid hold with strong fangs on my inwards. The lying in my little gipsy tent with everything damp and wet was sore against the grain. Frequent and most severe attacks of intermittent (fever) made me horribly weak but I never lay by for that."

He travelled, when he could, on a cross-grained brute of an ox which he called Sinbad, that had a nasty habit of prodding whenever opportunity offered. He would never allow his rider to hold up an umbrella and had a disconcerting habit of bolting suddenly under any tree that had branches low enough to scrape his master off. Once the ox pitched him into a river. But none the less, Livingstone valued him. He was a troublesome but useful servant, and carried a grateful master all the way west and nearly all the way home.

His carriers, though they served him well, grumbled constantly. The unending rain, the incessant mud and dark forest, and the complete lack of sunshine, depressed all heavily. One adventure, however, heartened their leader not a little. It showed their loyalty and affection. Crossing a river one morning, and intending to follow the native method of swimming by holding on to an ox's tail, he missed his grip, sank and had to strike out for the bank. The men had not seen him swim before and got such a fright that twenty of them dumped their loads and sprang into the water to rescue him. As he reached the bank one had him by the arm and another round the waist. It was well worth the ducking.

Food became an increasingly difficult problem. They had to kill, one by one, the oxen they had brought, but often the flesh had to be used as presents to the chiefs to smooth the way through. In a village called Njambi an unpleasant incident happened. Though a good lump of meat had been sent to its chief, next morning there came an impudent demand for a gun or a cloth or a man, and when these were refused the camp was surrounded with intent to plunder. Livingstone, with that deliberate slowness of manner which was so impressive among a shouting, dancing crowd, brought out his camp stool and sat down with his fowling-piece across his knees, and quietly asked what all the fuss was about. This calmed things for a moment, and then a youth, bolder than the rest, made a sudden charge at him from behind, only to retire even more suddenly when he found a gun poked into his face. Livingstone once more sat down deliberately and kept quietly looking around, fixing the more excited warriors with his strong eyes. His own men were strung up to fight, but their Leader's coolness kept them from losing their heads. Gradually Livingstone's intrepidity had its effect and the villagers, believing that conditions were growing dangerous, became less truculent. A bargain was, in the end, struck. An ox was bartered in exchange for food for the party. The bargain was poorly kept, it is true. Only a small portion of the flesh they themselves had presented came back. Still, Livingstone was well content. Arms had not been used. It was essential to his plan of introducing peaceful commerce that violence should be avoided.

Not long after he had an uncomfortable surprise of a different sort. He had, well as he understood the childish irresponsibility of his followers, never feared mutiny among them. But something of that sort occurred one Sunday. He was down with a bout of fever and had kept to his tent, but had given orders that one of the few remaining oxen should be killed. During the dividing of the meat a loud shouting was kept up that irritated the sick man past endurance. He ordered them to be quiet, but to the reproof they replied with impudent laughter. This unusual conduct seemed dangerously like mutiny. So he sprang to his feet, seized his revolver and, his eyes flashing, sprang out amongst the men. They were quiet at once and never again gave trouble.

7. *Portuguese West Africa*

The truth was that the poor fellows were losing heart. They had by that time been three months on an unending monotonous journey under conditions that were unfamiliar. The sun rarely shone, and when it did, the thick forest hid its light. Unfriendly tribes blocked the way, and a constant watch had to be kept against pilfering. At last their patience was exhausted. They came in a body and this time respectfully begged him to give up and return. He replied quietly that if they went back he would go on alone. To this there was but one answer. Patience was at last rewarded. They reached the valley of the Kwango, the eastern boundary of Portuguese West Africa, and found themselves to their delight in sunshine and in typical African park-land scenery, and the porters' spirits rose.

The relation to the tribes, however, did not improve. They became, on the contrary, more and more exacting. Barter goods were by now all gone and the Leader had by degrees to surrender to greedy demands his shirts, his razor and other personal effects, and the Makololo their copper ornaments. In his debilitated condition Livingstone found it increasingly hard to cope with these unfriendly chiefs, and confessed that a point came when he could hardly resist ordering his men to use their guns. On this occasion it was the porters who counselled patience. And then, as so often happened in Livingstone's story, deliverance came with dramatic suddenness.

They had been stopped by the wide river. Canoes were refused and a slave demanded as payment. Livingstone, exhausted by weakness, was on the point of surrendering his precious coat when, unexpectedly, a mulatto Portuguese sergeant appeared, used his authority with the tribe and had the party transported across. On the west side of this river a small garrison of militia was quartered, and by them exceeding kindness was shown to Livingstone and his men. They had still about five hundred miles to tramp—a third of the journey—but it was made much easier by the helpfulness of the Portuguese. Livingstone was so weak that, at first, he could hardly remember even his own name. He had for some time been forced to abandon his lunar observations. "I could not avoid confusion of times and distances," he says. "Nor could I hold an instrument steady or perform a simple calculation."

They were very hospitably housed at Cassange by the Commandant, and here Livingstone had his first square meal for months. He was ashamed of appearing so greedy, so much did he eat. Indeed he added, had his host not been present, he would have bought more food to devour at night. "For after fever the appetite is excessively keen and manioc (their staple food for months) was most unsatisfying." In addition to all this good food the Makololo had another reason for satisfaction. They had been able to barter, at what appeared to them a marvellous price, the ivory that Sekeletu had given them for sale and which they had so laboriously conveyed.

Not unnaturally the inhabitants were very curious about the purpose of Livingstone's errand and equally slow to accept his explanations. They could not believe him when he said he was a "Sacerdot." Had he not told them that he had a wife and children? He adds with a sly hit at some native priests of whom he had heard, that that was better than having children without a wife.

167

At Golungo Alto, an important town on the way, he was the grateful guest for some days of the Commandant—Antonio Canto e Castro—and here regained much strength. The scenery around this place is some of the finest in Africa—the country fruitful to an amazing degree, the beautiful hills being clothed up to their summits by crops and fruits of all sorts. It was soon after leaving this Land of Beulah that they had their first glimpse of the sea. As they crossed the hills, there it lay glistening in the distance. The Africans were thrilled. "We marched," they said, "along with our Father, believing that what the ancients had told us was true . . . that the world has no end. But all at once the world said to us, ' I am finished, there is no more of me.'"

There was also a certain pathos in the situation. Mr. Gabriel, the British Consul of Loanda, had received news of his approach and had sent an invitation to Livingstone to stay with him, but the letter had missed him and he, in his nervous condition, became greatly worried at the kind of reception that would meet him in a town of 12,000 people, amongst whom, he had learned, there was only one of his own race. The Africans on their part could not rid themselves of the dread that they might be kidnapped. To comfort them their leader gave assurance that what happened to them would happen to him.

Livingstone approached Loanda so weak in body that he could not sit on his ox for more than ten minutes at a time. This is his description of the welcome he received from the Consul, Mr. Edmund Gabriel:

"When I entered his porch I was delighted to see flowers cultivated carefully and inferred that he was what I discovered him to be, a real whole-hearted English gentleman. Seeing me ill he benevolently offered me his bed. Never shall I forget the luxurious pleasure I enjoyed of feeling myself in a good English couch after six months sleeping on the ground."

The date of arrival was May 31st, 1854. He had travelled 1,500 miles and it was two years since he had left Cape Town.

8. Rest and Return

Livingstone had seriously overtaxed his powers. Instead of feeling the benefit of Mr. Gabriel's unstinted hospitality, he began to grow worse. Severe dysentery supervened. Nothing could have exceeded the concern of his host or the consideration of the Portuguese Authorities. As far as his strength allowed, he passed the time in writing up his Diary, reports to the L.M.S. and letters to his family. So weak was he that he was glad to accept Mr. Gabriel's help in the actual writing.

By good fortune some small British cruisers, engaged in the suppression of the slave trade, were in the harbour at the time. The Commander of one of these, Captain Phillips of the H.M.S. *Polyphemus*, impressed by Livingstone's miserable condition, not only sent his ship's surgeon to treat him, but urged him to accept a passage home. The invitation must have been one of the sharpest temptations of his life. In his state of health the prospect of a return through that unfriendly jungle must have been appalling. He had confidently expected letters from his family at Loanda. It was now more than two years since he had heard of them. There were none. But he dismissed the tempting proposal in half a sentence as if refusal were a foregone conclusion, as no doubt it was. He had given his word to his Makololo and he knew they could not return without him. Besides, the journey had not solved his problem. The road to the West was too laborious to be extensively used as a trading route.

To his Africans Loanda had been a place of many marvels, and their belief in the Leader had been greatly increased by the honour with which he had, so obviously, been received. The large stone houses and churches had struck them with awe. But it was a visit to a warship that had impressed them most. "It is not a canoe," they said "It is a town!" One of them was given the great privilege of being allowed to fire a cannon. The sailors treated them with great good nature. They found easy employment too, in the city, and felt wealthy on the sixpence a day that they received for unloading coal for the cruisers.

Livingstone paid his respects to the Bishop, who was also the Acting Governor. This gentleman saw the value, from his town's point of view, of establishing trade relations with Sekeletu and promised his interest. He presented a horse and a colonel's uniform for the Chief, and clothes, in blue and red cloth, for each of the porters.

Livingstone was long enough in Loanda to realise how deeply the Portuguese authorities were committed to the slave traffic. The port had been a centre of the trade for centuries. It must be admitted that there was a certain magnanimity in the attitude of the Portuguese towards their visitor. The trade by which they had lived and thriven was being throttled by the pressure of the British cruisers. Livingstone they knew as a strong opponent of their trade, and yet they treated him as a good friend and helped him on his way. When on September 20th, 1854, the return journey began, he was full of gratitude for their hospitality and assistance.

The journey back took almost a year, twice the time that the westward route had required. In general his rate of travel was rapid judged by the practice of others. In a letter to the Royal Geographical Society he states that traders usually travelled ten days in a month and then made only seven miles a day, whereas his pace was twenty days a month at the rate of ten miles a day.

Painful news reached him at Pungo Andongo, where he was the guest of Colonel Pires, a rich merchant. He heard that the *Forerunner*, which had carried his dispatches, maps and much other correspondence, had been wrecked off Madeira and that all but one passenger had been lost. Had he accepted the berth that had been offered him he would have been on that ship.

He had to rewrite all his papers and redraw all his maps. This meant much delay. While staying here, however, he was delighted to receive a cutting from *The Times*, forwarded by Mr. Gabriel, which spoke of his journey to Loanda as one of the greatest geographical operations of the age. Later he was to hear with even greater pleasure that the Royal Geographical Society had presented him with its Gold Medal, its highest honour.

He was much impressed with the beauty and fertility of the country round Pungo Andongo and with the density of the population. Nevertheless the Colony did not prosper. He believed this to be a result of the debasing results of slavery, or what amounted to slavery, among them. Up to this point on his journey Livingstone was still in touch with the outside world. He hoped against hope that family letters might yet arrive, and Mr. Gabriel sent runners after him with mail. No such letters came, but instead national news that made him anxious. The Crimean War was at a critical stage. The last intelligence told of the charge of the Light Brigade and then he had to move on. The connection was broken, and he did not learn the sequel, nor indeed did he hear from his wife, till he reached the East Coast, twenty months later.

9. The Second Stage of the Great Journey

He said farewell in the beginning of 1855 to his most hospitable friend, Colonel Pires, and began the eastward journey in earnest. His caravan was well stocked. There were trade goods now in plenty. He carried, too, a strong tent that the British sailors had made for him, and his men had guns. He kept in the main to the track he had followed. He found, in general, the tribes more friendly, partly because of the good impression they had previously made and also, no doubt, because they carried more guns, though happily they did not need to use these. In spite of these favourable circumstances the going was slower. Livingstone had frequent bouts of malaria and his carriers suffered in the same way. The rainy season was again on. The tall grass through which they had to force their way was usually water-laden and the ground was swampy and difficult.

By now Livingstone had learned that he could not take the same liberties with his constitution that he had thus far done. Indeed he received, when near Cassange, a sharp reminder of this fact in a severe attack of rheumatic fever, accompanied by heavy loss of blood. The Doctor who had succoured so many, received on this occasion help from a Portuguese gentleman who fortunately arrived at the time. Relief was afforded by the application of leeches that swarmed in the streams around.

No lengthened account need be given of the return journey, since the incidents are in the main a repetition of what had gone before, except that travel was on the whole, perhaps, harder, because of the mud and morass. But one adventure which he tells vividly should not be omitted, since it might readily have led to his being killed.

It was while he was still weak from the rheumatic fever referred to that a headman of one of the villages was struck on the mouth by one of Livingstone's men. "My principal headman," he writes, "paid five pieces of cloth and a gun as an atonement, but the more they yielded the more exorbitant the Chief's demands became, and he sent round to the surrounding villages to aid him to revenge the affront of a blow on the beard. As their courage usually rises with success, I resolved to yield no more and departed.

"In passing through the forest, in the country beyond, we were startled by a body of men rushing at us. They began by knocking down the burdens from the hindermost of my men and several shots were fired, each party spreading out on both sides of the road. I, fortunately, had a six barrelled revolver and with this in my hand I staggered along the path with two or three of my men and fortunately encountered the Chief. The sight of my six barrels gaping into his stomach and my own ghastly visage looking daggers at his face, seemed to produce an instant revolution of his martial feelings, for he cried out 'Oh, I have only come to speak to you. I wish only peace.'

We examined his gun and found that it had been fired. Both parties crowded round the Chief.

"I requested all to sit down and said to the Chief, 'If you have come with a peaceful intention we have no other. Go home to your village.' He replied, 'I am afraid lest you should shoot me in the back.' I rejoined, 'If I wanted to kill you I could shoot you in the face as well.' Mosanto called out to me, 'That is only a Makalaka trick, don't give him your back.' But I said, 'Tell him to observe that I am not afraid of him,' and turning, mounted my ox and took my departure."[1]

And so with occasional excitement the journey went on monotonously. Month followed month in dull country over heavy spongy ground, shadowed by dense dripping forest. "These bogs are exceedingly trying to both cattle and men. The surface is covered with a kind of thick wiry grass, which is rooted in clods and floating on soft slush. If one can manage to tread on these they bear him up but one often steps on the side instead of the crown and the foot slips off down a foot or two, sometimes three, into the slush. I never got over one of these bogs without many such mishaps and many other people the same. The oxen found this much more difficult. They are always one or two feet in the mud and frequently all four, leaving them lying on their belly. So fatigued do they become by about quarter of a mile of this that they lie down disheartened and can be raised only by the people

[1] *Missionary Travels*, chap. XXII.

biting their tails." When rain ceased, white mists rose and it was like breathing steam. It was always difficult to get dry wood for fires. He records his twenty-seventh attack of malaria.

Throughout this never-ending trudge Livingstone, except when absolutely incapacitated, never relaxed his self-imposed discipline, but made observations, studied various languages and prepared reports for his scientific friends.

10. Back in Linyanti

By the middle of 1855 the Expedition was back in Katema's village, and Livingstone thanked God for familiar faces. Shinte and the amazon Manenko welcomed him as an old friend, a few weeks later, on his arrival at their town.

A small tragedy happened here. The ox Sinbad, ungracious till the end, was bitten by tsetse fly and died.

His main labour over, Livingstone had time to sum up the chief results of his travel. One that he puts high was its educative effect on the Makololo. The visit to the ships *Pluto* and *Philomel* had taught them more than he could have done in a year. "They had the idea that they would be kidnapped, but when I said, 'These are my countrymen and your friends,' and the jolly tars, who happened to be at dinner, freely gave them beef and biscuits, a world of prejudice vanished at once. I felt a foot higher myself." He knew that what his men had seen they would tell, and he believed that this would make the tribe generally more willing to give heed to his message. Further, he hoped that the wages they had earned, that seemed to them so lavish, would induce others to visit the Coast, and that the direct touch thus established would cut out the Mambari traders and thus help to stop the spread of the slave traffic. These results were admittedly only second best. In its main purpose the labour had been vain—"It had been found unpracticable," he has to admit, "to open up a carriageway to the Coast."

His bent of mind is shown in another—a small—matter. He had been impressed by the fruit trees in Angola. These had been introduced centuries before by Jesuit priests. So he felt himself in an apostolic succession, when he brought away with him cuttings of orange, fig and other trees and shrubs. He was afraid that if he took them further inland the climate might be too severe for them to thrive, so he had them planted under Shinte's care.

By the end of July they were back in the Makololo country, where they were received with a "demonstration of joy" such as the Missionary never saw before. They were as those who had risen from the dead. "The women came to meet us with their curious dancing gestures and shouts of 'lulliloos.' They kissed the hands and cheeks of the different persons of their acquaintance and the whole commotion of the moving cavalcade raised such a dust that it was a relief to reach the council room where the elders sat."

The following day a great thanksgiving service was held. "The men decked themselves out in their best and it was found that although all their goods were finished, they had managed somehow to save their suits of European clothing which being white, with their red caps, gave them a dashing appearance." They tried to walk like the soldiers they had seen at Loanda and called themselves his "braves." During the service they sat with guns over their shoulders and excited the unbounded admiration of the women and children. The Missionary spoke on the goodness of God "in preserving all from the dangers of strange tribes and diseases." Except for one man who had deserted on reaching his home country, he had brought them all back in safety—a marvellous achievement.

The progress down the Barotse valley was an ovation all the way. Every village sent an ox, with no thought of presents in return. They realised that Livingstone's prodigious efforts had been for their gain.

At Sesheke news was received that packages of goods were lying for him at the other side of the Zambezi. These had been left there by some of Mosilikatse's men, who said they were for "Nyaka" and had been sent by Dr. Moffat. The Makololo had feared a trap and had waited till the messengers were gone, and then brought them to an island in the middle of the stream and had built a hut over them. They had been there a year and the news they contained had lost interest. But the packages showed Mrs. Moffat's motherly care; for they held "white shirts and a blue waistcoat, woollen socks, lemon juice, quince jam and tea and coffee all the way from Hamilton."[1] But there was no word from Mrs. Livingstone.

Sekeletu was in no hurry to meet his friend. He had an uneasy conscience. He had been leading marauding parties against neighbours. They did at last meet, however, at Linyanti, where they arrived on 11th September, 1855, after an absence of two years.

Here again there were great rejoicings, and Livingstone handed over to the Chief the gifts sent by the Government of Loanda—the Colonel's dress coat, trousers and sash. These Sekeletu wore with much dignity and self-consciousness at the thanksgiving service and, the preacher adds with a smile, attracted much more attention than did the sermon.

The Chief was well pleased with the results of the journey and at once began to prepare another expedition. This in due course reached Loanda, where the men were again helped by Mr. Gabriel.

Livingstone was also gratified to find the wagon, that he had parked two years before near the town, safe. The guards had proved faithful. More important, the horses he had left were in good condition. This was encouraging because it

[1] *Blaikie*, chap. XXV.

proved that horses could live in that climate. These, Sir Harry Johnston thought, "were the forerunners of the establishment of the regular breed in the Barotse country."

The rest of two months that Livingstone gave himself before he started off again were only change of labour. He wrote many letters of great length. His Diary contains an elaborate review of the geology of Central Africa—the result of endless labour and observation—the first survey of these vast districts. In that connection, however, he found information in his mail that came as a shock. He had long been working at a theory to explain many phenomena that had puzzled him, such as the rapid drying up of the sources of water supply that was all too evident, and the apparently erratic behaviour of certain rivers. He had evolved the theory that the African Continent was, as he called it, "dish shaped." It was a brilliant conception now generally accepted. No doubt he had often toyed with the thought of the world-wide excitement that would be created when he announced his discovery. It must have been a keen disappointment, therefore, when he read in the papers sent him the announcement that Sir Roderick Murchison, Chairman of the Royal Geographical Society had, in the quiet of his study, already reached and had promulgated a similar conclusion. He accepted the inevitable with the best grace he could muster, and wrote to Sir Roderick an account of all the confirming facts that he himself had gathered. This led to a friendship that was one of the most fruitful of his life.

So, turning to his work, he used all the opportunity which the great popularity he then enjoyed gave him to proclaim his message. He was listened to with marked attention and he had visions of Linyanti as a mission station.

The people were urging him all the time to bring Ma–Robert—Mrs. Livingstone—to settle permanently among them, but he knew that was not to be. The yeast of a great new idea had begun to work. The curse of the slave traffic had become increasingly obvious to him. Its trail had been over all his journey west and now it was appearing in a yet more menacing form from the east, and the tribes about him were becoming affected.

It had been remarked already that it was not Livingstone's way to plan his life's path. Step by step he was led to more and more important tasks. His was the duty to be ready and to follow whatever might be the cost.

11. The Third Part of the Journey: The Route East

The eight weeks halt did the exhausted explorer much good and that not only physically. "In travelling the heart becomes benumbed. I feared much I was becoming a heathen myself, but a little rest has, thank God, quickened my spiritual feelings."

One of his visitors while at Linyanti was a far-travelled intelligent Arab named Ben Habib. With him Livingstone had many talks and was able to learn much of unexplored Africa and of districts that he himself was yet to know in after years. This man spoke of Lakes Nyasa and Tanganyika and another great lake beyond, and much else that stimulated Livingstone's passion for discovery.

He set out on the third of November, 1855, in the hot days before the rains, and Sekeletu went with him part of the way and supplied him abundantly with trade goods, including ivory and also a large company of free porters. A few days later he made the most spectacular of his discoveries, the great falls which he named the "Victoria Falls," after his Queen. He had heard of them many times, indeed their fame was over all Africa, but he was the first European to see and describe them. As he approached, the river Zambezi, here nearly a mile broad, was seen to his amazement to disappear and plunge out of sight with a stupendous roar into a narrow fissure hundreds of feet deep. Thence it churned its tumultuous course for thirty miles along a deep frowning gorge. Clouds of spray like pillars rose continuously.

This colossal phenomenon, called by the Natives Mosi-oa-tunya (the smoke that sounds), baffled even his powers of description. He makes a reference, not a comparison, it is true, to waterfalls near his own home town—a likeness so inadequate as to be almost amusing. If excuse for this failure be needed it might be urged that till then the Stonebyre Falls on the Clyde were the largest he had seen. But the failure has its value in that it emphasises the general reliability of his observations. His accounts had nothing in common with the tales of romantic travellers. His weakness, if he had one, was his fear of over-statement. Part of the reason for the inadequacy of his description came from the fact that the river was at the time low and that he did not cross to the south bank, from which much the best views are to be had. It may be mentioned that when, four years later, he revisited the place, the description then given was very much more adequate and his measurements of its gigantic dimensions much more nearly correct.

With rare courage he approached in a canoe the lip of the terrifying abyss. It was a nerve-racking experience. He says: "At one time we seemed to be going right into the gulf but though I felt a little tremor I said nothing, believing that I could face a difficulty as well as my guides." They floated swiftly to an island above the Falls and landed, and, lying flat on the brink, peered down into the awesome boiling cauldron. Next day he revisited the spot, made there a little garden, and planted some peach and apricot stones. Then, he adds shamefacedly: "I cut my name on a tree and the date 1856"—the only time he had committed "that piece of vandalism." Hippopotami soon spoiled the garden. The tree remains, but the initials have been overgrown.

Here Sekeletu took leave. The young chief had not been a good pupil, but his attachment to his "Father" was genuine, as had been shown by an incident only the night before. They had been caught in an unexpected thunderstorm and soaked. Livingstone's boxes had been sent ahead, and there being nothing else to do, he lay down on the ground, ruminating dismally on the probable consequences of the exposure. Sekeletu quietly spread over his sleeping friend his own blanket, and lay himself uncovered. This was a story that Livingstone loved to recall and he treasured the blanket. In spite of the obviously real devotion, however, he could not trust this kind-hearted youth, son of a great father, and his fears were well grounded. They met once more four years later, under pitiable circumstances.

Travel was this time more comfortable, though on occasion dangerous. His health was better, and this he ascribed to more suitable food. The tribes were on the whole friendly.

12. "The Word of a Gentleman"

The route in general followed the course of the Zambezi. Livingstone walked most of the way and benefited by the exercise.

It was at the borders of Portuguese territory, where the Loangwa, a large river, comes in from the North, that there happened perhaps the best-known adventure of his life. The river was broad and the company large. Several canoes were needed, but the Chief Mburuma would lend only two. His behaviour was ominous. "Coming after marauders," the Diary remarks, "we have all to bear suspicion." His warriors gathered from all sides, professing friendship but holding aloof. No women were to be seen. Their purpose was clearly to divide the party and attack them next morning while crossing the river. The entry in the Diary is much more explicit than the account he transferred afterwards to his book of travel—a characteristic illustration of his reserve. It shows deep perturbation of spirit. For the only time in his life, as far as our records go, Livingstone was afraid. His habitual courage was of the kind that paid no heed to danger. In this incident we see a supreme illustration of the higher courage which, being afraid, yet goes on without swerving.

The entry in the *Journal* is in two parts, written at an interval of some hours.

In the first he writes as if his last hour had come. He remembers his mercies and his sins, and renews his trust in God. "A guilty weak and helpless worm into Thine arms I fall," he quotes. He thinks sadly of his family. "They are thine: They are in the best of hands. I cast myself and all my cares down at Thy feet," and then with a sudden turn of thought: "It seems a pity that the important facts about two healthy longitudinal ridges should not become known to Christendom. Thy will be done." The handwriting is clearer and firmer even than usual, but the distress of spirit is obvious.

The next entry is in a completely different key. It is easy to imagine what has happened. The evening meal is finished. The groups of black figures have slipped away into the eerie dusk. Livingstone is seated outside his little tent reading and writing in the rapidly failing light. He has regained his poise, and the next entry gives the reason:

"Evening. Felt much turmoil of spirit in view of having all my plans for the welfare of this region and teeming population knocked on the head by savages to-morrow. But I read that Jesus came and said 'All power is given unto me in Heaven and on Earth. Go ye therefore and teach all nations and (heavily underlined) *Lo I am with you always even unto the end of the world.*' It is the word of a gentleman of the most sacred and strictest honour and there's an end on't. I will not cross furtively by night as intended. It would appear as flight and should such a man as I flee? Nay verily. I shall take observation for Lat. and Long. to-night though they may be my last. I am quite calm now. Thank God."

In the morning things look blacker than ever. The warriors have been reinforced from neighbouring villages. Women and children have been sent away, even the Chief's wife chased out of sight. Only one canoe has been produced though others can be seen. It is a critical moment but the leader is his reliant self again and the company are influenced by his calm. Camp is struck and the goods packed without haste according to the usual routine. Then Livingstone quietly shepherds his porters to the bank and into the single canoe, first the goods, then the cattle and then the men. The single canoe plies back and forward, so progress is slow, but there is an island in mid-stream that serves as a useful half-way stop. Livingstone stands on the bank. At times the armed men crowd round him and he keeps them amused with his watch, his mirror and his burning-glass. Then, when the last man is safe in the canoe, he thanks the Chief politely for his kindness and steps aboard. Next day he sends back gifts.

The qualities that make this man great appear perhaps more clearly in this story than in any other event in his life. The sentence with which the account in the Diary closes illustrates in a most characteristic fashion his fear of appearing to brag, and his charity. "Perhaps," he says, "after all they were influenced only by a desire to be ready in case I should play them some false trick. They have reason to be suspicious of whites." The sentence, "Should such a man as I flee?" which seems to have an air of bravado, was clearly influenced by no such thought. It is an outcrop of Livingstone's fundamental faith. He is thinking of himself not as a man, but as an Ambassador.

¹ Nehemiah vi. 11.

13. Nearing the Coast

Portuguese territory was reached at Zumbo, and they found there the ruins of well-built houses and of a church, nearby which lay a broken bell with the inscription I.H.S. and a cross. This station was a memorial of the past glory of the Portuguese Empire and the devotion of Jesuit Fathers. The colony had gradually declined, the effect of climate and the pressure of virile tribes. Zumbo has since been reoccupied.

The journey towards Tete had some very difficult moments. Above all things, the leader dreaded being forced to use arms for he felt that even a skirmish would ruin his work and purposes. But at times it was made very difficult for him. They had hoped to be able to do much of the journey by canoe, but there were several powerful river lords on the route, all jealous of their rights and all most grasping. His men on their side were difficult to hold in hand. They were well armed and had grown militant. Time and again it was only Livingstone's tact and patience that averted bloodshed, but he succeeded.

His approach had been made known to the Governor of Tete, and before he reached that town he was met by a company of soldiers with a machila (hammock) which he was glad to use. His health had been poor of late. Fever had attacked him once more.

He was detained some time at Tete and was

there the guest of Major Sicard, a Portuguese gentleman of a fine type, who became a staunch friend.

The eastward tour had been satisfactory. The road had proved much easier than that to the West, but its real value, as a solution of his special problem, depended on whether or not the Zambezi were navigable throughout all its course, up to the Falls. He believed that it was, but there was doubt. There were cataracts above Tete. If these were passable by boats there would be easy access to the interior through which "Christian Commerce" could penetrate. If not, some other way must be found. He could not spare the time to explore the Rapids—there were urgent reasons why he should go Home—but he planned to make only a short stay in Britain—not more than a few months.

When he returned he would still need the help of Sekeletu's men. An immediate problem, therefore, was to make some temporary arrangement for his porters. Here Major Sicard's help was invaluable. Land was set aside that they might cultivate and thus support themselves till he came back. Having thus settled them in safety, he promised an early return and said good-bye. When on May 20th he arrived at Quilimane he learnt that the Government vessel, the *Dart*, had been on the outlook for him but had gone on. He also learned that she had lost a lieutenant and five seamen while attempting to cross the bar of the river. He felt somehow responsible for this disaster and it upset him not a little.

189

There were letters waiting for him, but alas still none from his wife. He had to wait six weeks before the next ship, the *Frolic*, called, but when she came she brought abundant supplies, many letters—some from his family—and much needed money.

Among the many pleasant communications that the mails brought there was one that wounded him sorely. It was from Dr. Tidman, Secretary of the L.M.S. It began by expressing in the warmest terms admiration for his magnificent efforts, but went on to say that the Society's financial position prevented it from promising "within any definite period to enter into any remote, untried and difficult fields of labour."

The phrasing was perhaps unfortunate, and Livingstone read into it more than was intended. It seemed to the travel-weary man to be a revoking of the promise given him to push north from Kolobeng. Further, it seemed to cast doubt on the value of his unparalleled efforts and even to back up the criticism of some of his colleagues in the comfortable South, that exploration was not missionary work. That touched him to the quick. Any suggestion that he was less a missionary than the "dumpy man" in the long coat with a book under his arm, that he was fond of poking fun at, hurt him deeply. Had he not "in season and out of season" preached the Gospel? Had he not spread it more widely than any man alive? Had he not discovered a belt of elevated land, eastward of the Makololo country, well suited for the residence of missionaries? "Viewed," he exclaimed, "in relation to my calling, the geographical feat is the beginning of the missionary enterprise."

The difference so far as it existed was, on his arrival home, quickly adjusted. The Directors had not meant all that in his tired state he had understood, but still this was one of the causes of his resignation from their service.

No missionary of modern days has done so much as he to commend the Christian faith to the world, not by his preaching, not even by his exploration, but by the shining example of his life.

After six weary weeks in Quilimane he boarded the H.M. brig *Frolic* and sailed for Mauritius. Here he rested and was helped back to health. He sailed for Southampton, but even on the way home adventure pursued him, for he was wrecked off Tunis and, in the end, reached England via Marseilles and Dover, on the 9th December, 1856. At Cairo he received the unexpected news of the death of his father. This was a very heavy blow.

His journey across Africa was, without doubt, one of the greatest achievements in geographical records. It lasted, counting the start from the Cape, just under four years. The distance covered, a considerable part on foot, was six thousand miles.

The claim that Livingstone was the first white traveller to cross the Continent has been strenuously disputed by Portuguese authorities. They assert that two half-caste Portuguese traders, Pedro Jean Baptista and Amaro José, performed the feat in 1806-11. Livingstone asserted that he had evidence to prove that they had not completed the journey. If they did what is claimed for them, they certainly did nothing to add to geographical knowledge. The Portuguese maps remained fantastic, based obviously on mere hearsay, for half a century after.

FAITH

CONFLICT WITH SUPERSTITION

(*Gift of the Congregational Church of Scotland*)

MERCY

FREEING A SLAVE GANG

(*Gift of the Anti-Slavery Society*)

THIRD INTERLUDE

FAME

THE FIRST VISIT HOME
1856 to 1857

LONDON.   SCOTLAND

"*One thing for which he is admired by his countrymen is that lofty and enduring courage, that British pluck which has sustained him for years through the deserts and swamps of Africa.*"
DUKE OF ARGYLE.   18th February, 1857.

"*While endeavouring to spread the blessings of Christianity through lands never before trodden by a British subject, he has made discoveries of incalculable importance.*"
SIR RODERICK MURCHISON.
15th December, 1856.

"*I say that what this man has done is unprecedented.   You could go to any point across the entire Continent along Livingstone's track and feel certain of your position.*"
SIR THOMAS MACLEAR,
Astronomer Royal, Cape Town.
12th November, 1856.

1. A National Figure

Livingstone's first action on landing was to hurry to Southampton where, he learned, his wife was awaiting him.

The past four years had been a time of great strain for Mrs. Livingstone. She had lived chiefly in a London suburb, a lonely anxious woman. She had good friends, but she was by nature reserved and she had depended so much upon her husband's strength that without him she felt lost. In those early days Livingstone had many critics and even a few enemies, and malicious rumours had somehow gained circulation. The husband, it was whispered, had been glad to be rid of his wife, he was consoling himself with Native women, had even, indeed, married an African princess. Such tittle-tattle sounds in modern ears ridiculous, but it had, at that time, some amount of currency and Mrs. Livingstone knew about it and felt it keenly.

Then, letters were rare. They came years apart. Many, both his and hers, went astray. No one knew better than she the dangers of the African forest. She wrote: "I never passed a dreamless night, nor knew an easy day." She had counted on one year of separation, then two. Actually it stretched, as we have seen, to four. Only the quiet, heroic courage, to which Mr. Oswell often testified, enabled her to face life. The joy of their reunion must have been in proportion to the length of their separation.

Always it was their fate, however, to have family interests circumscribed by public duty. They had not more than a day or two together when he was back in London at the call of the Royal Geographical Society, to attend a great welcome meeting. Thus there began a whirl of public engagements that, except for the months when he was working furiously at his first book, left him with hardly any rest, during the fifteen months of his furlough.

The tremendous enthusiasm that his return evoked is almost as surprising to look back upon as it was to him to experience. He had left home fifteen years before a quite insignificant person. Few had noticed in him more than mediocre gifts. In the intervening years he had been buried in Africa out of touch with the world save by letters to a few outstanding men of science and by reports to the London Missionary and Royal Geographical Societies—institutions that do not usually bulk largely in the eye of the general public.

It is true that the discovery of Lake Ngami and his appearance and disappearance at Loanda had put him "in the news" for short periods. Word of his crossing of Africa had no doubt once again created interest, but the public that concerns itself in matters of this sort is, ordinarily, not large. Yet his arrival home was an event of the first importance and he became forthwith, what he has ever since remained, a National Figure of

195

heroic proportions. Before long he was so well known that he hesitated to appear in the streets of London lest he should be mobbed by the curious. Once in Regent Street he had to take refuge in a cab. In church he had at times to seek an obscure corner lest his presence should be known and interfere with the devotion of the worshippers.

No doubt, the times were propitious. The Crimean War, recently concluded, had been fought in a manner that did credit to few except the common soldier. In India there were ominous signs of troubles to come. Times were bad and the country depressed. Then there came this man who seemed to embody all the virtues by which the British, as a people, believe themselves to be distinguished; a man without fear who had faced dangers innumerable and hardships inconceivable, and all for a noble disinterested purpose; a man, too, of the people, who owed help to no one, but had won his way by dint of native grit.

There was much, too, in his very look. His story was written plain upon his face. A sturdy, somewhat emaciated figure, a sallow complexion that showed the effects of exposure, an inanimated face that in its deep lines bore the marks of suffering; a strong mouth and grim expression, all combined with a simplicity of manner that gave confidence and set the seal of truth on all he said. It was not merely or mainly the intrepidity he had shown that attracted. Other travellers had been equally brave. It was perhaps chiefly a recognition of those rare gifts of understanding and sympathy with which he had captivated barbarous people, and of the spirit of Christian grace shown in all his dealings with them, that won for him the place in the hearts of the British public that he has never lost.

The hope of imperial expansion did not enter at all into the country's interest. The passion which led to the "Scramble for Africa" was not then born. But Africa was "in the air." Curiosity as to its uncharted spaces had grown from the stories of many travellers. Further, the revelation by Livingstone, that Central Africa was not, as had till then been believed, a sandy waste, but a fertile and thickly populated land, raised in the mind of the mercantile community high hopes of lucrative trade that might do much to counteract the after-war depression from which they were suffering.

Add to this the revived enthusiasm of all supporters of Foreign Missions and of the Philanthropic Societies, and the amazing warmth of the welcome becomes understandable.

At the meeting of the Royal Geographical Society referred to, Livingstone listened to a speech by its Chairman, Sir Roderick Murchison, in which he emphasised in unqualified terms the value of his discoveries. He found there also an equal, or perhaps greater, pleasure in seeing again his hunter friends, Steele and Vardon and Oswell.

Next day, at a great gathering called by the L.M.S. over which Lord Shaftesbury presided, he was again lauded to the skies.

Livingstone's speeches in reply were very short

and halting. He excused his lack of fluency on the ground of long disuse of his native tongue. His manner was notably modest, and he kept on reiterating that he had done no more than his duty. He made it plain that he considered his work as only begun, and announced, as the purpose of his life, the determination to abolish the slave traffic and to open Africa up to "Commerce and Christianity." It is worth remarking that the first meeting in his honour—it took place two months before that in London—was held in Cape Town. The new Governor, Sir George Grey, who presided, was himself an explorer and an official of wide experience. The speakers united in a pæan of praise that could not but be gratifying to Livingstone when he heard of it, by its contrast to what had happened only four years before. The change in feeling was due in good measure to the influence of his friend Maclear, the Astronomer Royal.

2. The Penalty of Fame

Livingstone would have been less than human if he had not received keen pleasure from all this appreciation; but at the same time it was a trial to one so shy to be the central figure in so many public gatherings. To be lauded till, as he says, he felt he had to shut his eyes; to be lionised by people so imposing, in circles so brilliant was embarrassing to a degree. In Society he and his

wife were described as "shy." He rarely spoke
unless addressed, and never of his experiences
unless drawn out, though when he did he showed
a sense of "lively humour." When he told of his
achievements he always used the pronoun "we."

He was received by Queen Victoria and amused
her by saying that when Africans inquired after
her wealth, the query always took the form of a
question as to how many cows she had. All these
glittering excitements, however, interfered with
what he longed for most, a quiet time with his
own people and an opportunity to get to know his
children. They had been living in Hamilton. The
family had left the Shuttle Row soon after he
sailed for Africa. As soon as he could break free
he hurried North. He was delighted to find his
mother well and was affected to tears when they
spoke of the father's death.

It is in curious contrast to Livingstone's dislike
of publicity—a fact of which there can be no
question—that he wore everywhere the gold-
braided cap that is now so closely associated with
him that it is quite impossible to think of him
in any other headgear. It must have made him
"kenspeckle" wherever he went, but none the less
he persisted. This seems to indicate a rather
delightful little human failing, a spice of obstinacy
or perhaps even a trifle of vanity. It is customary
to call this his "Consular cap." This is a mistake.
(See Appendix III.)

Early in 1856 the proposal was made to him that
he should write a book on his travels. He felt this

to be a duty, but the task itself he found very irksome. He had all the necessary material in his Diary, but he was distrustful of his own gift as a writer. It was not that he had any lack of experience. The few short articles he had written to various magazines had, it is true, not been accepted, but his private correspondence was enormous, and each letter was the size of a small pamphlet. (See Appendix IV.)

The book took several months to complete. He found it an uncongenial task. He used to say he would rather cross Africa than write another book. The work had, however, one great compensation. It could be written in the midst of his family. It was indeed so written in a literal sense, in a London lodging, with his children shouting and tumbling around him. Their noise did not perturb him. From early youth he had learned the discipline of concentration. As a family they were a merry crowd—and Robert, the eldest, was a stirring lad. The father, when free, was full of fun. He had the most wonderful stories and knew how to tell them. His custom was to take the children to the Barnet Woods and there act hunting scenes and teach them scout-craft as practised by the Makololo. Sometimes, as a special treat, he would show them the marks of the lion's teeth on his arm!

The book, *Missionary Travels and Researches in South Africa*, was an immediate success. It was published by John Murray at a guinea, and seven large editions were quickly taken up. Reviewers were unanimous and enthusiastic. Livingstone showed an almost boyish delight, by scattering signed copies around to all his friends. Murray's terms were generous, and the financial result to a man who had lived for so long on £100 a year seemed a fortune, but, as we shall see, he gave away what came to him lavishly. He built a small cottage in Hamilton and this became the family home.

The book still retains its place as a classic. It is a perfect mine of accurate information on native customs, the habits of beasts and birds, and very much else. As a story of travel it is less successful. The mass of other material interferes with the flow of the narrative. The style, though somewhat Johnsonian, is simple and clear, with often a happy, memorable phrase. The tone is restrained as if he feared exaggeration. It is not often that he allows his innate love of beauty to appear, but when he does he shows that he can paint a lovely picture.

3. The Wider Task

This exacting work finished, Livingstone was at liberty to accept some of the numberless invitations that had come to him, to lecture and to speak. He was a guest of honour at the British Association meetings in Dublin. He met the Manchester Chamber of Commerce, showed to the members twenty different kinds of African products that he had brought home with him, and discussed for their benefit the openings for trade in Africa.

Degrees and honours were showered upon him. He was made Freeman of London and Glasgow, and in the latter city was presented with £2000. Nothing was too high for this man who had begun life as a "piecer" in a Blantyre mill. There is the best evidence, however, to believe that he was not in the least spoiled by all this fêting. Sir Roderick Murchison, at a public banquet, declared: "After eighteen months of laudation . . . and after receiving all the honours which the Universities and cities could shower upon him, he is still the same honest true-hearted David Livingstone as when he issued from the wilds of Africa." The truth is that he soon tired of these public functions and grudged every moment spent away from his home.

The question of his future had to be considered. He had decided that he must separate himself from the London Missionary Society. Relations with it had been throughout pleasant, but there were some among its supporters who had expressed the opinion that the work he was best fitted to do was not real missionary work, and though he knew that this was the opinion of a few only, he felt that to accept any longer a salary from the Society would restrain his freedom of action. Some of his most respected friends advised him against thus separating himself from a definitely religious organisation. They valued his influence in the country as a national asset and feared any weakening of his Christian witness. How little they understood the man.

Livingstone's many lectures had naturally greatly increased the interest of politicians and merchants in the development of Africa, especially of the valley of the Zambezi, to the unexplored wealth of which he had called attention. The Portuguese had for centuries held the coastline, but though they made a claim also to an interior of indefinite extent, they had explored it little. A suggestion was therefore made that the British Government, in concert with the Portuguese, might provide Livingstone with facilities for further exploration in that region. It is somewhat doubtful with whom the idea originated and it is not a matter of moment. To Lord Clarendon, the Foreign Secretary of the time, the credit is usually given, but a letter exists, dated May 2nd, 1857, in which Livingstone wrote to his Lordship offering to accept, if so desired, an appointment as "an agent of Her Majesty, for the promotion of Commerce and Civilisation with a view to the extinction of the slave trade." It is quite probable that the proposal originated with Sir Roderick Murchison.

Government took up the suggestion promptly, and Livingstone was appointed British Consul at Quilimane on a salary of £500. The Royal Navy was to co-operate. £5000 was voted for the purpose of equipment.

No plan could have been more attractive. He had come to feel more and more deeply on the subject of the slave trade. Sir Risdon Bennett wrote: "The all-pervading deadly evils of slavery

and the atrocities of the slave trade, never failed
to excite his righteous indignation. If ever he was
betrayed into unmeasured language, it was when
referring to these topics." Here was the very
opportunity he wished. Here was a fight to which
he might dedicate himself body and soul. So he
accepted.

The Zambezi Expedition differed in many ways
from Livingstone's other journeys, but chiefly in
that he had with him European assistants. Of
these there were six, besides many Naval men
who joined him from time to time. Government
was prepared to equip the party generously, but
Livingstone did not take full advantage of these
offers, and probably, as events showed, made a
mistake in over-economy. He was painfully conscientious in the spending of public funds, but his
previous experience of financing travel on a meagre
pay of £100 a year was not the best introduction
to the outfitting of a Government enterprise.

A word should be said here about the new
Consul's relations to the Portuguese Authorities
—a problem which had a momentous influence
on the fate of the Expedition. Livingstone had,
in Africa, as has been said, met several Portuguese
officials whom he admired and who had treated
him with unstinted kindness. He had studied the
economic problems of their Colonies and was
convinced that slavery was the main reason for their
poor condition. He had found, too, expressions of
sympathy with these views among many Portuguese officers. But at the time he does not seem

to have realised that slavery was a basic fact in
the economic order of these Colonies and that
many of the officials were themselves deeply involved in the traffic. Before he had left Quilimane
he had written a letter to the King of Portugal
thanking him for the kindness of his officers,
giving advice as to the conduct of the Colony, and
laying stress on what he had seen of the debasing
effects of the whole slave system. The letter had
been politely acknowledged and he had no reason
to doubt that his advice had been welcomed. The
Ambassador in London, Count de Livadio, had
expressed himself as most appreciative, and arrangements had been made, which however fell through,
for Livingstone to visit the King of Portugal.
Every one was most polite—that was their strong
suit—but he had not been long on the Zambezi
before he realised that in spite of this urbanity
they were working against him, quietly, all the
time.

It was most natural that the Portuguese Government should have been suspicious of a British
Expedition bent on exploring hinterland that they
had counted for centuries their special preserve. It
was equally natural that, considering the profits
that the trade yielded them, they should be appre-
hensive of so strong a man's butting into their
concerns. Still they smiled and were polite. It
was a type of character that Livingstone had not
yet fathomed. There was no subtlety in *his* make-
up. He was soon to be enlightened.

Judging by its consequences, much the most

important speech that he ever made was that
delivered to the University of Cambridge towards
the end of 1857. Professor Sedgwick, a venerable
figure, presided, and Livingstone was rapturously
received by the undergraduates. He was no
polished speaker. His voice was hard and somewhat unmusical, and his few actions stiff. In
short, jerky, almost unconnected sentences, he
described Africa, its people and customs. It was
like an extract from his book. Towards the end
he made a personal appeal, ending with the well-
remembered words: "I direct your attention to
Africa. I know in a few years I shall be cut off in
that country which is now open. Do not let it
be shut again. I go back to Africa to try to make an
open path for Commerce and Christianity. *Do you
carry out the work I have begun. I leave it with you!*"
The final two sentences were spoken with a sudden
rise in voice that became a shout and stopped
suddenly. The effect was dramatic in the highest
degree. It was largely as a result of this speech
that the Universities' Mission, with the tragic
history of which, three years later, he was to have
such close connection, was formed.

A great final banquet in Livingstone's honour
was given in February, 1858, at which there were
gathered, in the Chairman Murchison's words,
"Men of real distinction in all the great classes
of the British public." It was a worthy termination
to a wonderful welcome.

PART FOUR

THE CONSUL

The Battle Joined

The Zambezi Expedition
1858–1863

"*Let us state what we know of one portion of Africa. Nineteen thousand slaves from the Nyassa country alone pass annually through the custom house (at Zanzibar). Besides those actually captured thousands are killed or die of wounds or famine. Thousands perish in the internecine war waged for slaves. It is our deliberate opinion that not one fifth of the victims ever become slaves. Taking the Shire Valley on the average we should say not even one tenth arrive at their destination.*"

"The Zambezi and its Tributaries," Chap. xix.

SIMPLIFIED MAP

showing Livingstone's Journeys as described in

PART FOUR

A Brief Account of the African Slave Traffic

FOR sheer brutality probably nothing in the history of the world has equalled this trade, more especially in the form in which Livingstone was, from now on, to encounter it.

Africa had been from time immemorial the great reservoir for slaves and the traffic had been conducted, in the main, by Arabs. Cruel as slavery always is, in those earlier days it had been mainly a domestic institution in which the victims were often well treated—though their capture must have involved great suffering. With the imperial expansion of the European powers, dating from the beginning of the seventeenth century, however, there grew up a demand for labour to work new plantations; and when in the eighteenth century the Americas joined in, the traffic assumed prodigious proportions. Various nations had their share in the responsibility, but it must be admitted that, latterly, the British people secured a shameful predominance.[1]

At that period the principal markets for slaves were on the West Coast of Africa and it can be claimed, as a slight mitigation, that here the trade was, in general, conducted by barter and not by violence and the only excuse, if indeed it can be so accepted, is that at that date, Negroes were

[1] See *The British Anti-Slavery Movement*, by Prof. R. Coupland.

regarded more as a race of highly-developed monkeys, than as men. It can further be claimed that, when at long last, the British conscience was aroused, the nation lavished its financial and other resources on an attempt to make good the damage it had done. In addition to the £20,000,000 voted for the emancipation of the slaves of the Empire, many hundreds of thousands of pounds were poured out, over a long course of years, in maintaining a fleet of small men-of-war on the East and West coasts, whose purpose it was to end the traffic by the capture of Arab dhows and the freeing of the victims. In the forties, of the whole British Navy no less than a sixth part was employed in African patrol work. Livingstone met those ships at Loanda, and their help was to be indispensable to him on the Zambezi. The chief function of the British Consuls, too, placed at various ports, was to make control by these ships effective, and many of them, as for instance, Dr. John Kirk and Livingstone's younger brother Charles, did noble work in trying to right this old wrong. The other Powers, naturally, were apt to resent this campaign as a piece of hypocritical interference, and again and again it came near to causing international complications. Lecky says that this crusade of Britain against slavery may probably be regarded as amongst the two or three most perfectly virtuous pages in the history of nations.[1]

The particular form of this inhuman traffic which Livingstone was from now forward to

[1] Quoted in Fisher's *A History of Europe*, page 1033.

meet, was a comparatively recent development. It may be said to have happened in two stages.

First : In the early part of the nineteenth century ivory abounded, but transport was difficult. The tsetse fly made the use of cattle for this purpose impossible, but the human animal was always there in abundance, and the possession of firearms made their capture safe. A village would be surrounded before dawn and attacked. All who resisted were shot; the able-bodied men and women seized and the old left to their fate. Of those who remained gangs were formed and round the necks of all likely to give trouble slave sticks were fixed. These were thick tree branches with forked ends that were bolted round the neck. Two were then jointed together thus making a shackle that could not be detached. For all who proved intractable or who malingered, there were leather whips and other summary methods.

The second stage was, however, worse. The degradation resulting from this bestial business soon spread among the tribes. Guns gave a power almost irresistible, so the desire to possess firearms grew rapidly. Inevitably tribe began to attack tribe; the well-armed raided the weak. Ivory might grow scarce but for human flesh there was always a profitable and easy market. Thus in a lamentably short space of time prosperous countrysides became devastated and reverted to forest.

From the time of the discovery of Lake Nyasa onwards the full havoc of this traffic became clear to Livingstone. Arabs and half-caste Portuguese were the culprits—that was well known—but when it dawned upon him that the Portuguese Authorities not only winked at, but apparently promoted this horrible thing, his fury flamed, and he gave expression to his indignation in uncompromising terms.

1. The Zambesi

Livingstone was forty-five years of age when he accepted the post of Leader of the Zambezi Expedition. It occupied five years and was the most exacting period of his life.

He took with him six European assistants. More had been suggested, but he was content with a few. A naval officer, Commander Bedingfeld, volunteered and as Livingstone had known him at Loanda, he was glad to have him appointed. His work was to take charge of the river boats. Dr. John Kirk, a young man, the best of the group, went as botanist and physician, and Richard Thornton as geologist. There was also Thomas Baines, a middle-aged man of varied and wide experience, to act as artist and storekeeper, and George Rae, a Scots engineer. Finally, there was Charles Livingstone, David's brother, younger by eight years. This man had been a minister in the United States. His position on the staff was somewhat indefinite. He was officially the photographer of the party and the chief assistant, and was given the title "Moral Agent." He had special knowledge of cotton production which was expected to prove useful.

The company sailed on March 10th, 1858, from Liverpool, in the *Pearl*, a steamer of 200 tons, bound for Ceylon. Mrs. Livingstone and Oswell,

the youngest boy, went with them. It had been her
hope to go with the party to the Zambezi but
unfortunately she became ill on the voyage and
"grew thin as a lath." Her husband was so concerned about her that he was relieved to be able to
put her in charge of the Moffats who had come to
Cape Town to meet them. With them she went on
to Kuruman. Her absence was to prove a serious
loss to the Expedition.

The voyage was uneventful. Each member was
given instructions in writing as to his special
duties. In those to Kirk, which have been preserved,
there appears much characteristic advice.[1] "You
will understand that Her Majesty's Government
attaches much importance to the moral influence
that may be exerted on the minds of the natives
by a well regulated household, setting an example
of consistent moral conduct, treating the people
with kindness, relieving their wants, teaching
them to make experiments in agriculture, explain-
ing to them the more simple arts, imparting to
them religious instruction as far as they are
capable to receive it, and inculcating peace and
goodwill to each other."

As to his professional work, Kirk was advised to
be on good terms with the native medical men, not
to disparage their methods of treatment, and never
neglect the opportunity which the bed of sickness
presents of saying a few kind words "in a respectful manner." "Depend on it a kind word or deed
is never lost." It was one of Livingstone's favourite

[1] *Kirk on the Zambezi*, page 113.

themes, that if Natives were not elevated by contact with Europeans they were sure to deteriorate.

At the Cape the Consul met with an enthusiastic reception, especially from the Governor, Sir George Grey, and his old friend Maclear. A silver box containing eight hundred guineas was presented to him.

The general purpose of the Expedition was the exploration of the Zambezi valley and of its commercial possibilities. If the trip up the Zambezi to repatriate Makololo be excepted (and that was not really within the purpose or scope of their instructions), it will be seen that its movements were confined to a comparatively narrow compass.

2 The Zambesi Delta

In the middle of May, 1858, the *Pearl* was off the mouth of the river and the newcomers had their first impressions of a scene they were to know all too well. It was not an attractive picture. Long sandy stretches covered with grass; miles and miles of unwholesome-looking mangroves; innumerable channels choked with weeds running everywhere.

Search had first to be made for a suitable entrance into the river. So their specially constructed launch, the *Ma-Robert* (called by Mrs. Livingstone's African name) was disembarked, her three compartments bolted together, and a promising-looking opening carefully examined, but in vain.

There was no penetrating the thick banks of weeds. So return had to be made to the ship. After three days of search the Kongone mouth was discovered and the *Pearl* found her way through.

These, and the days that immediately followed, were a time of exceptional anxiety for Livingstone. He was suffering from a painful internal trouble but his main care was for the health of his party. He had not had time to grow accustomed to the responsibility of having charge of European colleagues. He knew well that the delta was saturated with malaria and he took what precautions he could—quinine was dealt out copiously —but, as his diary shows, he was haunted with the memory of the tragic fate of the great Niger Expedition (page 50), and dreaded some similar catastrophe. So he worked night and day to get his people moved as quickly as possible out of this unhealthy belt. One of his pet theories was that the best protection against malaria was vigorous daily exercise—advice not very welcome to people made languid by fever.

He was worried, too, about his duty as regards the *Pearl*. The captain would gladly have taken her the 300 miles up the river to Tete, the Portuguese fort, and nothing would have pleased Livingstone more; there the district was comparatively healthy. But the river was dangerously full of shoals and he had been instructed to do nothing to delay the ship. With all haste, therefore, he put up on a small island forty miles from the mouth an iron shed that they had brought.

Here stores could be dumped and taken up later, gradually as occasion offered. They gave the place the name of Expedition Island.

There was a further reason for anxiety. It was reported that the country ahead was in insurrection and that the Portuguese were at war with a notorious robber and murderer called Mariano. This rascal had been actually insolent enough to interfere with their slave-trading! Fighting had resulted. It was not long before the Expedition came into contact with this freebooter—a momentary excitement—for when it was made clear that they were English, arms were laid aside. It was thus only by stages and with tantalising slowness that their goods were moved up from the coast. It was six months before they reached Tete, which Livingstone intended to make the base of operations.

In the meantime, various members had had more or less serious attacks of fever, and the Leader had had a foretaste of two difficulties that were to embitter so many months of the first two years; differences with his colleagues and the maddening ineffectiveness of the *Ma-Robert*. Of these something should, at this point, be said.

It must be admitted frankly that while Livingstone was supremely gifted in his management of Africans, he was not in his right place as a leader of Europeans. It may be that the gifts are incompatible. He was himself quite conscious of this weakness and would, had Government allowed, have gladly worked alone.

He never had collaborated with other Whites, and he was not a good "mixer." In this respect his very strength of character was his weakness. He could not discuss his plans with others and thus carry his men along with him. The trait that Oswell had remarked upon persisted (see page 90), and the fact that he now held a Government post added to the difficulty. The standard he set himself in work and conduct was most exacting, and he did not realise that it was not quite reasonable to expect equal devotion in others. A sympathetic physician, in cases of severe illness, he disregarded in himself all the minor complaints that cause so much discomfort in tropical climates—"prickly heat" and the like—and had but little patience with those who gave in to them.

He had, in short, the defects of his high qualities, and his restless energy must often have made him a trying companion. He was "dour"—determined —undeviating in all his plans. Had he been less so he would not have been Livingstone, but, engulfed in the never-ending worries of the Zambezi period, he was apt to be "dour" in the less admirable sense, self-contained and unapproachable, and if Kirk, who admired him greatly, is to be believed, at times even morose.

In considering the frequent bickerings of this time, full weight must be allowed to the effects of the climate. Malaria seems to have been always present, more or less. Speaking of the depressing effects of this disease, Livingstone wrote : "The whole mental horizon (becomes) overcast with black clouds of gloom and sadness. A man feels very much a fool, if he does not act like one. He is peevishly prone to find fault and to contradict. In fact a man unfit for society."

The publicity given, mainly in South Africa, to these differences must, to one so lately deluged with adulation, have been a rough experience. A recent biographer has said truly that the Expedition suffered a genuine loss by the absence of Mrs. Livingstone. Her presence would have soothed her husband and kept all on their best behaviour.

It must, in fairness to Livingstone, however, be remembered that these dissensions were passing phases; his personal magnetism held. All but two of his colleagues remained, to the end of their lives, devoted admirers.

3. *The* Ma-Robert

More than any other single cause that contributed to the distresses of the Expedition was the failure of the *Ma-Robert*—the first steam-boat on the river. She had been specially designed to simplify the problem of river transport, and she was thus, in a sense, the centre of the expedition. Actually she held up progress times innumerable and was much less efficient than native canoes would have been.

She had been constructed in Liverpool by Macgregor Laird, who had used a similar type of boat on the Niger. She was like a flat-bottomed canoe, seventy feet long and built in three water-tight divisions. She was driven by paddle wheels, but her engine power—twelve horse—was utterly insufficient to overcome the currents she had to face. Her plates were only one-sixteenth of an inch thick, and unfortunately they were made of a kind of steel, still in the experimental stage, upon which the river water had some chemical action, and it was not long before she became pitted with tiny holes and leaked like a sieve. The holes had to be stopped with clay. She burnt wood but it was found that steam pressure could be kept up only by the use of the hardest kinds—lignum vitæ was used when available; but fuel cut with immense labour in a day and a half was consumed in one day's sailing. Native canoes could pass her easily. She was clumsy to handle and the main task of most days was to keep her off sandbanks and refloat her when she stuck. How every one came to loathe her! The "Old Asthmatic" was her nickname. "Engines fit to grind coffee in a shop window" was one of Livingstone's sarcastic remarks, and many were the grumbles at the greed of the builder.

Very early in the journey the naval officer took umbrage at his conditions of service, showed insubordination and resigned. As this action seemed a reflection on his leadership, Livingstone felt the matter keenly. At first he refused to consider the resignation and then, on its being renewed a little later, accepted with obvious relief. It was a painful business, especially as

Bedingfeld did not fail to make his grievances public.

If Livingstone had any blame in this first unpleasantness it was lack of judgment in recommending the appointment. He had met this man at Loanda and was, no doubt, gratified at an offer of service from one of his position. But to think that a commander of a ship of war would be content in charge of a tub like the *Ma-Robert*; take his share in the physical labours of unloading cargo, and accept—in a muggy feverish atmosphere—instructions from a civilian, was expecting service that only a very exceptional man could give, and Bedingfeld was not of that type. Indeed, a little caution in investigating his record would have revealed that he had been under discipline in the Service for insubordination more than once.

What irked Livingstone especially was that Bedingfeld had thought himself indispensable and presumed on this, and in his reports, and even in his published book, the Leader showed irritation in a way not quite consistent with his usual kindliness.

He took charge of the navigation himself, though it added much to his already heavy burdens, and as he wrote later he "conducted the steamer over 1600 miles, though as far as my likings go, I would as soon have driven a cab in a November fog in London."

It will be remembered that Sekeletu's men had been left at Tete, and that the Governor—Major Sicard—had made himself responsible for their care. Livingstone had promised to return in six months and conduct them home, and when he found that his preoccupations made that impossible, he had secured a promise from the Portuguese Authorities to provide for their maintenance—an engagement that was not kept. Major Sicard, however, had stood by his word and the men had been fairly content. There had been casualties among them. Six had been killed by an unfriendly chief, and small-pox had taken toll of others. Many had acquired wives.

This is how they received their Master. "The men rushed into the water up to their necks in their eagerness to see their white father. Their joy was perfectly frantic. They seized the boat and nearly upset it and carried the Doctor ashore singing all the time that their Father was alive again."[1] The people had taunted them saying that their great Bwana had failed them and they had suffered loss of face in consequence. Now they could hold their heads high.

Tete became the base of the Expedition, and here the iron house found its permanent position. The Governor continued all through courteous and indeed friendly. He put a substantial stone house at their disposal. While the official attitude to the slave trade remained always a barrier between them, Livingstone thought well of the Governor and was most grateful for much kindness.

[1] Rae. Article in *Chambers's Journal*, March 30th, 1861.

4. *The Kebrabasa and Murchison Cataracts*

The vexatious delay due, in the main, to the low horse-power of the steam launch made Livingstone eager to investigate without further loss of time the great problem that was then absorbing his thoughts. Did the Zambezi provide a navigable highway into the interior? Could the Kebrabasa Rapids be passed? The fate of Central Africa seemed to him in his eagerness to depend on the answer.

The Portuguese replied emphatically in the negative and they should have known, since the Cataracts ended only thirty miles above Tete. But Livingstone distrusted them. He suspected that they wished for their own advantage to keep the country closed.

Conditions were favourable. The river was low and so, resting only two days, he took with him young Kirk and a few of the Makololo and set out upon a preliminary survey. At first the task seemed simple. The *Ma-Robert* took them most of the way. It turned out, however, " as tough a bit of travel" as Livingstone had ever tackled. At times they had to wade up to their waists. The bank of the stream—a hundred yards broad at this point—was covered with dense thorn scrub that made rags of their clothes. They had to spring from rock to rock and from crag to boulder. The wriggling round projections wore them all out. The deep trough-like shape of the valley focused the sun's rays, so that even the leathery soles of the feet of the Makololo were blistered. Still Livingstone persevered. The porters' protests grew loud but no heed was paid to them. "We always thought he had a heart," they grumbled to Kirk. "Now we believe he is mad." Kirk's comment was—"the heat was fearful, like Hell if that place is what I imagine it." It was his first taste of Livingstone's powers and pertinacity. In the end they were beaten and had to return.

Livingstone was deeply disappointed but not discouraged. "Try again" was always his favourite motto. He had built too much on this confidence in a navigable passage to surrender easily. His Diary shows the kind of religious fervour with which he faced this special task. "If we can blast the rocks which obstruct, how thankful I shall feel. It will be like opening wide the gates that have barred the interior for ages. Will the good spirit of the Lord grant this honour to us, His servants, in this expedition? If it is to promote the good of my fellows I will turn quarry-man next." The scheme had completely captured his imagination. He was convinced that by blasting a passage might be made. None of the others, however, believed this feasible, and were inclined to grumble at hardships that he ignored.

He made a second and a third attempt. Never was his native stubbornness so clearly shown or so poorly rewarded. It was with bitter disappointment that at last he gave up this plan upon which he had built so much. Not even then did he relinquish it entirely. He wrote to the Home Government for a boat of higher engine power than the *Ma-Robert* had. He meant probably, when that arrived, to try once more.

Foiled at this point, and set upon finding another route into the interior, they decided to try the Shire—a river that joins the Zambezi, coming from the North, at a point a hundred and fifty miles below Tete. It was practically unexplored country. The Portuguese had left it carefully alone. The reason they gave for so doing was that it was, they alleged, impenetrable because of vast banks of duckweed. The more credible reason was because it was known to be inhabited by warlike tribes of Manganja who used poisoned arrows.

The first of many trips on the Shire was begun in January 1859. Duckweed was met for three miles up but not much afterwards. The tribes showed excitement. Especially were they amazed at the ship that moved without hand paddles. As hitherto their only visitors had been slave-traders they were naturally suspicious. They thronged the banks, dodged behind trees, and armed with poisoned arrows prepared to resist.

It was in moments like these that Livingstone's amazing nerve showed itself. With deliberate slowness he stepped into the water and calmly walked ashore, calling out that they were English and had come neither to fight nor to make slaves. His imperturbability disarmed the Natives. Presents were given and friendly contacts made that were helpful later.

L.L.   225   H

The river animals also found the "puffing monster" hard to understand. The hippopotami dived, but the crocodiles, mistaking it for some strange swimming beast, sometimes rushed at them with open jaws and at great speed. The "Asthmatic" behaved well and for all it was a pleasant rest. Livingstone speaks of the thrill of "meandering over two hundred miles of unexplored country." They steamed on till they reached the great Cataract that Livingstone has named after his friend Murchison. There the weather broke, so they turned and dropped downstream. As a reconnaissance the short trip had been most successful and they had left behind them good impressions. One friendship proved particularly useful. The chief Chibisa, whose village lay at the foot of the Rapids, showed himself ever after a staunch ally. Livingstone liked and trusted him because of his hearty laugh. This he always judged a good sign.

The valley was noted as being wide and fertile. Cotton and indigo "Superior to that of America" could be grown and they were once again impressed by the opportunities that the Portuguese, by their lack of enterprise, were missing.

5. Towards the Great Lake

The result of their wise treatment of the tribes was seen when, three months later, they made their second approach, for they found the people

friendly. This time their aim was to reach
Lake Nyasa. The launch had to be left at the
foot of the Rapids, and for its protection they
took with them two naval men—Walker and
Rowe.

Livingstone and Kirk, with a few Makololo, disembarked on the left bank and faced the steep
incline towards the North-East. Guides, for some
reason, were hard to get, indeed only crazy men
would accompany them. It was, without doubt,
risky travel. The Manganja, through whose land
they must pass, were an independent type of people,
who did not respond to friendly overtures. They
signalled from village to village by drumming and
the sound had an uncomfortably defiant note.
There was fear of attack night and day. Progress
was so slow that it took a fortnight to cover
distance that was, as the crow flies, not more than
forty miles. But they pushed forward steadily,
climbing steeply all the way, and at last were rewarded by the sight of a wide sheet of water—
Lake Shirwa. This lake was somewhat disappoint-
ing. The water was bitter. But the country round,
however, was exceedingly beautiful. Great mountains could be seen toward the north and west—
with the impressive massif of Mount Zomba
towering up to 7000 feet. Unfortunately the tribes
were unfriendly and their attitude became so
threatening that Livingstone, realising that his
own show of force was unimpressive, thought it
wise to retrace his steps. The return was timely.
They found Walker, who had been left in charge of

the *Ma-Robert*, so ill with malaria that, without treatment, he would have died.

This journey, though interrupted, was one of Livingstone's most fortunate attempts. He and Kirk had been the first Europeans to view the country now known as Nyasaland. At last he had discovered what for years he had sought with such inspired tenacity—healthy uplands where white people might settle and live in comfort.

There followed one of those runs down to Kongone for stores and possible mails, that absorbed so much time and energy. They were usually unpleasant experiences—delay, fresh infections of malaria, and all the unrelieved aggravations of the *Ma-Robert*. On this particular occasion the discomforts were even worse than usual. The weather had broken and "in addition to the leakage below, rain poured, through the roof." The cabin became a breeding-place for cockroaches and of mosquitoes of a specially vicious type. Everything was soaked. No wonder that tempers were often sadly frayed.

6. *Lake Nyasa and the "Lady Nyasa"*

After a month's rest, Livingstone and his brother with Kirk and Rae disembarked once more at Chibisa—at the foot of the Rapids, keyed up for the excitement of a great discovery. They had with them thirty Makololo, all armed, but for impression merely, since none could shoot. The device succeeded. For that reason as also, no doubt, because of the good impression they had already made, there was no opposition. The route taken was that already followed, and once more they were struck with the fertility of the district. The tribes had thus far escaped the slavers' blight and were industrious; expert in agriculture and skilled in iron work. They were, however, inveterate drunkards. Never had Livingstone seen such heavy drinking.

The expedition passed round Mount Zomba and Lake Shirwa and then turned down into the Shire valley above the Rapids. Soon after, they were rewarded on September 16th, 1859, by a first view of Lake Nyasa—the second largest of the inland seas of Africa—350 miles long. It was one of Livingstone's major discoveries. He anticipated by only two months the unfortunate German explorer, Dr. Rocher, who had approached from the East. This man was murdered near the Rovuma river on the way back.

At this point Livingstone realised as never before the wide ramifications and the growing menace of the slave traffic. One of the great slave routes from the interior passed round and across the Lake. Chained gangs were seen frequently. They were themselves approached by a villainous-looking set of fellows armed with long muskets, who offered them children for sale. The Ajawa tribe, with whom before long the Explorer was to come into sharp conflict, was raiding far and wide. Little ivory remained in those parts, but there were people in plenty. Four yards of calico could be got for a man, three for a woman, and two for a child. Victims of war were an easy prey to those who held guns. All these revelations, the burnt villages, the numerous skeletons, the floating corpses, and all the other horrors that they saw caused the Consul furiously to think and everything strengthened his conviction that there was only one cure for this anarchy—the introduction of honourably-conducted trade that would make dealing in slaves unprofitable.

Out of this turmoil of spirit there grew one of his many plans. It seemed to him obvious that a steamship placed on the Lake, and the trade it would make possible, would soon cut the feet from under the revolting traffic that now ruled. Livingstone's plans never rusted from waiting. He wrote at once to his friend Young, in Scotland, giving him authority to spend £2000 of his own money on this project. Rae, who had had experience as engineer on a transatlantic steamer, was warned to be ready to go home to supervise the building of the boat.

How Livingstone intended to work the little ship when she reached the Lake is not clear. Her building was an impulse as generous in conception as it was extravagant in execution. The result was —to look ahead—an excellently-designed and built little vessel—though, alas, once more too deep in draught for the shallow Shire. She was constructed at the Meadowside Yard, Partick, but at the cost, not of £2000 but of £6000—half the profits of his book. She never saw the Lake, but was fated to become only one more of the many burdens under which, in the end, the Expedition foundered.

7. Colonisation Schemes

At this time, too, a larger plan that had long been germinating becomes prominent in his letters. The discovery of the healthy high lands he had just seen brought it again into prominence.

In his Diary, dated August, 1859, there stands this entry, "I have a very strong desire to commence a system of colonisation of the honest poor. I would give £2000 or £3000 for the purpose and intend to write to my friend Young about it. The project seems feasible. The Lord remember my desire. . . ."

His proposal was that an experimental colony should be tried in these uplands; that twenty or thirty worthy people now in poverty in Scotland should be helped to settle in this fertile region. By colonising, he did not mean farming in the Canadian sense but superintendence of African labour and guidance in discovery of the capacity of the country. The splendour of the idea filled his mind. He wrote to Young, Murchison and others. In a letter to Oswell this passage appears: "I never saw any part better supplied with running water. Cotton is cultivated extensively. The Shire valley was hot and stifling but no sooner did we ascend to the second terrace, than we had a feeling of freshness.

231

On the three thousand feet terrace, it was delight-fully cool and on Zomba it was cold. Europeans, without doubt, could live there." It is another illustration of Livingstone's prevision that just here there now exists a prosperous settlement, where Colonists, mostly Scots, have introduced flourishing industries.

When replies came they were disappointingly critical. Young, no doubt had his eye on the rapidly evaporating bank balance, and was thinking of the family. Sir Roderick wrote that it would be necessary to have a much more secure hold in the country, else there "was danger that the settlers might die off and become a burden on you and all concerned, like the settlers of old at Darien." Keen though the disappointment was, Livingstone clung to hope, as phrases like "Death alone will stop my efforts," common in his letters at this time, show. It is evident that he was working under a heavy sense of strain. He returned to Chibisa's village in very poor health.

He had plenty that was unpleasant to occupy his mind. Dissensions had come to a crisis and drastic action seemed called for. The *Ma-Robert* had grown so rotten that it was no longer safe to sleep on board for fear that she should sink in the night. Further, for twenty months he had had no word from his family. Mails had been lost by the capsizing of a boat belonging to the H.M.S. *Lynx*. Indeed, it was not until a year after the event had happened that he heard of the birth at Kuruman of his youngest child—Anna Mary.

8. Dissensions in the Camp

A short time before the events recorded in the last chapter the conduct of two of the party had seemed to the leader so unsatisfactory that he had felt it necessary to dismiss both. It was a painful business and much public criticism resulted, in the case of Baines especially. Most biographers incline to the opinion that Livingstone's action was, in these cases, unduly severe, if not unfair. Certain facts recently come to light have done something to clear up obscurities, especially in the case of Thornton. This man's papers, after lying in private hands for seventy years, were sold recently and some of them, now in the Blantyre Memorial, revealed the facts of a story that in the end reflected credit upon both men.

Richard Thornton, who was evidently an attractive young man, joined the Expedition on a two years' engagement as geologist. With the others he reached Tete but took no part in the Kebrabasa trip. Like the rest he suffered from malaria but unlike the others he did not stand up to it, but, on the contrary, in those early days showed a complete lack of stamina. He made no attempt to carry out the specified tasks set him and apparently, for no other reason than that he had given in to the climate and "gone lazy." Livingstone's entries in his Diary show concern about him. "Thornton doing nothing. Invariably lazy and wants good sense." "This is a case of complete collapse. He has several times had hysteria." Thornton frequently complained of illness but Kirk records, "I cannot prescribe for his anomalous symptoms, many of which are only expressive of giving way to feelings of lassitude which we all have felt." This put the Leader in a very difficult position. He could not allow slackness of one to affect the general morale, and so, after several warnings, Thornton was "separated from the expedition" and his salary stopped. Almost immediately after the dismissal, the Lake Nyasa explorers started out and were absent for six months.

The shock of this disciplinary action seems to have had effect, for soon after Thornton was at work. He did some exploration on his own account and showed a new spirit of enterprise by leaving the Zambezi and joining up with Baron von der Decken and, with him, exploring the Kilimanjaro region. When Livingstone returned to Tete he examined the records of what Thornton had accomplished in his absence, and finding them of value, tempered justice with mercy by writing to the Foreign Secretary suggesting that in the circumstances the forfeited pay might be restored, and this was done. He wrote also to Thornton in the same strain.

This good news took many months to reach the geologist but by 1862 Thornton was back on the Zambezi where, at his own request, he was restored to his old position. Kirk speaks of enjoying his pleasant company.

He died tragically. He found the Universities'
Mission—whose story we shall reach soon—suffering from lack of animal food, and undertook,
unknown to his Leader, an overland journey to
Tete to fetch sheep and goats. It was a terrible
experience. There was no water. He arrived back
exhausted and died of dysentery.

Most of Livingstone's biographers take the
restoration and repayment of salary as an admission on his part that he had been over severe. This
new information, on the contrary, shows that he
dealt with a difficult situation in a way worthy of
him.

The matter of Baines is more complicated. This
man was an experienced traveller, with a good
record. He was the artist and also, somewhat
incongruously, and as it happened, unfortunately,
the storekeeper. A large number of his canvases
are now in South Africa. They show him to have
been a skilful draughtsman but hardly a great
artist.

Kirk calls him a "good-natured soul." He was
notably a hard worker, never shirking, as Charles
Livingstone and Thornton often did, disagreeable
drudgery. Indeed, he was warned by the Leader
against over-exertion in that treacherous climate.

He was soon prostrate with malaria. He had
previously suffered from sunstroke and probably
as a result, when his temperature ran high, he
became lightheaded and for a time thereafter was
apparently somewhat irresponsible.

Not long after Tete was reached, complaints

were made to Livingstone that, in his absence, Baines had made free with the Expedition's stores; had used Government material and time, in painting portraits, and was consorting with the less reputable Portuguese. Charles Livingstone was no doubt the informant. There was a strong antipathy between the two. Baines admitted some irregularity, though he afterwards withdrew the confession, alleging that he had been lightheaded when he made it.

There is sufficient evidence to believe that these charges were not without some justification. A man of Baines's easy temperament may readily have become openhanded with Government property. He was not a trained storekeeper. At worst, however, the offences were trivial and might well, considering the good work that he had done, have been passed over with a reprimand. But Livingstone took a very serious view of the position and dismissed him. Baines demanded an inquiry at Tete, where the irregularities were alleged to have happened, but Livingstone refused to interrupt his exploration for that purpose and Baines departed, angrily asserting his innocence. Kirk and Rae believed him "not guilty," and in the Cape he had many friends who supported him. He appealed to the Home Authorities, but they stood by the Consul.

Professor Wallis[1] puts the blame of the incident, firstly upon Charles and secondly on Livingstone, for giving too ready an ear to his brother's insinu-

[1] *Life of Thomas Baines* (in preparation), by Prof. J. Wallis.

ations. Charles had certainly added little of value
to the Expedition and had contrived to make himself generally disliked.

Livingstone had to suffer, to some extent
deservedly, much adverse criticism, especially at
the Cape. After all allowances have been made, it
must be admitted that he did not treat Baines with
the fairness that would have been expected of him.
It is difficult to excuse his refusal to allow his
assistant the opportunity of the inquiry he
demanded. There was a streak of obstinacy in
Livingstone's character that made it difficult for
him to change a decision after it had once been
made.

9. Taking the Makololo Home

Part of the trouble dealt with in the last chapter
was due to the fact that Livingstone was in low
health. He had his share of malaria, and suffered
from hæmorrhoids and other disorders. Add to
this, the whole company had been badly upset,
poisoned by the mistake of an incompetent cook.

It had become necessary, once more, to go down
to Kongone. Temporary repairs were needed to the
launch, though it was clear that she could not be
kept much longer afloat. Until the new boat that the
Government had despatched in response to Livingstone's appeal, should arrive, exploration by river
was out of the question. So the Leader used the
intervening time to fulfil the promise made to Chief
Sekeletu and lead his Makololo back to the tribe.

He did not find them over willing to go. Indeed after the march had begun several deserted.

They left Tete and passed by easy stages the now familiar Kebrabasa Gorge and were much struck by the grandeur of the scenery. Livingstone still clung to his conviction that in times of flood navigation might be possible. Kirk and Charles, who made up the party, thought otherwise. It was an intense pleasure to be back to the freedom of bush travel and Livingstone was pleased to find that he could still out-walk his Africans. To the student of his Diary it is a relief to pass from the monotonous daily record of the faults of the *Ma-Robert* to lively descriptions such as this:

"There must be something in the appearance of white men frightfully repulsive to the unsophisticated natives of Africa on entering a village previously unvisited by Europeans. If we met a child coming unsuspectingly towards us, the moment he raised his eyes and saw men in "bags" he would take to his heels in an agony of terror such as we might feel if we saw a live Egyptian mummy at the door of the British Museum. Alarmed at the child's wild outcries, the mother rushes out of her hut, but back again at the first glimpse of the same fearful apparition. Dogs turn tail and scour off in dismay and hens abandoning their chickens fly screaming to the tops of the houses. And so the lately peaceful village becomes the scene of confusion and hubbub until calmed by the laughing assurance of our men, that white people do not eat black folk ; a joke being often, in Africa, greater assurance than a solemn assertion."

There was little that was unusual on the journey. The tribes were more friendly and trustful. After ten weeks of travel they reached the Victoria Falls. Here they learned with dismay of the fate of the L.M.S. party that had been sent to occupy Linyanti. It was a tragedy even more poignant than that which was to befall the Universities' Mission.

The suggestion had been Livingstone's. He had offered to pay the salary of one of the men to act as his substitute and had promised to meet and help to settle them. Helmore and Roger Price with their wives and six young children formed the party. The season was unpropitious and they had endured terrible distress in the Kalahari desert. When they reached the Makololo country there was no word of Livingstone and Sekeletu proved treacherous. He robbed them of food and clothes. While they waited, one after another sickened and died. Fever was the probable cause but poison was even suspected. Last of all Helmore and Mrs. Price succumbed, and poor Roger Price accompanied by the two Helmore children struggled back to Kuruman to tell the tale. Six deaths in as few months![1] Livingstone arrived five months too late. News of the plans for the party had not reached him. Mails had been lost. He was deeply distressed. It is strange how trouble and tragedy were to dog his footsteps all through these Zambezi years.

[1] See *Isabella Price, Pioneer*." Slater. Livingstone Press.

This was the last hope for the Makololo people. Nemesis befell the Chief. Four years later his nation was annihilated by an uprising of the tribes. Had the Mission been established their extinction might have been averted.

The Victoria Falls was examined with care and found to be of far greater extent than Livingstone had previously judged, and his description was this time much more adequate.

A day or two after Sesheke, Sekeletu's town, was reached. The young man who had promised so well was now a pitiful object. He had contracted some kind of leprous trouble and had become in other ways a degenerate. The doctors treated his disease with immediate good, but only temporary, results. He died four years later. Through his mismanagement Sebituane's empire was fast crumbling. The Missionary was deeply disappointed but the Chief's personal attachment to his "Father" was impressive.

The party pushed on to Linyanti a hundred miles distant to visit the graves of the Mission band, and here also Livingstone found the wagon, with all its contents intact, which he had left in charge of the tribe seven years before. Since this territory had already been explored, the journey had not been properly within the scope of the work of the Expedition. Hence they could not prolong their stay. The return began on the 17th September, 1860.

10. Adventures by Water

The Explorers were keen to test on their way back the navigability of the river from the great Falls downwards. So they bought canoes and engaged two young Makololo as guides. The undertaking was much more risky than they had realised.

The Kariba Rapids were negotiated without difficulty, but the party nearly came to grief in the narrows near Mburume. These they reached without any inkling of danger. Big "jobbing" waves splashed suddenly aboard. It was only the pluck of their Africans that saved them. Two sprang overboard and shouted to another to do the same. "I can't swim," the man cried. "Jump in then and hold on. The white men must be saved," was the reply. It was only by strong swimming and dexterous guidance that the Africans kept the canoes afloat, till the foot of the rapids was reached. It had been a terrifyingly narrow escape.

But worse was to follow in the Kebrabasa Cataracts. The road among the rocks was appallingly difficult so they decided to take the risk of shooting the rapids. A somewhat abbreviated account of Kirk's story of this adventure is here given. It was, in after years, his favourite yarn.[1]

"Started in the canoes. For two miles we found the way good: the current very strong. Then the river was divided by a long mass of rock: the sides

[1] *Kirk on the Zambezi*, page 177.

of the island and of the river were perpendicular and only at a few places could we land. We got up on one of these and examined the part in front. On the left the entrance seemed bad. To the right it was very bad. The danger was from being dashed against the opposite bank. We crossed to the north bank to examine. In attempting this one canoe was taken out into the current and almost lost. The men, however, managed to paddle back and leap on a rock thus saving their lives although the canoe and all the cargo was swept down. In it went my Enfield rifle.

"The cook's canoe was abandoned as it was small and unsafe. The things were taken out and it was left to float down. On the left bank we found an entrance not so bad as it looked. As usual my canoe went first for mine was the crew with most dash. We cleared in fine style and had complete command of the canoe.

"I said ' Now avoid that rock. The water runs hard on it.' They bent the head round and had given one stroke ahead. But at this moment we saw Livingstone's canoe carried up to the rock on the right. Every second we expected to see it upset and all in the boiling water. To make things worse Charles Livingstone's canoe was running as if into them. Both would be upset. The only hope was from us. We all looked. Had we paddled on we should have saved ourselves easily, but had the others upset there was no hope of saving them for the water boiled up and curved in eddies so that no man could hope to survive.

We lost a few strokes while looking at the almost inevitable destruction of the others.

"The next thing I saw was the water rushing over our canoe. We were upset and all in the water. We struck with a loud crack. Dr. L. occupied with his own danger, looked up. Before he could direct his eyes we were all in the water or clinging on. The water boiled and rushed past, coming up in heavy masses at times and then subsiding.

"The man at the stern got hold of a rock and held the canoe, which was pressed against it, from going down. Sometimes it was sucked under. The man at the bow at once jumped into the water. His position was most dangerous, but he held on to the canoe.

"I found myself in the water with my body sucked under the canoe which was on its side. Having ascertained that the bow man was all right, we got a few bundles on to a crevice of rock. By that time Dr. L.'s canoe, which had escaped by a miracle, had come up after landing her goods. We passed what we could catch into her, but most things had gone. We got our canoe dragged up and bailed out. I had not the least feeling of danger to life and yet there have not been many escapes more miraculous. The loss of goods, but especially of valuable notes and specimens, was serious." No lives were lost. The rest of the journey to Tete was done on foot. The Expedition's stores were now running short. So, in the hope that one of the naval ships might have replenished the cache at Kongone a trip thither was decided upon.

The *Ma-Robert* was now, in spite of constant tinkering, past repair. New leaks appeared each morning; the engine pump gave way; the bridge kept collapsing; the cabins were constantly full of water. At last, on December 21st, she finally grounded and filled. The river rose in the night and by daybreak she was completely submerged. They had to leave her, and there were emphatically no regrets.

With stores almost exhausted they prepared to spend an uncomfortable Christmas on a small island near Sena. Once more, however, the kindly Portuguese came to their relief. It cannot have been easy for Livingstone, being the proud man he was, to have accepted gifts from these people, however generously offered. The clash of interests had grown obvious. Livingstone was coming to see more and more clearly that these courteous gentlemen were all the time trying to put a spoke in his wheel, and it was never easy for him to hide his feelings. But this was only one among a host of worries that besieged him at this time. It is fair to him to remember, however, that kindness had by no means been all on the one side. Livingstone had acted as doctor to many of them and had saved the lives of some.

11. *The Arrival of the Universities' Mission*

The beginning of 1861, however, brought much brighter prospects. The new steamer—the *Pioneer*

—sent out by the Home Authorities, arrived. She was a well-built little boat and had a long life on the Coast.

But the outstanding event of these days was the arrival of the Universities' Mission. This Society was the direct result of his famous "I leave it with you" speech at Cambridge five years before and there were few, if any, things, in his life that gave him, at first, so much joy. The mission was to be conducted upon lines that he had advised; it was to combine industrial training with spiritual work.

The leader was Bishop Mackenzie and he had with him five Englishmen and five coloured men, of various qualifications, but it was noted, with some apprehension, that they had among them no doctor. They were to occupy Livingstone's newly-discovered health resort, the Shire Highlands.

Mackenzie was a man after Livingstone's own heart; a Scot from the Border Country; a man of ability and devotion; handsome and of attractive personality, and absolutely free from clerical "side." He showed himself ready to put his hand to anything. He had had already many years of experience of mission work in Natal, and knew the ways of the country.

Livingstone wrote enthusiastically to Maclear and among other things expressed his satisfaction that the mission was under a Bishop. He had seen, he said, such idleness and folly result from lack of supervision. Those who remember his prickly youth may well smile. Dr. Philip was not to be allowed to play the bishop over *him*. He wrote to Drummond, the friend of his student days, "I always determined not to submit to any bishop." It would be hard to think of any one less likely to work happily under episcopal or any other control, nor for that matter, to exercise such authority himself!

To Mackenzie on his part, it was a profound satisfaction to meet with and accept guidance from Livingstone. He had a way, which Stanley also referred to, of encouraging inexperienced people. "How excellent," the Bishop remarked, "is his way of offering help—not as if he were indispensable but as if he might be of some use. This is the way in which real strength and real knowledge always speaks." Their relationship was of the most pleasant.

Of Kirk, Mackenzie wrote, "We are the greatest possible cronies. He encouraged me to try my hand at botanising." No enterprise could have had a happier introduction. None the less the friendship began with a severe disappointment for the Bishop. He was behind his time schedule already and his people were waiting, impatient to begin work. He had been delayed at the Cape. His consecration ceremony was of special importance in that he was the first missionary bishop of his Church to be ordained since the Reformation. The four bishops who shared in the ceremony had to come from afar and much time had been absorbed by the arrangements.

Livingstone had promised to accompany and

help to settle them. But they found him deep in a "secret" plan for the circumvention of the Portuguese Authorities. He was growing increasingly suspicious of their ways and they of his motives. Free access to the Zambezi and free trade with the interior were essential to his plans, and now he learned that they had established custom houses at the ports and were levying dues. They, on their part and perhaps not unnaturally, had come to regard him as a British Agent with unfriendly intentions. They were beginning to suspect that his missionary garb was only a cloak for deep designs and even for the annexation of their territory. The Zambezi was their preserve. They could not or would not develop the district, but they had ample means to hinder those who wished to do so.

The Kebrabasa rapids effectively shut one door into the hinterland, but Livingstone believed there was another. He was convinced that the river Rovuma, which reaches the sea three hundred miles north of Mozambique, came from Lake Nyasa. If he could show this to be navigable throughout it would open another way, with which the Portuguese could not interfere, into the territory he had recently discovered. The new boat, the *Pioneer*, which had now arrived, made this investigation possible, and he had determined to begin the exploration without delay.

When this purpose was unfolded to him, Mackenzie was much upset. It involved him in more months of irksome and unprofitable waiting.

Rather than delay he was prepared to proceed up country alone, but to this Livingstone objected, pointing out that there was no reliable chief in the Shire Highlands to whom they could be commended. This was a difficulty that could not be overcome, so Mackenzie consented to go with him and arranged to send his missionaries to Johanna, one of the islands of the Comoro group, there to wait.

The expedition to the Rovuma was a failure. Entrance was easy but the water was low and rapidly falling, and after they had steamed thirty miles up, the unpleasant conclusion was forced upon the Doctor that if they did not turn, the *Pioneer* would be trapped and held prisoner for many months. Had Livingstone been alone he would have persisted and gone forward on foot. To every one else the retreat came as a most welcome relief. Kirk's opinion of the Rovuma held no qualification. "This is hell on earth, if ever I saw one. Such a place and such a people!" Return had become additionally urgent, because the naval officers in control of the *Pioneer* were all down with malaria. Livingstone had to take charge of the navigation. He got much satisfaction out of the sturdy strength of the little ship, so happy a contrast to the late unlamented *Ma-Robert*.

Back in the Shire he set himself with all the fire of his infectious enthusiasm to forward the cause of the Mission. He greatly admired not the Bishop only but also certain other members of the party, especially Scudamore and Horace Waller.

This latter became a close friend and eventually the editor of his *Last Journals*. It was for Livingstone a happy time. It may indeed be said, as regards the Zambezi Expedition, his last happy time. After this the tide of fortune seemed definitely to set in heavily against him. He was from now on to become hemmed in by disappointment and pursued by tragedy.

Looking back on this period, he himself judged it as a kind of watershed of his life. Hitherto there had come to him success heaped on success. He had achieved a celebrity second to none. Gratifying as his popularity, doubtless, had been, he was not comfortable in the rôle of hero. The Celtic melancholy had shown itself at times. But from now on he was to taste repeated failure: to see his favourite schemes go all awry. It is, however, just in such times of misfortune that the real greatness of the man becomes more and more evident. Nothing could shake his belief that he had been predestined to rid his beloved Africa of some of her greatest evils.

An increasing anxiety of these days, a sickening fear that would have paralysed any man of lighter calibre, was the growing dread lest, after all, his explorations should become for Africa a curse and not a blessing. He was finding out that the slave dealers were the first to profit by his discoveries, and were, along the paths that he had blazed, penetrating into districts that before his coming they had feared to enter; had at times even the effrontery to use his name and call themselves his children. So that all too often the sequel to his visits was, not the smiling valleys of his dream, made prosperous by honourable trading, but ruined villages, scattered tribes, and a devastated countryside.

These doubts made no iota of difference to his ultimate aims, but joy, to a considerable degree, went out of his life. He had to fall back on his own deep reserves of power. He drew, more and more, in upon himself. His mission to become the liberator of the slaves became not less but more definitely plain. Nothing must divert him. No hardship, no sacrifice must count. So in spite of many chilling disappointments he consecrated himself afresh in a noble concentration to the hard task that he believed God had made his special care.

One other matter may be mentioned here. Livingstone has often been criticised as having been warped and uncharitable in his judgment of the Portuguese in spite of all their courtesy and help-fulness to him. That may be to some extent true, but if so, the reason is not far to seek. He was discovering unquestionable proof that the recrud-escence of the evil that was multiplying in spite of all his efforts had its origin in the Portuguese headquarters at Tete and among some of the very people who treated him with such polite consider-ation.

12. May Missionaries use Fire-arms?

For the moment, however, Livingstone was enjoying the fellowship of Bishop Mackenzie. He needed indeed all the distraction he could get, for every day seemed to bring its new worry.

The *Pioneer*, an otherwise admirable little boat, had one defect. She was designed to draw three feet of water. With machinery and fuel aboard her draught was five—at least one foot too much. She grounded constantly, so that the laying of anchors straining at the capstan became a daily toil, a continual grind. In all these unpleasant tasks the Bishop took his full share, but, as Livingstone notes, not all his assistants were equally active. The amount of time and force wasted on sheer slogging drudgery is unpleasant to contemplate. It was fortunate that the tribes had been won to friendliness.

On ascending the Shire, when they reached Chibesa's village, disconcerting news awaited them. An aggressive movement, characteristic of the African tribal life of those days, was in progress. The Ajawas or Yaos—they had various names— were pressing down from the North, working hand in hand with the slavers and laying waste the country, and the weaker tribes, including the Manganja of the Shire valley and the Highlands, were in deadly fear.

A deputation from a Chief near Mount Zomba met the party on landing and invited Mackenzie to settle in his country. Though fear of the Ajawa was plainly the purpose of the request, the opportunity seemed a good one and led by Livingstone they set themselves to the climb. On the second day word was sent them that a large slave gang was coming in their direction en route for Tete. This proved beyond question Livingstone's suspicions. If any confirmation were needed the proof was plain; the leader of the gang was recognised as a well-known slave of the Commandant of Tete. It was a critical situation. If they released the captives there was fear that the Portuguese might retaliate by destroying valuable private property lying in their town. If they let them go through, it would seem as if they condoned the outrage "promoted," he wrote, "under the pretence of being ' our children,' of setting one tribe against another and thus securing slaves."

They did not hesitate and what followed is given in one of the Explorer's most vividly-drawn narratives (see picture opposite page 257). "A few minutes after, a long line of manacled men, women and children came winding their way round the hill and into the valley. The black drivers, armed with muskets and bedecked with various articles of finery, marched jauntily in the front, middle and rear of the line. Some of them blowing exultant notes out of long tin horns. They seemed to feel that they were doing a very noble thing. But the instant the fellows caught a glimpse of the English, they darted like mad into the forest, so fast indeed, that we caught but a glimpse of their red caps and the soles of their feet. The chief of the party alone remained and he had his hand tightly grasped by a Makololo." " The captives knelt down and in their way of expressing thanks clapped their hands with great energy. Knives were soon busy cutting the women and children loose. It was more difficult to get the men adrift as each had his neck in a fork of stout stick six or seven feet long and kept in by an iron rod which was riveted at both ends across the throat. With a saw luckily in the Bishop's baggage, one by one the men were sawn out into liberty."[1]

Eighty-four persons, chiefly women and children, were thus freed. Mackenzie had been absent at the time and was at first doubtful of the wisdom of what had been done, but agreed later and attached them to his mission.

This dramatic act gave rise to much indignation, but it is difficult to conceive of Livingstone's acting otherwise. He knew that the clash was bound to come and to have failed to take up the challenge would have been to have surrendered all that he was fighting for. But serious consequences were to follow for all concerned.

The local authorities made no protest. To have done that would have made their complicity too obvious, but influences were set to work against Livingstone in Lisbon and London. He was charged with exceeding his powers as Consul, with using his status to the detriment of Portugal

---

[1] *The Zambezi and its Territories*, chap. XVIII.

and to the advantage of Britain. This charge was not fair. Livingstone had in him nothing of the Imperialist in the modern sense. It is true that a few years subsequently when he had completely lost faith in the Portuguese honesty and when no other remedy seemed possible, he did suggest, to the Home Authority, annexation, but his interests were entirely humanitarian and in no sense political. Inevitably, however, his opponents took an opposite view. He became to them a troublesome intruder and various schemes were set agoing that brought about, in the end, the recall of the Expedition.

As regards the Mission the effect of the complications that followed the release of the slave gang were soon evident. The rescued slaves and some fifty others gave Mackenzie a nucleus with which to begin work and he accepted the responsibility of their protection. On the invitation of Chigunda the local Chief, Magomero, a spot about ten miles from the modern town of Zomba was selected as a place suitable for a station. While the company was on the way thither, however, a most unfortunate incident occurred.

News was brought that the marauding Ajawa were approaching, and it was thought wise to interview their chief and try to persuade him to abandon his kidnapping. So Livingstone and some others moved out to interview him. They were met on the way by a crowd of Manganja refugees fleeing for their lives. The wail of terrified women was heard, and behind, there rose the smoke of burning

254

villages, then suddenly, round the hill there swept
Ajawa warriors in hot pursuit. They stopped dead
when they found white people in front of them
and Livingstone went forward and called them to
a palaver. It looked as if they might listen when,
most unfortunately, there was heard behind,
among the Mission party, the shout, "Our Chibisa
is come." This ill-advised slogan spoiled any
chance of peace. The name had an ominous sound.
Chibisa was widely feared as a general and sorcerer.
Turmoil broke out forthwith. The Ajawa darted
away yelling, "War, War!" and the captives
pitched their loads to the ground and made for the
hills. But the enemy quickly rallied and in a few
moments the small group of Whites was all but
surrounded by frenzied fighters armed with bows
and poisoned arrows. Four of them had muskets
and used them.

The missionaries gave ground slowly but prompt
action was imperative. They were being rapidly
enveloped. Very reluctantly, therefore, and for the
first time in his life, Livingstone gave the word to
fire. Six of the Ajawa fell. The effect was immediate. The long range of the rifles frightened
them and they bolted.

It was a black day for the Leader. He had often
been in danger from armed enemies, but he had
hitherto always been able to control the situation
and never before, though he habitually carried a
revolver, had he had to use it in self-defence. On
this particular occasion he was, probably purposely,
unarmed, and had taken no part in the firing, but

still, it was he who had given the command and he was therefore responsible.

The consequences on the fortunes of the Mission were of the utmost seriousness. In protecting the Manganja they had antagonised the aggressive Ajawa, and the matter could not rest there. The Bishop and his assistants were keen to follow up their success, to pursue the enemy and release the slaves that had been recaptured; but Livingstone advised caution and waiting till the effect of the first check could be judged.

Content that the missionaries were now in a position to do without his further help, Livingstone prepared to proceed with the exploration of Lake Nyasa. Before he left his advice was asked as to what should be done in the probable event of the Manganjas' craving protection against their formidable opponents. The counsel he gave was, not to interfere in tribal quarrels.

The advice was sound but it was hard to follow. Applications for protection, backed by lurid tales of atrocities soon followed, and that from two of the biggest chiefs of the district. The Mission party had meanwhile been strengthened by the arrival of two officers from the *Pioneer* and was now a compact little body of ten white and three black men.

The decision that this group, composed mainly of clergymen, was now called upon to make was most embarrassing. To found a Mission of Peace on rifle butts; to carry, as the Bishop pictured himself doing, a crosier in the one hand and a loaded gun in the other, was most incongruous in their own eyes, but they knew that it would appear ten times more so in the eyes of their supporters in England. Yet there was no difference of opinion among them. They felt it a Christian duty to use force, if necessary, to release the captives. A skirmish resulted and the Ajawa were dispersed.

As can be readily understood Mackenzie's action in thus passing from defence to attack met with much criticism in England and Livingstone came in for his full share. While it was true that the Bishop had acted against the Consul's considered advice, yet it was he who in the first brush had given the command to fire. After a little hesitation Livingstone defended his friend and stated publicly his opinion that the missionaries were justified in using arms to protect those who had sought shelter with them, many of whom would otherwise have been slaughtered. Both men had been thus forced into action thoroughly uncongenial to them. But to Livingstone it must have been especially grievous since it had made him break a rule that he had been able to follow till then, in spite of a thousand risks.

At Magomero there was soon gathered, as a nucleus for work, a large number of liberated slaves. The village was laid out and the missionaries settled down to learn the language and begin other congenial tasks. With exception of the enmity of the Ajawa, which they hoped would soon pass, the prospects were excellent.

13. The Second Expedition to Lake Nyasa

Meanwhile the Explorer was progressing North. Time was short, Mrs. Livingstone, a sister of the Bishop, and others were expected at the mouth of the Zambezi before long. The immediate plan was to carry a boat past the cataracts, which cover thirty-five miles, and explore the lake country as widely as time permitted.

The track by the Rapids was most laborious but once they were passed the going was easy. Before long they were on the Lake. But all the way the travellers were horror-stricken to see the effects of the murderous methods of the Ajawa. Tribes fleeing in thousands, homeless and starving; the marauders, backed by the Arab traders, securing without effort all the slaves they needed for the transport of their ivory; everywhere devastation.

The tragedy burnt itself into Livingstone's soul and filled him with a consuming righteous anger. He realised for the first time how desperately urgent the problem had become. A wide territory that had teemed with people was being emptied and he estimated that for one wretch who reached Zanzibar, five, and probably more, died or were killed on the road. He had prayed fervently for the safe arrival of the little ship he had ordered. He would station it here in this centre of iniquity. He was more sure than ever that it would, as he puts it, "break the neck of the infamous traffic in this quarter."

Though the country was new and exploration had always its fascination, it was throughout a most depressing and physically exacting trip. There was not room in the boat for the whole party and as the porters were afraid of being left among strangers in a country so excited, the expedition had to be divided into two. One took the shore and the other the Lake. It was most difficult to keep in sight of each other and six miles a day was all the distance they could cover. They found the Lake subject to sudden and dangerous squalls. Wind was often heavy and long continued.

The attitude of the Natives varied from the extremes of hostile suspicion to uncomfortable curiosity and Livingstone had his first experience of a tent robbery, the effect of which was to deprive them of essential stores and thus shorten the voyage. They heard rumours of the Mazitu (Angoni), a Zulu tribe whose name was as terrifying to the people on the Lake shores as that of the Ajawa further South.

They had to turn before they reached the northern end of the Lake, but they went far enough to see an appalling sight—a country swept clean of its inhabitants, shores covered with skulls and sands with decomposing bodies. It was a horrible spectacle impossible to forget. Livingstone climbed one of the heights to the North-West and by the lie of the mountain ranges beyond, made a guess, and as the map in the keeping of the London Missionary Society shows, an underestimate, of the length of the Lake. They had covered only about five-sevenths of its sweep and there was still about a hundred miles unvisited, but food supplies had now run dangerously low.

Livingstone was sorely disappointed with what he had seen, especially with the character of the country as judged from the shore. It was emphatically no place for colonisation. But in this instance his prophetic sense failed him. There was much he had not seen. Quite near, but beyond the steep sides of the Lake, lies the country that now bears his own name—Livingstonia, of which Professor Coupland writes, "Within thirty years that Coast was to be dotted with the stations of a British Company trading up and down the Lake 'with a steamer on the water' and dotted also with the stations of a British mission. And to-day, on the mountain plateau about forty miles beyond the point that Kirk's little boat had reached, stands the great church of Livingstonia, its lofty tower visible far up and down the Lake, an eternal monument to the faith and works of the man it honours."[1]

It had been, at least so it seemed to the travellers, a somewhat unsatisfactory excursion, the most nerve-racking of their experiences and they arrived back at Chibisa at the beginning of November (1861), weak, undernourished and depressed.

Their spirits were restored by a cheery visit from the Bishop. His news was most gratifying. The work had begun well. His vigorous methods against the Ajawa seemed to have been justified by

[1] *Kirk on the Zambezi*, page 210.

subsequent events. Reinforcements were arriving. An energetic young colleague, Burrup by name, had made a surprisingly rapid run up the Shire by canoe. Miss Mackenzie and Mrs. Burrup were expected in January. Everything promised well.

One of the most tantalising of his experiences of these months was that, through no fault of his own but through the unreliability of his men— scantiness of rain—or trouble with his boats, he was so frequently "too late." The most exasperating of these detentions happened just at this urgent moment. The *Pioneer* was marooned for "five weary weeks" below Chibisa, so that when H.M.S. *Gorgon* with Mrs. Livingstone and the other ladies on board, arrived off the Zambezi, there was no one to meet them. There was nothing for it but to put to sea again and, as it happened, to chance into a tornado on the way to Mozambique, from which they had "an all but miraculous" escape. In three weeks they were back to find, this time, the *Pioneer* in sight.

14. Reunion and Tragedy

"I have steamboat on the brig," semaphored the Captain of the *Gorgon*, a dull wit surely! "Welcome news," was Livingstone's reply. "Wife on board," was the *second* message. "Accept my thanks," came the matter-of-fact answer. "The most interesting conversation he had enjoyed for many a day," was his comment later. It was almost four years since husband and wife had met. Her illness had upset their original plans. In the meantime Anna Mary had been born and there had been a short visit to the children in Scotland.

His wife's return brought Livingstone new life. The opportunity she gave him of free discussion of plans, promised a counteraction to the taciturnity that was steadily closing in upon him. It was a sad pity that she had not been able to come four years before and a tragedy she was to stay with him so short a time.

To make land porterage easy, the *Lady Nyasa*, the steamboat of the captain's message, had been constructed in twenty-four sections. She was a fine piece of work and Livingstone rejoiced over her. There was a broad hint of future trouble, however, in the fact, quickly discovered, that when the sections were loaded on the *Pioneer* that little vessel could not clear the shoals of the river. That was only the beginning of the delay, for it was soon found that the *Pioneer's* engines had been carelessly looked after and badly needed overhaul. Their packing had not been renewed for twenty months, and so Livingstone, in order that there the *Lady Nyasa* might be put together, had to order a halt at Shupanga, a place only about fifty miles from the delta. Nothing could have been more unwelcome than this delay. Livingstone was desperately anxious to have his wife transferred out of the malarial low country to some healthier spot.

Miss Mackenzie and Mrs. Burrup were naturally anxious to push forward and gladly accepted an offer from Captain Wilson (of the *Gorgon*) to conduct them in his ship's gig up the Shire river as far as the mouth of the Ruo, that is to about sixty miles below the Cataracts. Dr. Kirk fortunately, went with them. The journey proved exhausting to Miss Mackenzie, who was elderly and far from strong. Mrs. Burrup, a young bride, is described as "lively."

At the Ruo there was no one to greet them and there was no news. Made anxious by this ominous silence they hurried on to Chibisa. Here they had to listen to a tale that, for pathos, has few equals. It runs, briefly, thus:

The Bishop and some of his colleagues had made a successful effort to recover a number of their people who had been captured, and had returned with them to Magomero. Though Mackenzie and Burrup were both in poor health they were anxious not to miss their appointment at the Ruo and most imprudently started out via Chibisa. The walking overtaxed their strength but they secured a canoe, intent on a hurried journey by river. They encamped for the night at the Elephant's Marsh—a terribly malarial spot, on the farther side of the stream. Here mosquitoes were intolerable; so, foolishly, they attempted to continue the voyage by night. They ran on to a sandbank, were upset and soaked: luggage and medicines were lost. They reached the island of Malo utterly worn out.

Fever soon attacked Mackenzie and after three weeks of struggle, handicapped by lack of drugs and proper food, they gallant man died. Burrup buried him and, with his Africans, forced his way through incredible difficulties back to Magomero, where, his strength exhausted he, too, expired, within a month of his Bishop's death.[1]

This was the news that met the poor women. Prostrate with grief and shock they were taken back to the *Gorgon*. Livingstone was well-nigh heartbroken. He felt the catastrophe almost as heavily as did the relatives. He had admired and loved Mackenzie and the feeling had been reciprocated. He foresaw that as the Mission had resulted from his inspiration and was partly in his charge, he would come once more under censure. He was accustomed by now to criticism of many kinds, and the personal aspect of the matter did not greatly trouble him, but he trembled for the fate of the Mission upon which such high hopes had been built. "This will hurt us all," was his comment and then, with the characteristic recoil of his thought, came the resolution, "I shall not swerve a hairbreadth from my work, while life is spared."

And suffer the Mission did. The recruits that the *Gorgon* had brought retired, and only one—Horace Waller, continued to work in the Shire Highlands. This failure of his favourite plan was among the severest blows of Livingstone's life. It was not made easier when he learned that another hopeful visitor who had also arrived by the *Gorgon* had come to the same conclusion and was preparing to depart.

This was Dr. James Stewart, who had been sent

[1] See Goodwin Memoir of *Bishop Mackenzie*. 338 et seq.

out by the Free Church of Scotland in the hope of beginning a mission under Livingstone's direction. The disasters of which he had been a sympathetic witness had forced upon this man also the conviction that the time was not yet opportune. He returned later, however, to Nyasaland, and became renowned in after days as the founder of the great Lovedale Mission in South Africa.

And so there fell upon Livingstone's devoted head stroke upon stroke; but the heaviest was yet to come.

15. The Valley of the Shadow

It had been Livingstone's intention, as soon as was possible, to remove his wife from the unhealthy river country to the Shire uplands, but the tragic occurrences, just described, had absorbed every one's attention. Her health had suffered and she had had several slight feverish attacks, but neither Livingstone nor Kirk had thought them serious. Ship life had seemed to suit her and she had grown stout.

About the middle of April, however, she grew suddenly worse and so ill did she become, that she had to be removed from the *Pioneer*, where she had been living, to a house at Shupanga. There her condition grew quickly more serious. Medicines had no effect. She became comatose and on the evening of the 27th of April, 1862, she died. They had been reunited only three months. She was buried under a large baobab tree near the house.

Livingstone was utterly broken. "For the first time in my life," he says, "I am willing to die." Dr. Stewart, who was with them, speaks of his weeping like a child. Mary Moffat, aged only 41 when she died, had been a wife worthy of a heroic husband and her sacrifices were hardly less than his. Latterly she had grown over-introspective and had become obsessed by her own unfitness and lack of faith. His replies to her letters show him at his deepest and tenderest.

The profundity of his grief made expression necessary, and Livingstone, for once, lays aside his reticence, when in his Diary, he records this incident. "In our intercourse in private there was more than would be thought by some as a decorous amount of merriment and play. I said to her a few days before her fatal illness. ' We old bodies ought to be more sober and not play so much.' ' Oh no,' she said. ' You must always be playful, as you always have been. I would not like you to be grave as some folks I have seen.' This led me to feel what I have always believed to be the true way, to let the head grow wise but keep the heart always young and playful."

In the days that immediately followed, Livingstone found an outlet to his grief in letters to his children, to his relatives, and many of his intimate friends. He seems to have received much comfort in the writing. He was of those who find it easier to write than to speak of their deepest emotions.

The thought of his motherless bairns, especially of the youngest girl, was never far from his mind. He sent letters to each of his older children and opened his heart to them in a way that would have been impossible in their presence.

To Oswell, aged eleven, he wrote:

"With many tears running down my cheeks I have to tell you that your dearly beloved mamma died last night about seven o'clock.

"I was with her night and day and trust she was tended by the all powerful arms. She was so deaf from quinine that I could not converse with her about the rest of her soul, but on asking aloud if she rested on Jesus, she looked up towards heaven thoughtfully. I think she meant 'Yes.' She saw me shedding many tears at the prospect of parting from my dear companion of eighteen years and must have known that her bodily case was hopeless.

"She loved you dearly and often spoke of you and all the family, especially little baby. You must think of her now as beckoning you from heaven."[1]

He gave himself only a few days respite and then turned again, with ever sterner intent, to his work of exploration. He became even less sociable than he had been and lived a life of his own. His already grim face grew grimmer and assumed that look of rigid determination that becomes so marked in his later photographs.

The first task was the fitting together of the

[1] An unpublished letter.

sections of the *Lady Nyasa*. This took longer than had been counted upon, and once more it was a case of "too late," for before she could be made ready to take the water, the stream had grown too shallow and for six months she could not be used.

This further delay was most vexatious. The Expedition had already passed its time limit and the Leader felt keenly that there was not much to show for its work. So once more he turned to the scheme that had become almost an obsession—the attempt to find a free waterway up the Rovuma. No one else favoured the idea but that fact had no influence on Livingstone's purpose.

The *Pioneer* carried them to the mouth of the river. After that boats were to be used. It was a very irksome journey. Livingstone worked under heavy depression. He is described by Kirk as being uncomfortable at sea and throughout more than usually unapproachable. "When the weather gets foul or anything goes wrong it is well to give him a wide berth, especially when he sings to himself. But the air is some indication. If it is the ' Happy Land' then look out for squalls and stand clear! If ' Scots wha hae' there is some grand vision before his mind."[1]

Up the Rovuma, therefore, they forced their way and the farther they went the more unpromising prospects became. But Livingstone would not turn. The tribes were ill-disposed and on one occasion, the second and last time in his long career, arms had to be used in self-defence, but

[1] *Kirk on the Zambezi*, page 240.

Livingstone took no part in the shooting. At last, after 150 miles of unremitting struggle, a point was reached where the stream became narrow and full of rocks and where information that could not be ignored made it certain that further passage would soon become impossible. Here, accepting defeat at last, the Leader gave up and ordered the return.

It had been an exhausting and fruitless fight. All were worn-out and nervy. Kirk and the others were weary of what they considered Livingstone's reasonless pertinacity. And so back to the Zambezi and to the problem of the *Lady Nyasa*.

16. A Land of the Dead

After the customary delay the *Lady Nyasa*, now ready for the river and the water being suitable, was taken in tow by the *Pioneer* and, after some very difficult navigation she arrived at Chibisa. It was proposed to take her to pieces at this point and carry her past the Cataract to the level of the Lake.

All along the banks the most terrible sights met them. The havoc had been the work of the half-caste rebel, Mariano, a scoundrel of unique ferocity. There was a smell of decaying flesh everywhere. Dead bodies floated past them and at times blocked their paddles. The river banks that only three years before they had seen thickly populated and prosperous, were silent; all the villages were destroyed. Here and there a fisherman could be seen laying his traps to save himself from starvation. "Ghastly living forms of boys and girls with dull, dead eyes were seen crouching near some of the huts. A few days more and all would be dead." The scene burnt itself into Livingstone's mind. It took its place in his memory with the massacre he was to witness later in the Manyuema country. What made his distress the more keen was that he could not rid himself of the unreasonable feeling that he was in a sense to blame. It was he who had opened up the river and thus given to the brutal marauders an entry that before they had feared to take.

The condition of the staff, too, had become serious. Every one was depressed. Charles Livingstone and Kirk were so ill that arrangements had to be made to send them home. And then the Leader himself became so reduced by a severe attack of dysentery that he was not fit to be left alone, whereupon Kirk insisted on postponing his own departure. None the less, Livingstone held on to his purpose of transporting his little steamer beyond the Rapids. A gallant attempt was made but it was soon evident that the labour was quite beyond their strength. The cutting of a forty-mile track was necessary — over rough country covered with forest. Because of the slave raids native porters were almost impossible to get. Every one was more or less ill. Was he to be baulked in this plan also; this that looking so promising had cost him so heavily?

At that point, 2nd July 1863, there came the final, but not unexpected blow—a despatch from Earl Russell recalling the Expedition. The time limit was long passed: the expense, including the co-operation of the Navy, had been heavy, and the immediate gain not apparently great. All this was undeniable, but political motives also entered into the decision. The Portuguese Government was becoming increasingly restive and the British Cabinet had no wish to provoke international complications.

Livingstone could, of course, do nothing but submit. He had no grievance against the Foreign Office. They had treated him generously. But the reverse made him only the more determined to "bide his time" and continue the fight. "Please the Supreme," he wrote to James Young, "I shall work some other part yet. In leaving, it is bitter to see some 900 miles of coast abandoned to those who were the first to begin the slave trade and seem determined to be the last to abandon it."

The failure to place the *Lady Nyasa* on the Lake was the final disappointment. He had always hoped that the Government would pay half of the cost, but that could not now be expected. The little ship was left on his hands. The *Pioneer* had to be returned to the delta as soon as was practicable but, as it happened, because of the seasonal fall in the level of the river, she had to remain at Chibisa for some months. So Livingstone, indomitable as ever, and in spite of the series of hardships that had worn out every European under his charge, resolved to use the time by one more examination of the lake country. His brother and Kirk had, for urgent reasons of health, gone home, and he himself was very far from well.

He took with him a ship steward and a few Makololo. The purpose of this final trip was to gain information as to the slave routes into the interior. It was for this reason that instead of completing the survey of the Lake itself, at Kota-Kota, about half-way up, he turned west in the direction of the Loangwa River and for a hundred miles or more followed the great slave road to Central Africa along which captives innumerable had been led.

One important result of this all too brief journey was that he learned of great lakes and rivers that lay beyond. Indeed, he came within only ten days travel of Bangweulu, the lake that was to become the fatal magnet of his last months—and by no means the least of the many regrets of this tantalising time, was the knowledge that, if only a few of the wretched months of which his boats had robbed him, could now have been recaptured, he could have achieved exploration so brilliant that it would have redeemed his Expedition of all possible imputations of failure.

Time could not, however, be spared. All salaries ceased on December 31st, and he felt that to delay would be unfair to his assistants, including the naval men, many of whom had served him most enthusiastically. The journey had done his health good, as open travel usually did. He had recovered to a considerable extent his good spirits and the

272

thought of an early meeting with his children cheered him greatly.

One grateful act that he did at this time was to name a chain of hills, west of the Cataract, "Kirk's Range." It was a compliment that his friend greatly appreciated. There had been times when the young botanist had doubted whether his laconic Leader had really appreciated his service and, indeed, there had even been moments, during the Thornton-Baines trouble, when he had feared that he might be the next to receive his congé.[1]

A good illustration of Livingstone's Scots difficulty in saying "thanks" is provided by a little chit that Kirk treasured and which remains among his papers. It is dated June, 1863, and was sent from the "Cataract." It runs:

"MY DEAR KIRK

"I am sure I wish you every success in your future life. You were always a right hand to me and I never trusted you in vain. God bless and prosper you.

"Ever yours with sincere affection
"DAVID LIVINGSTONE"

If these words had been spoken months before they would have saved Kirk many uncomfortable moments, but Livingstone's friends had to take him as they found him.

They were back on the Shire by the first of November and on its final run the *Pioneer* picked

[1] *Kirk on the Zambezi*, page 168.

up the remaining members of the ill-fated Universities' Mission. Their withdrawal had been gradual. For a short time some of the missionaries had established themselves on Mount Morumbala but for various reasons, chiefly because there was no prospect of restraint being put on the slave traders, this, too, was relinquished and finally Bishop Tozer, Mackenzie's successor, without any reference to Livingstone, recalled them to Zanzibar. This surrender, as it appeared to him, affected Livingstone acutely. It seemed to him like the desertion of a key position. He appealed to Tozer to reconsider; to think of the impression the retreat would make on the native tribes if the "sole hope of these wretched downtrodden people were removed"; of the encouragement it would give the forces of evil. When the appeal failed he expressed his disapproval of the move freely and strongly. Tozer "bolted out of the country" was a phrase he used repeatedly.

His censure was perhaps harsh but his disappointment was almost overwhelming. Probably, however, all things considered, the decision was wise. The Mission could hardly have kept its hold without a continued use of force and that would have been most undesirable.

Later, from Zanzibar as base, the Mission advanced gradually into the interior and it now occupies part of the country round Lake Nyasa, and its Cathedral stands on the site of the old Slave Market.

274

17. The End of the Expedition

When he looked back on its six years, Livingstone must have felt that the Expedition had not fulfilled expectations. Lord Russell had said bluntly that it had cost much and had not achieved its purpose. Even Murchison spoke of "little success." Friendly Lord Clarendon wrote, "The information we have gained is rather scant." From his own special point of view there was even less room for satisfaction. Not only had he not crippled the slave traffic; he seemed to have given it a new lease of life. The Universities' Mission had withdrawn and his colonisation scheme had received the cold shoulder. For all his exhausting toil there was little to show.

Time has reversed the verdict, however. There was, it is true, little that was spectacular in his discoveries, but their consequences far exceeded in importance those of his first journey. The Expedition made history by discovering the central part of that great highland back-bone which, beginning at the Red Sea, stretches to Cape Town. Out of this discovery all later colonisation has grown.

Though he would have denounced with all his old fire much that has gone on since under the name of "Imperialism," Livingstone was second only to Rhodes as a founder of the British Empire in Africa, and it is mainly on the results of the Zambezi Expedition that this claim rests. Further, even where he felt himself to have failed most grievously, later events falsified his fears.

In 1874 the Free Church of Scotland began its work in Livingstonia and Dr. Robert Laws,[1] a man only less notable than Livingstone himself, with the help of E. D. Young, put the first steamboat, the *Ilala*, on the Lake. Soon after, the Established Church of Scotland occupied the Shire Highlands and named their head station "Blantyre." Close behind them—in 1878—came the African Lakes Company,[2] whose definite purpose was to realise Livingstone's dream, "Christianity and Commerce," and their steamer, the second *Lady Nyasa*, did much of what Livingstone's boat had been built to do. Further, the steady pressure that was soon to be exercised by Dr. Kirk as British Consul at Zanzibar may fairly be claimed to have had its origin in those years that held for the heroic Leader so much of apparently useless agony of soul. Professor Coupland sums up the situation thus: "History must award the honour of the final overthrow of the Arab slave trade in the first place to two men, Livingstone who did most to inspire the attack, Kirk who did most to carry it through."[3]

But all these things were hidden in the future as Livingstone, feeling himself for the first time beaten, took his way down the river he was not to see again. A hurried and uncomfortable visit was

---

[1] *Laws of Livingstonia.* W. P. Livingstone.
[2] *After Livingstone.* F. L. M. Moir.
[3] *The Exploitation of East Africa*, page 232.

paid to Sena where certain business obligations to the Portuguese had to be settled. He was received with characteristic suavity. They had admired and wondered at him, but no doubt they were devoutly glad to see him go.

18. A Master Mariner

There remained one embarrassing problem— the disposal of the *Lady Nyasa*. He resolved to sell her in Zanzibar and the Captain of the H.M.S. *Ariel* offered to take her in tow as far as Mozambique. On the way they had a terrifying adventure.

A hurricane struck the *Ariel* with such force that she was whirled right round so that a hawser became twisted about the screw propeller, putting the engines out of action. Then, helpless, she was turned bow towards the *Lady Nyasa*, and it looked at one moment as if she would ride right on to the little boat. Livingstone made ready to catch hold of one of the flying ropes but she passed safely and they breathed again.

There followed a terrible night. Close beside the frail vessel—only two hundred feet away—plunged the cruiser, "so as to show a large portion of the copper on her bottom, and then down behind, so as to have the sea level with the top of her bulwarks." The man-of-war's crew thought that any moment the *Lady Nyasa* must founder and offered to send a boat to transfer them to the *Ariel*, but Livingstone would not agree. He feared the danger

277

to so many lives and thought it his duty to stay by his Africans. Happily, the *Lady Nyasa* behaved admirably, never once shipping a green sea. After three days tossing he was glad to accept the hospitality of the bigger ship but even then, so rough was the water, that a boat was damaged in the crossing.

Some weeks were needed for repairs and then they sailed to Zanzibar. Here the ship could have been sold if he could have satisfied himself that she would not fall into the hands of slavers. He would have sunk her rather than that. The only alternative was to navigate her across the Indian Ocean to Bombay—2,500 miles of open sea with himself as skipper.

Amongst all Livingstone's exploits none was more intrepid and indeed more foolhardy than this one. The little vessel was not built for the open sea. She had no adequate deck protection. She had engines, but she carried only fourteen tons of coal. Her sea-going quality was seen by her behaviour when struck by a sharp squall. She turned broadside to the wind and "nearly rolled quite over." As crew he had three white men—a sailor, a carpenter, and a stoker. There were nine Zambezi lads (one of whom was Chuma), who had till then never even seen the "Big Water." Rae, the engineer, upon whose technical knowledge he had counted, accepted a post on shore and left him in the lurch. Who but Livingstone would have braved such a risk?

They set out on April 30th. The monsoon winds

were due by the end of May. He calculated on being able to cross in eighteen days. Actually it took forty-five, for twenty-five of which they were becalmed, and at best the sailing pace was very slow. Two of the white men fell ill and for a time steam could not be used. Even when the engines worked she was able only to crawl.

The Captain had plenty of time to regret his temerity. The entries in the diary are frank in their anxiety. Water began to give out. Would they reach Bombay before the monsoon broke?

By the 28th of May they had a foretaste of the monsoon. The morning was wet and scowling. "A poor weak creature, permit me to lean on an all powerful arm," runs the entry. Good seamanship was needed but the crew were untrained. "The squalls usually came up against the wind and cast all our sails back. This makes them dangerous."

Then comes the brief entry. "We sighted land a little before twelve"—115 miles from Bombay. Monsoon conditions had established themselves. The boat was only just in time. As it was, entry into the harbour was difficult. The insignificant little ship, because of a sea fog, slipped into Bombay quite unnoticed, but when his arrival was known every attention was paid him. He became the guest of the Governor, Sir Bartle Frere. His visit created some stir among the Indian merchants who controlled so much of the East African trade. He was encouraged by their interest and entertained the hope that they would assist in the establishment of honest commerce.

He reached London in July, 1864. He had no definite plans for the future, but some resolutions were clear. He had said a year before, "I do not know if I am to go on the shelf, but if so, I will make the shelf Africa." That decision still held. Another, equally definite, was to make plain before all the world the connection of the Portuguese Authorities with the horrors of the slave traffic of which he had seen so much.

FOURTH INTERLUDE

THE SECOND VISIT HOME

THE LURE OF AFRICA
1864-65

LONDON   SCOTLAND

" To be debarred from spending most of my time in travelling, in exploration, in continual intercourse with the natives . . . giving them some idea of our religion, I always felt to be a severe deprivation."

LETTER TO SIR RODERICK MURCHISON.

" I feel in a strait—duty calling me to my family."

TO THE ROYAL GEOGRAPHICAL SOCIETY.

1. Concern for the Family

Livingstone's immediate purpose on reaching London was to see his old mother and get to know his children. Since his wife's death, particularly since he had received disturbing news about his eldest boy, Robert—whose romantic story will be told presently, they had been constantly on his mind.

The family, two girls and three boys lived

chiefly in Hamilton in his house, Ulva Cottage (called after the island from which his grandfather had come). He found the eldest daughter, Agnes (later Mrs. Livingstone Bruce), grown into a delightfully companionable girl of sixteen. He became obviously proud of her as she was of him. The youngest child, Anna Mary (Mrs. Livingstone Wilson), he had not seen before. He thought her a "nice sprightly child." She was then six years of age and, naturally, at first very shy of this stranger. Of the three boys, Thomas was in poor health; neither he nor Oswell was ever really robust, and both died in early manhood.

He had the deep satisfaction, denied him in the case of his father, of seeing his mother before her death. She was eighty-two years of age and grown so old that she did not recognise him. During the months that followed she gradually failed. Her mind ran on "that puir laddie Robert." Her great remaining wish was that one of her sons might "lay her head in the grave," and this was granted. Livingstone was in Oxford when news reached him of her death.

This is a suitable place to tell the story of Robert, the shadow of which remained over his father to the end, and no doubt largely accounted for the lament that occurs so frequently after this time in his Diary and his private letters, "Oh why did I not play more with my children in the Kolobeng days? Why was I so busy that I had so little time for my bairns. Now I have none to play with——"

With regard to Robert, it is not easy for those

our day to understand how deeply the Livingstone family felt the disgrace of a story that seems to hold little, if anything, worse than headstrong insubordination. But clearly, Robert was looked on as the family scapegrace; the younger children were forbidden to speak of him.

The lad had shown from early years, as was to be expected from a son of his father, great strength, and indeed stubbornness of character. W. C. Oswell, who was fond of playing with the Livingstone children, remembered him at the age of four as a determined little fellow with his father's tenacity of purpose and his mother's quiet endurance, and speaks of his dangerous habit of wandering too far from the wagons, in spite of constant warnings that he might be "poked by a borila[1] or nibbled by an alligator." Livingstone speaks of him at this period as being excessively stubborn at times: "I never saw one so very determined."

The unsettled life, with its fragmentary schooling, had been bad for a lad of his temper. When he reached Scotland he showed at once (probably because his education was behind that of his classmates) a dislike of school and an instability of purpose. "I fear," his father wrote him, "you will need to strive against fickleness. Everyone has his besetting fault . . . that is no disgrace to him, but it is a disgrace if he do not find it out, and by God's grace, overcome it."

It was, however, after the parents had sailed, that the trouble came to a head. The children

[1] Native name for the Black Rhinoceros.

were left in charge of two maiden Livingstone Aunts, very excellent women, but of stiff puritanical type, not fitted to handle a headstrong boy of the difficult age of fifteen. He was tried at various schools, amongst others the Quaker School in Kendal, but he would not settle.

Eventually, since he had his father's love of travel, and as Livingstone feelingly put it, "a good deal of the vagabond nature of his father,"[1] he was sent out to South Africa, that he might join his parents on the Zambezi. He got no farther than Natal, where he stayed with one of the Moffat families at Isipingo. Here they found his restless high spirits disturbing, but they had no greater fault to find with him than that he played the martinet over other youths. Livingstone wrote to Kirk when his friend was leaving the Zambezi, "My son Robert is in Natal. If you see him, say a kind word to him and advise him to work. I fear he may become a ne'er-do-weel."

But no chance of going up-country presented itself and he was shipped back to Liverpool, where, to the great concern of the family, trace of him was lost. That he was the son of so distinguished a father made his disappearance a matter of public remark and thus, to the family, a sad disgrace.

Of what further occurred to him only fragments are known. He went to the United States. The Civil War was in progress and he enlisted in the Northern Army in October, 1863, as a "substitute"

[1] "Whatever of the donkey he has in him, he inherits from me." Letter to Waller, February 7th, 1865.

284

in an Infantry regiment of the New Hampshire Volunteers, under the somewhat flamboyant name of "Rupert Vincent." He saw hot service. He is entered in the official records as having "deserted," but, in as much as he returned six weeks later and was readmitted, he must either have been lost or have taken unofficial leave. He was wounded in a battle near Laurel Hill, Virginia, captured, and died of wounds in a prisoners' camp at Salisbury, N. Carolina, on December 5th, 1864, at the age of 18. Blaikie reports that before he died he wrote to his sister regretting the pain he had given his parents, adding that he still hoped to travel. The same authority states that he was buried at the National Cemetery at Gettysburg, but this, owing to the distance from Salisbury, cannot be accepted as true.

Whether or not the lad did so of set purpose, it fell out that he died fighting in America the same battle for which his father gave his life in Africa. There are indications that Livingstone found consolation in this thought, as well he might. H. M. Stanley tells how one evening, in a moment of confidence arising from thoughts of his dead wife, "when the tent door was down and the interior had been made cheerful by the light of a paraffin candle," the old warrior opened his heart and told the tragic story of his vagrant boy.[2]

---

[1] Rupert Vincent, private, Third New Hampshire Regiment, Co. H. Serial No. 3263. October, 1863. He gave his age as 20.
[2] H. M. Stanley. *How I Found Livingstone*, page 601.

2. *Concern for the Slaves*

Livingstone did not find himself quite so much the lion that he had been on his first visit. There was not the same halo of success about him. He was, it is true, received with great cordiality in many circles of distinguished people, and mentions with satisfaction that, in spite of his seven years of jungle life he felt much at home in their company. He visited Mr. W. E. Gladstone, who had supported the Universities' Mission and was specially interested in what he had to tell of its troubles. But at the Foreign Office, he was received by Lord Russell in a "very cold manner."

He was, however, more widely known to the general public. Working folk had grown proud of him and he became, what he still remains, a people's hero. No doubt such popularity gratified him, but public notice was always uncongenial. This sensitiveness explained a tragically serious mistake that he made. He had suffered for years from hæmorrhoids. The famous surgeon, Syme, strongly recommended operation, but Livingstone, mainly because he dreaded the public's knowing of his infirmities, persisted in refusing. It was a blunder that he was most bitterly to regret.

One of the brightest experiences of this period was a short visit to the Duke of Argyle at Inveraray. Livingstone had a Highlander's clan loyalty and was much gratified with the warmth of his reception. A young divinity student, Caie, then

286

tutor at the Castle, has left a vivid glimpse of him at this date. Of his deep-lined, sunburnt face; of his black (sic) piercing eye, firmly set shoulders, medium height, and of the arm that hung idle; in manner, reserved, and a modest talker—a pleasant picture. Livingstone calls his days with the Duke "the most delightful visit I ever made."

He took the opportunity of seeing Ulva, but found that the island had lost most of its population. No relatives could be discovered and of the old home only the walls remained. But he learned, to his delight, that he was well known in the Highlands. The people claimed him and "cheered him as a man and brother."

The chief event of the furlough, an opportunity to which he had long looked forward, was his address on the slavery problem before the British Association at Bath, in September, 1864. He had been very nervous while preparing. "A cold shiver comes over me when I think of my speech. I am labouring with coat off and sleeves tucked up."[1] But he gained confidence during delivery. He spoke under great stress of feeling, with much energy and excitement. His theme was the Portuguese connection with the slave traffic. He spoke his mind uncompromisingly. Bishop Colenso, at the time because of his heterodoxy, much in the public eye, proposed the vote of thanks.

The Portuguese took great umbrage and were quick to give an official reply. Senor Lacerda, their spokesman, made a most bitter personal

[1] Letter to Waller (1st September, 1864).

attack upon him accusing him of hypocrisy; of
"ardour to aggrandize his own nation and perhaps,
no less to do honour to himself"; of under the
pretext of propagating "the Word of God exploring
for no other purpose than to drive the Portuguese
out of Africa"; of "machinations no longer concealed against the indisputable rights of the
Portuguese Crown"—and much else in a similar
strain[1] All this pleased rather than disturbed
Livingstone. It showed that his shot had got
below waterline. He was not, however, quite so
complacent about their claim to have forestalled
him in many of his discoveries. This was a point
on which he was always naturally sensitive. He
pointed to their maps which were, he showed, fantastic, and had been obviously written from hearsay.

He straightway set himself to write his second
book. It was intended to be a "trumpet blast"
against his antagonists; but once he settled down
to it its main purpose was quickly forgotten, or
rather became subsidiary, and it grew to be a
detailed account of the work of the Expedition.

It was written under ideal circumstances. For
the eight months of its composition he and his
daughter, Agnes, were guests of Mr. W. F. Webb,
his hunting friend, at Newstead Abbey—Lord
Byron's lovely old home. It was supposed to be
composed in co-operation with his brother Charles,
who soon after became British Consul in Fernando
Po. Both diaries were used but the joint arrangement proved awkward and this in part, no doubt,

[1] Portuguese African Territories. D. José de Lacerda, 1865.

explains why the book had not the interest, or vitality, of his earlier volume. He found the writing a laborious business into which Agnes and all the Webb family were roped.

The book, which was called *The Zambezi and its Tributaries*, was not published till after he left the country. It did not have the immense popularity of *Missionary Travels* but still it met a gratifying reception and about 10,000 copies were sold.[1]

The days passed most pleasantly. No one could appreciate better than Livingstone the smooth orderliness of a cultured home. Playfulness came back to him. "He regained an almost boyish flow of animal spirits and revelled in fun and frolic." Livingstone's photographs rarely do him justice. They are much too sombre. A grim mask hides him. In the home and among congenial friends, he brimmed over with humour and even occasional boisterousness.

Happy and busy as in these days he was, the burden of Africa, the appeal of the slave, was always the background of his mind. Hence he was ready to listen to a proposal that came to him through the President of the R. G. S. that he should take charge of an expedition to explore the watersheds of the three great rivers, the Nile, the Congo, and the Zambezi.

[1] *Note.*—Of *Missionary Travels* there were fourteen editions, totalling 70,000 copies. It is still in print and still selling. Of the *Zambezi and its Tributaries* 10,000 copies were sold in five editions. Of the *Last Journals* there were two editions, with a total circulation of 10,000 copies. The last two books are out of print.

Nothing could have suited him better. It would afford him the chance to test the truth of his theory regarding the Rovuma, to explore the country of great lakes and rivers on the edge of which he had stood on his last interrupted trip to Lake Nyasa; and by far the most fascinating, it would give him the opportunity to crown his life as an explorer by solving that eternal enigma—the source of the Nile. Not the least attraction of the proposal was that he could go alone and, though he was still to be consul, as a missionary. Sir Roderick did not approve of the combination of exploration and missionary work, but on this point Livingstone was adamant.

One defect of the scheme was that the financial provision offered was quite inadequate. Government granted £500 and the R. G. S. a similar sum. Few eminent men have been so shabbily treated financially as was Livingstone. He was actually called to the Foreign Office to listen to the magnanimous proposal that he should accept authority over all the chiefs in the vast region that lay between the Portuguese Territory and Abyssinia, and work, as it was carefully explained, without any salary and with no prospect of pension![1] Nor was the R. G. S. more open-handed. A few years later, to Joseph Thomson—a great traveller in the true Livingstone tradition—they voted £3000 for a much smaller piece of work, but for Living-

---

[1] A pension of £350 was granted him in June, 1873. He had died a month before! Provision was made for his children, however.

stone, who had brought their society so great prestige, £500 was judged adequate. Their grant, too, was accompanied by certain conditions as to maps and reports that irked him greatly, as his letters frequently indicate, but which he consistently ignored . . . Had it not been for the generosity of his old friend Young, the scheme would have fallen through.

That the great man was lacking in business acumen there is much in his life to show, and nowhere so much as in his inability to look after his own interests. It is told that while he was still in Newstead, an inquiry reached him from Lord Palmerston asking if there were anything he could do for him. A decoration may have been meant, or more probably, a pension. Any ordinary man would have sensed that, but not Livingstone. His request was that a guarantee should be got from the Portuguese of free access for trade to the Shire Highlands. This consent was in the end given, but what could a man of the world like Palmerston make of one so unselfregarding? Looking back on this offer in 1871, in a letter to Kirk, from the Manyuema country, he remarks regretfully, "I could only think of my work in Africa. It never occurred to me that it meant ought for myself or my children till I was out here and Lord Palmerston dead."

Livingstone left Britain for the last time, in August, 1865. Before sailing he travelled to Hamilton to bid farewell to his children. He paid a last visit to Blantyre and gave to the young people there a brief sentence that is an epitome of his own life. "Fear God and work hard."

He left his family to the care of his two sisters and of James Young of Kelly. This man would have put half his fortune at Livingstone's service, had he been willing to accept it. His friendship was one of the great comforts of the Explorer's life—the certain knowledge that whatever might happen to him or his family, there was always Young to fall back upon.

He spent a few days in Paris, where he put Agnes to school, and passed eastward through Alexandria. He saw the beginning of the canal that M. de Lesseps—in vision and enterprise a kindred soul—had begun, and reached Bombay.

His chief business was to dispose of the *Lady Nyasa*. The price he got was disappointingly small, £2,600—less than half her cost. But as it transpired the price did not matter, for the Indian Bank in which he invested the money failed soon after. There is no evidence that the loss troubled him much. Money was never one of his main interests.

He was now fifty-two years of age, but actually older than his years. To all appearances his furlough had restored him to full health, but the extreme hardships that he had exposed himself to had depleted his reserves of strength. "I am very old and grey," he had told Oswell. "My face is wrinkled like a gridiron. A barber offered to dye my hair for ten and six! I must be very good-tempered for I did not offer to fight him."

PART FIVE

THE MARTYR

An Epic of Endurance
1866 to 1873

Central Africa

Commit thy way unto the Lord; trust also in Him; and He will bring it to pass.
                                                    Psalm 37, 5.

"The text present in my mind in every difficulty."
                    Letter to a Young Friend.
                    D. L. 24-2- —.

"*His immense labour and sacrifice have been amply justified by time. But great as his work and results have been, the man himself is greater still. His heroic figure looms over the Continent showing to Dark Africa the true character and shining example of a Christian Gentleman.*"
                                        General Smuts.

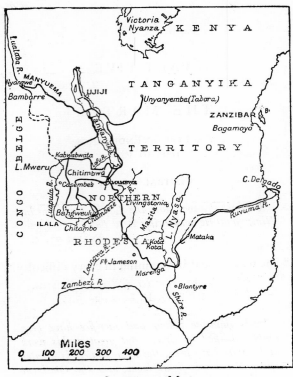

SIMPLIFIED MAP

showing Livingstone's Journeys as described in

PART FIVE

THE LAST EXPEDITION

1. Back to old ways, with a difference

LIVINGSTONE spent four agreeable months in Bombay. The Governor, Sir Bartle Frere, was more than sympathetic. Zanzibar had an old business connection with India, and for that and more personal reasons he was concerned that his friend should arrive there with adequate prestige. So he made him his official representative and gave him a passage on a luxuriously fitted vessel, the *Thule*, with instructions that the ship was to be handed over by him personally to the Sultan, as the Governor's gift. The Sultan was delighted. He received the temporary ambassador with all honour, and gave him a firman which commended him to the care of all his Highness's subjects.

Livingstone took the opportunity of visiting the famous Slave Market, where he was distressed to notice that of the three hundred men and women exposed that day for sale, the majority were from Lake Nyasa territory. He was so familiar with their tribal markings and tattooings that he almost expected them to recognise him.

The members of the Expedition formed a heterogeneous group. Their leader had brought with him from Bombay thirteen sepoys of the Marine Battalion, specially commended as being well seasoned to hardship. Their duty was the care of the draught animals. All except the havildar—the corporal—soon showed themselves to be lazy rascals. Nine others came from India—the so-called "Nazik boys"—freed negro slaves who had been trained at Nazik. They proved themselves to be hardly less unreliable than the sepoys. Then there were ten men recruited on the Island of Johanna. Of these Musa had been with him before, as sailor on the Shire. There were two from Shupanga—Susi and Amoda, and there were two Yaos, of whom one was Chuma.

It was a most unfortunate selection, but probably no better men were available. There was no unity and little loyalty. They were to cause their leader endless vexation.

With his mind set upon making an experiment in African transport, he assembled in Zanzibar perhaps as mixed a collection of draught animals as were ever gathered in one caravan. There were camels, Indian water buffaloes, mules and donkeys. His hope was to discover some beast of burden that, by being immune to the poison of the tsetse fly, might make human porterage, but particularly slave porterage, unnecessary.

The experiment did not succeed, though it must be admitted that, because of the carelessness and cruelty of the attendants, it did not have a fair chance. None of the animals proved that they could pass unscathed through tsetse fly country. Much was hoped from the water buffalo. This is a humble and phlegmatic brother of the

African buffalo—one of the terrors of its forests. Livingstone tells how when he saw them first in Bombay his immediate impulse was to take cover! He believed, without grounds however, that their thick dull grey hides would provide protection against the poisonous proboscis of the fly. The camels proved themselves too tall for the tree-covered tracks of the interior. The donkeys and mules lasted longest but succumbed, apparently in the main to the ferocity of their drivers. Soon the caravan was back to the customary human porterage; but Livingstone's faith in the donkey was justified years later in the experience of Major Lugard.[1]

The general plan of the Expedition was to explore the Rovuma River and discover its relation to Lake Nyasa; next, to cross round or pass over that lake and, turning north, to find out the connection, if any, between Nyasa and Tanganyika; then to examine the unknown territory around Lakes Mweru and Bangweulu, of which he had heard many accounts, and finally and most important, to reach the sources of the Nile.

It was a very ambitious programme, but he thought he could complete it within two years. In order that he need have no fear of being stranded for lack of necessary stores, he arranged through the British Consul in Zanzibar for an advance depôt to be established at Ujiji, on the east side of Lake Tanganyika.

Livingstone looked forward to the prospect of

[1] Authority, Sir H. H. Johnstone. *Lugard at Lake Ngami.*

this journey with keen enjoyment. From nothing did he derive so much pleasure as from the life of the forest and the camp-fire. The panegyric on the joys of travel quoted on page 135 date from this period, but the phrases about "the humble hardy companions" and "the community of interests" soon lost their relish in the worries that were to follow. The truth was that he was to traverse an Africa different from anything he had known: a land in which the fruits of the slave traffic had become tragically clear: a land of all but universal suspicion and hatred: a land of scattered tribes, of villages so poor that the barter goods they carried no longer attracted, and through much of which, on that account, they were to pass half-starved.

Further, it will soon be apparent that Livingstone himself was no longer the dominating personality he had been, and that from now on, physically at least, he lived upon a lower key. While there was still the same inflexible resolve and dogged pertinacity, the old exuberant energy, that taxed the patience of Kirk and his fellows, rarely, if ever, appeared. The old dæmonic force that by a flash from his masterful eyes could subdue crowds of excited savages, seems to have passed out of him. His old method of controlling his porters—courtesy backed by inflexible purpose —no longer worked. Indeed there were not a few moments on this journey when it was they and not he who controlled.

The main reason for this change was, of course,

his diminished physical vitality. His powers of endurance were still marvellous, but there was little joy in their exercise. It was a struggle most of the way, and only his indomitable will carried him on. He had for years systematically over-taxed his strength and the price had to be paid now. He was subject to a variety of ailments, and so dependent was he on his medicine chest that when it was stolen the news of the loss sounded to him like a death knell.

The weakening of the physical frame, however, in no way lessened the power of the spiritual urge, or his passion for the cause for which he fought, but his resoluteness was tempered by an increasing gentleness and restraint. It is from now on that his moral qualities stand out most convincingly, their effect, no doubt, heightened by the drabness of the background. It is the Livingstone of this period who is given by universal acclaim a place amongst the heroes as a supreme example of a life dedicated with utter selflessness and unalterable determination to a great purpose. Towards the end, it becomes an epic of endurance, a long drawn-out struggle the equal of which is hardly to be found in history.

2. *The Rovuma River and Beyond*

The journey began on the 4th of April, 1866, at Mikindani Bay, twenty-five miles north of the Rovuma River, and the road lay at first through a land of great fertility and then through jungle so dense that Livingstone laments that he was "no more capable of taking bearings than if he had been in a hogshead observing through the bunghole." It was not long before the buffaloes and camels began to disappoint his optimism by showing signs of the attacks of the dreaded tsetse fly, whose bite is so virulent that two or three are enough to destroy the victims in a few weeks.

Nor was it long before trouble occurred with his men. Livingstone had to walk ahead in order that he might keep a watch on the movements of Somali, the guide, who had an awkward habit of diverting the course to suit his own gallantries. The result was a long straggling line over which the Leader could exercise practically no control. Had the tribes been unfriendly his men would have kept together for protection. As it was, at times the company was distributed over almost a hundred miles.

The men from India were always behind, often far behind, and were completely undisciplined. They heaped their packages on the poor draught animals, and when unobserved, beat them without mercy, so that one by one they died. All the time Livingstone was worried and puzzled to know how much of their poor condition was due to the fly and how much to cruelty and neglect. Though food was scarce, the sepoys ate greedily and even stole from their comrades. They schemed against him and used their influence successfully to sow disaffection among the Nazik boys. The havildar was the only one whom he could trust, but he had little influence with his men.

Livingstone was curiously hesitant in his treatment of these malingerers. This may be partly accounted for by the fact that they were a new type to him, and that they were not his own employees but were paid by the Indian Government. "I shall try to feel as charitable as I can," is his comment. Moral suasion did not work, however, and once, in punishment of a more than usually heinous act of cruelty, he himself beat one of them with a cane, but felt this so degrading that he did not repeat the tonic. At last, worn out by the anxiety they caused, he sent them back to the coast and engaged local labour in their place.

The Nazik boys were less truculent, but no more satisfactory. They were bone lazy and rid themselves, on various pretexts, of their loads. One went so far, because of its weight, as to strip the tinfoil wrapping from a package of tea that he was carrying, and later threw away three-quarters of the precious leaf.

As the road climbed higher, conditions as to food grew steadily worse. Ghastly evidences of the slave trade were seen by the wayside. Women stabbed or shot through the body and left by the path to die. Others lying with slave sticks still round their necks, sick and starving and unable to move. "Too weak to be able to speak or say where they came from." Livingstone never got hardened to these terrible sights. They always sickened him.

In general, in curious contrast to the last visit, the tribes along the Rovuma were friendly and some indeed craved protection. At Mataka, on the high ground above the Lake, they were entertained most hospitably by a friendly Yao Chief and picked up strength, but on most of the latter part of the way they were half-starved. The impoverished tribes had little food to sell, and the leader had to barter, on occasion, for needed supplies with even articles of personal clothing. Light is thrown on their difficulties by an incident not mentioned in the *Journal* that came to light later.

In 1877 Bishop Chauncey Maples met at Newala on the upper end of the Rovuma Valley an old man who, with much ceremony, presented to him a coat "mouldy, partially eaten, but of decidedly English material, that had been given him, he said, ten years before by ' a white man who treated black men as brothers and whose memory would be cherished along the Rovuma after we were all dead. A short man with a bushy moustache and a keen piercing eye whose words were always gentle and whose manners were always kind, whom as a leader it was a privilege to follow, and who knew the way to the heart of all men.'" The coat had been given him, he said, at Makatla, and he gave it to the Bishop as to one of Livingstone's brothers. A marvellous testimony it was to Livingstone's influence and an extraordinarily accurate description of the man.[1]

By the month of August (1866) they struck the Lake about sixty miles from its southern end. The journey had extinguished any last flicker of hope that may have remained that the Rovuma might provide a safe way into the interior. As far as this long cherished plan was concerned, the Portuguese might sleep in peace. The travel had taken four months, whereas the Shire route, under favourable circumstances, need not take more than as many weeks. Further, they had had to climb a track that mounted to 3,400 feet.

3. Lake Nyasa once more

Livingstone had expected to have his caravan ferried over to Kota-Kota, but the Arabs knew his reputation and feared and avoided him, and no ferry could be got. But a rest of ten days was much enjoyed. They had reached a land of plenty and the people were generous. It felt like coming home to a place he had not expected to see again. It was very pleasant to bathe in the delicious waters of the Lake once more. Inevitably at times his thoughts strayed down the Shire valley, so full of memories, and to Shupanga, where "lies

[1] This old coat, which is of a thick blue serge material, is full of holes made by rats and white ants. It was given to Charterhouse School by Bishop Maples, and later, by the generosity of the school authorities, to the Blantyre Memorial, where it may now be seen.

the dust of her whose death changed all my future prospects." He wrote to Waller[1]: "I cannot tell you how sad I feel looking back at the (Shire) Highlands. Instead of the steamer I did my best to get on the Lake, two Arab dhows ply their calling as slavers. The owner of one has swept a large tract of the western side bare of people."

They travelled down to the south end of the Lake and then crossed the river and over the mountainous Peninsula of Cape Maclear to Marenga. Here the Chief, dressed in grandeur in a red silk shawl and attended by his court beauties, received them in state. It was at this point that they began to hear fearsome stories of the Angoni Zulus, the Mazitu, as Livingstone calls them, of whose unbridled brutality he had seen such horrible signs on his previous visits to Lake Nyasa.

The Johanna men took fright immediately. Their leader Musa's eyes "*stood out*" with terror. They refused to go farther, threw down their loads and decamped. Livingstone, though his party became thereby inconveniently reduced, was glad to see their heels. They had proved inveterate thieves. They would even extract the flints from their guns.

Their departure had, however, an unfortunate sequel, which, though Livingstone did not learn of it for over five years, may be told briefly now.

When Musa and his men reached Zanzibar, in order to cover their desertion and escape punishment, they produced a carefully concocted and

[1] Waller Papers. Rhodes House, Oxford.

most circumstantial tale. They described how that after they had passed Marenga's village their small party of twenty had been attacked by a band of Mazitu, and how Livingstone, after shooting two men, had been struck down by a blow from behind; and how they, escaping to the bush, had come back stealthily and had buried the body in a shallow grave dug with sharpened sticks. So skilfully was the story woven that even Dr. Kirk accepted it as true. When it reached England it was almost universally believed, and obituary notices appeared in all newspapers.

There were, however, a few who doubted. E. D. Young, a gunner in the Royal Navy, who had served on the *Pioneer*, had had Musa working under him and knew him to be a liar of genius. Horace Waller and Murchison also refused to credit the story. The result was an expedition led by Young. In a steel boat called, appropriately, the *Search*, he made an astonishingly rapid trip up the Shire, and in Marenga's country had no difficulty in collecting evidence to disprove Musa's falsehood. But Livingstone, unconscious of all this flurry, had gone far beyond their reach.

To return to our story. After passing the south end of Lake Nyasa, the caravan struck north towards the high land between the two great inland seas. This was the first objective. They passed through the country of the Ba-Bisa. It was fine open land with long sweeping slopes. The rainy season had begun and everything was refreshingly beautiful. They climbed to a level

of 4000 feet. Once again the *Journal* grows
eloquent as Livingstone describes and revels in
the beauty of the flowers, the grasses and the trees.
The drawback, however, was the terror inspired
by the Mazitu. It overspread the countryside.
"Everything is Mazitu." Even the noise of a hunt
after a hyena set every one's nerves on edge.
Livingstone, therefore, thought it wise to steer
wide of their territory.

If the map of his journeys during the next six
years be glanced at casually, so irregular and
without obvious plan does it appear that it gives
the impression of an almost purposeless meandering over vast spaces. The truth is that while
circumstances frequently compelled him to change
his plans, their main objectives were clear. But
the difficulties as compared with his previous
journeys were enormous. He found generally
that he could not go where he planned, as had
been his wont, but only where he was permitted.
Hostile tribes often barred the way; wars made
certain districts dangerous; porters rebelled;
stores and medicines gave out, and food became
frequently well-nigh unprocurable. Many, very
many months were spent in fruitless waiting. He
needed patience as never before.

After the Johanna men left he had to work with
such carriers as the chiefs would grant him.
Sometimes help was refused; often grudgingly
given. Frequently the porters were too afraid to
be of use. Once to shame them a chief put the
burdens on the heads of his own wives, and a

very jolly crowd they proved. And so, although on the map the path looks strangely irregular, the Expedition moved steadily northward. All the routine activities were pursued with unfailing regularity. The *Journal* has some entry on most days, and the notes in their fullness and vividness recall the enthusiasm of his early years. In addition to Sunday services for his porters, he held public preachings whenever opportunity offered. The caravan passed to the north of the Zalanyama Range and reached the Loangwa River and near the point where Fort Jameson now stands. The distance in a direct line is only about 120 miles from Marenga. The slowness of the travel may be judged by the fact that it took them three months, that is till the end of 1866. It was the river that Livingstone remembered so well at its confluence with the Zambezi.

Here the food problem became unusually acute. The fear of Mazitu marauders had discouraged cultivation and no one would sell. They had to depend upon what Livingstone shot, and never did he feel the handicap of his damaged arm more keenly. It was a season when game was scarce. The ground was heavy from rain and the high grass made shooting difficult, and he returned from the hunt exhausted and not infrequently unsuccessful.

They spent Christmas day uncomfortably. The goats on which Livingstone depended so much for the milk diet that he required had been stolen. All the party were suffering from lack of food,

307

and all, but especially Livingstone, were much reduced in health.

4. A Loss and a Catastrophe

Early in January Livingstone had to face two losses, one unimportant, except to himself, and one that can without exaggeration be called a disaster.

He had enjoyed the company, since the coast, of a little dog, a French poodle, Chitane by name. He had been amused many a time at the efficient way it took charge of the caravan and drove off the country curs. None dared approach or steal, and Chitane never stole himself. He had a great shock of reddish hair, so abundant that it puzzled the village dogs. They were never sure which end might bite!

Then, on January 15th, came the crossing of the Chambezí River and this entry: "The water was waist deep, the bottom soft peaty stuff infested with leeches. I neglected to give orders about the poor little dog. The 'boys' were—like myself —all too much engaged with preserving their balance. He must have swam till he sank, poor thing." Livingstone missed his loyal companionship.

The second misfortune fell near a place called Lisunga. He had engaged on the Rovuma uplands two additional porters of the Yao tribe. They had thus far done well; had been useful as inter-

preters and had come to be considered trustworthy. Then, without any hint, in dense forest
and in tropical rain that obliterated their footsteps, they had deserted, carrying with them a
load that was full of essential articles; guns,
dishes, some very precious flour, and far more
important, the indispensable medicine chest. This
was the last thing he had ever expected to be
deprived of. The loss of the other articles he took
philosophically as was his custom. "This was
just a part of the undercurrent of vexations that
are not wanting even in the smoothest life." But
the theft of the drugs made him feel for the
moment as if he had received a sentence of death.
He remembered what had happened to Bishop
Mackenzie after a similar catastrophe.

Vigorous search was made, but neither the men
nor their plunder could be traced. Quinine had
become to Livingstone almost a necessity of life.
He knew that without it the attacks of malaria
from which he now so frequently suffered would
be much more severe, and in their bad effects
more permanent. Had he consulted his health
and comfort he would have turned back there and
then, but retreat was never possible to him.

He writes: "Everything of this kind happens
by permission of One who watches over us all
with the most tender care and this may turn out
for the best." He summoned all the charity he
could muster but did not find it easy. "It is
difficult to say from the heart ' Thy will be done,'
but I shall try. These Yao had few advantages as

they were sold into slavery in early life, they were in the worst possible school for learning to be honest and they behaved well for a long time." And so on, for half a page, the Diary continues to find reasons for kindly judgment. But when he comes to the final word there is a flop back on hard realities. "True! Yet this loss of the medicine case gnaws at the heart terribly."

Sympathetic students of the *Last Journals* cannot fail to be impressed with the growth in him during those long years of depression and loneliness of a spirit of humility and charity. Meekness was not a virtue that by any stretch of imagination could be applied to the Livingstone of Kolobeng or the Zambezi, but this, too, begins from now on to take its place. A consciousness of his own failings is often evident, and from it there grows something deeper—a gentleness that comes very near to saintliness.

Even his friends at home felt the change. Oswell, when later he read the *Journal* of this time, wrote thus to Agnes Livingstone: "The dear old fellow, how quiet and gentle he has grown in these last *Journals*. Though his unflinching courage and determination remain where they ever were, his gentleness seems to have become more and more diffused through all he did." As Canon Campbell[1] points out, he became a severer censor of his own conduct than of the misconduct of others. "Nothing is commoner in his diaries subjoined to bald narratives of poltroonery or pure scoundrel-

[1] R. J. Campbell's *Livingstone*, page 344

ism of which he has been a victim than expressions like ' The recollection of my own shortcomings makes me charitable,' or ' Consciousness of my own defects makes me lenient.'" It must be noted, however, that while he carried his mildness of method almost to an extreme on this journey and allowed himself at times to be "put upon," he would permit no such liberty to his followers. "My own men walk into houses in which we pass the night and steal cassava without shame. I have to threaten to thrash them to keep them honest. Where the natives are pugnacious they (his men) are meek as sucking doves."[1]

The consequences of the lack of medicines soon became evident. Entries like the following— mostly written in the laconic fashion with which he always refers to his bodily ailments, begin to appear frequently. "In changing my dress this morning I was frightened at my own emaciation." "I am ill with fever. Every step I take jars in the chest. I am very weak. I can scarcely keep up with the march." The most disturbing of all, a month later: "After I had been a few days here I had a fit of insensibility, which shows the power of fever without medicine. I found myself floundering outside my hut and unable to get in. I tried to lift myself from my back by laying hold of the posts at the entrance, but when I got nearly upright, I let them go and fell back heavily on my head on a box. The boys had seen the wretched state I was in, and hung a blanket at the entrance

[1] *Last Journals*, Vol. II, page 256.

of the hut that no stranger might see my help-
lessness. Some hours elapsed before I could recognise where I was." Add to all this the pregnant
sentence: "Incessant hunger teases me; real
biting hunger, and faintness," and some understanding may be reached of the trials of this time.

5. *Great new Rivers and Lakes*

On January 28th, 1867, the Expedition crossed
the Chambezi—a river not by any means to be
confused with the Zambezi. This mistake—
Livingstone chuckled—the Portuguese so-called
"explorers" had made.

This great stream is important in the story
because it was to the vast watershed of which it
is a part that the Explorer's labours were to be
largely confined during his remaining five years.
It rises in the Nyasa-Tanganyika plateau and
flows south-west through marshy land to Lake
Bangweulu; then from the southern end of that
lake, under the name of the Luapula, it passes
through Lake Mweru to become the Lualaba—
and finally the Congo. When Livingstone first
crossed this river in its upper reaches the rains
were relentless and he describes the district as a
land of dripping forests and oozing bogs.

North of the river lay the territory of Chita-
pangwa, a wily and rather unpleasant person
who followed up an apparently kindly reception
by insistent and exorbitant demands. He frightened

the porters so that they could hardly control their voices. A prolonged bargaining contest followed, conducted with good humour on both sides. The Chief had the whiphand, however, and knew it, and in the end Livingstone had to surrender a valued tin trunk that the man coveted and was quite relieved to be able to pass on unscathed. As a compensation, the enforced delay, however, and adequate food had temporarily improved his health.

They were fortunate at this place to come across a gang of Swahili slave-traders on the road to the coast. For a small sum they took charge of mail and saw them delivered. These were, with one exception, the only letters of Livingstone that reached the outside world in the five years between this date and that of H. M. Stanley's arrival. There is good reason to believe that all his correspondence was systematically interfered with by the slave-traders, who dreaded his influence. In the mail that did get through he was able to order stores and fresh drugs to be sent to await him at Ujiji.

Pushing laboriously northward through the Ulungu country, they reached by April the south end of Lake Tanganyika, which Livingstone calls the Liemba. Even though once more ill, he describes with enthusiasm the extreme beauty of the scenery round him. A short journey from this point convinced him that there was no connection between the two great inland seas. He found that the level of the northern lake was some hundreds of feet above that of Nyasa. This settled one problem that had been referred to him for elucidation by the Royal Geographical Society.

It had been his intention to continue north-west, to explore the great lake further, but the ubiquitous Mazitu were once more afoot. Some friendly Arab traders he had met urged him strongly not to run the risk involved. They, on their part, were at loggerheads with a powerful chief called Nsama, and the country was so disturbed that the Expedition had to wait three months till peace was restored.

Progress northward being difficult, if not impossible, he took the opportunity, naturally not a congenial one, of the protection offered by a gang of Arabs, to visit Mweru. That this lake might well be one of the headwaters of the Nile, was a conception that was already beginning to take shape in his mind. The Arabs were friendly but most dilatory, and they took three months to cover two hundred miles. So at their headquarters at Kabwabwata he left them and turned southward alone. On November 8th he discovered Lake Mweru. It was an important event, sufficient to have made the reputation of any ordinary traveller, but it gave Livingstone nothing of the joyful thrill that Ngami and Nyasa had done. The record is prosaic. "It seems a goodly size and is flanked by ranges of mountains on the East and West." He contented himself with a partial examination of the east side and continued south.

There was no district through which he had

passed that did not show more or less the devastations of the slave traffic. So common were these signs that Livingstone ceased to mention them, but now and again incidents occurred that impressed him specially. Here is one. "Six men slaves were singing as if they did not feel the weight or the degradation of the slave sticks. I asked the cause of their mirth and was told that they were rejoicing at the idea of coming back after death and hunting and killing those who had sold them."

Before long he reached the town of the great Chief Casembe, a man well known for his cruel, despotic rule. He interested Livingstone none the less. He is described in some detail, as a man of heavy face, somewhat Chinese in type, and with an outward squint. It was a thoroughly barbaric court. By the Chief's side stood the executioner, a ferocious-looking fellow holding a broad sword and, on his arm, a curious scissor-like implement. The prevalence in the people standing around of cropped ears and lopped wrists, proved that the weapon was not worn as a mere ornament. The Chief was attended by a jester—a dwarf, three feet high, whose antics alone could make the tyrant smile. The stockade around was decorated by human skulls, and the people were, in general, more savage than any he had seen.

Revolting though the surroundings were, Livingstone stayed a month with this unattractive individual, and seems to have had some influence upon him. He was well treated. It was a fine country, and there was abundance of food. From here he turned back to Lake Mweru and stayed some time at Kabwabwata. His intention was still to proceed to Ujiji, some 250 miles North-east. There was, however, no prospect of an immediate start, and so he used ten days of the time, on a visit to the Lualaba iver, as it runs out of Lake Mweru. The importance of this great stream must have impressed him as he, apparently suddenly, determined to do some exploration round Lake Bemba (or, as it is more usually called, Lake Bangweulu) from which, there named the Luapula, the river flows. The decision was very unpopular. The Arabs objected strongly and, probably due to their influence, the Nazik boys mutinied and refused to accompany him. Opposition, as usual, only stiffened his resolve. "What are difficulties for but to be surmounted?" he once wrote to Waller. To visit the Lake became a duty that must be fulfilled. Five men were faithful, and they were enough. Bangweulu was reached in July, 1868.

The people of these parts were, because of the spongy nature of the country, among the most isolated he had met. They had never even heard of a white man, so everything he did was a marvel in their eyes. For a month he worked out observations on the Lake. Travel was usually by canoe, and canoes were hard to get, and the full task could not be completed in the time he could spare.

He writes at great length in the Journal about the bogs, oozing "sponges," the innumerable "burns" and water channels of this district.

Clearly this must be the "secondary source" of a vast river system—probably, he believes, ultimately the Nile. This opinion became conviction that was, in the last months of his life, to change his plans completely.

There follows, at this point in the Journal, a gap of six weeks. Up to this date, with few exceptions, every day had its entry, often long and usually full of a wonderfully varied interest. The reason was that he had suddenly become helplessly embroiled in a tribal fight in which Casembe, the Mazitu, and the Arabs, were mixed up in the erratic fashion of African tribal warfare. At one point, Livingstone came uncomfortably near to losing his life. The delay became intolerable. It took him three months to get back to Kabwabwata. He was consumed with anxiety to reach Ujiji, where mails and stores were certain to be awaiting him. It was three years since he had left Zanzibar, and not a single letter had thus far reached him. The Nazik boys, voluble in their glib professions of penitence, were waiting him at the Arab headquarters. They were an unsatisfactory crowd, capable of any meanness or treachery, but, probably because no others were procurable, he re-engaged them. But his comment is, "I had my own faults."

The country that lay between Lakes Mweru and Tanganyika was still in a most disturbed condition. For him with his small party to have travelled alone would have been almost suicidal, and there was no alternative but to go in company with a slave gang. Even that meant weeks of delay. In general he was respectfully treated by the tribes, but he must have been in their eyes a strange enigma. This emaciated old man who wandered about for no understandable purpose, with complete disregard of rain and storm; always moving patiently on, asking innumerable questions, and writing everything in a book; gentle to every one and doing no one harm; speaking of a God whose name was new to them and praying a great deal. Probably, in their eyes, he was more or less mad, and therefore to be respected! The Africans often bullied him and extracted what they could out of him but there was in him something strong, though gentle, and so they let him pass unharmed.

And the Arabs? It is noticeable that Livingstone did not denounce them with the heat that he did the Portuguese, and yet they were greater sinners. There were among them a few who do seem to have understood him to some extent; devout followers of the Prophet, men better than their trade, who had a valuable knowledge of Africa. They realised clearly that he was working against them, yet they admired and sometimes helped him, generously. In the average, however, these traders were brutal, sensual, and degraded below the level of the slaves they tortured.

It will be noted that at this part of his career Livingstone's missionary and philanthropic aims were almost completely in abeyance. He had become an explorer pure and simple. If that thought troubled him, his defence would no doubt have been that he had done all that was

possible to him in the situation, and that for the
rest he must wait his time.

6. *Ujiji at Last*

At this juncture, however, Livingstone had no
strength left to worry either about the people's
opinion of him or about the value of his work. He
was at the end of his health and patience. Would
those Arabs *never* move? They were procrastina-
tion incarnate. The prospect of having to travel
with a slave-gang was most obnoxious but it had
come to be that, or, most probably, death. But
the degradation of it! Here is Waller's vivid
description: "Mahomed and his friends, a gang
of hangers on, and strings of wretched slaves
yoked together by heavy slave sticks. Some carry
ivory, some copper, some food, whilst hope, fear,
misery and villainy may be read on various faces."
To have to watch the despair of these poor wretches
as they toiled along in rain and mud, many
tortured by dysentery and forced to lie anywhere
they could, often in the wet! To see them die and
be glad to die! Livingstone never grew hardened
to the horrors of which he saw so much. Here his
powers of mind abstraction served him not at all.

The first entry in the Journal for 1869 is brief
but ominous. "I have been wet times without
number, but the wetting of yesterday was once too
often. I felt very ill, but fearing the Lofuku
might flood, I resolved to cross it. Cold up to the

319

waist, which made me worse." And then, next day:
"Very ill all over."

Severe pneumonia followed. He was acutely ill
for sixteen days. Had it not been for the generous
care and skill of the Arab Leader, Mahomed Bogharib, he certainly would have died. A machila or
hammock, slung on a pole, was made, and he was
carried. The jolting was terribly painful. The sun
blistered and burnt. He had a serious relapse but,
at long last, after six weeks of torture, he reached
Lake Tanganyika.

There, happily, canoes were available, and the
travel became much easier, and he gradually
gained in strength. His thoughts were all of the
"medicine food and milk" that he would find at
Ujiji. But when, in the middle of March, having
crossed the Lake, he arrived there, it was only to
discover with blank dismay that his stores had
been plundered and that there were no letters!

The disappointment to a man in Livingstone's
state of health must have been shattering. His
medicines were at Tabora (Unyanyembe), one
hundred and fifty miles away, and there was a war
raging in the territory lying between. Even milk
was hard to procure. "The cows had not calved."
Sixty out of his eighty pieces of goods, and all his
beads had been stolen. Happily, things did not
turn out to be quite so solidly black as at the first
blow they looked. Some coffee and tea were un-
touched, also a little sugar and some cloth. "I
found great benefit from the tea and coffee and
still more from the flannel on the skin."

COURAGE

MEETING AN ANGONI IMPI

(*Gift of the Geographical Societies*)

RENUNCIATION

PARTING FROM STANLEY

(*Gift of the " Daily Telegraph"*)

The Arabs of Ujiji, as was inevitable, considering that they lived by the slave trade, were a particularly bad lot, and Livingstone allowed himself to be bullied and imposed upon in a way that can be understood only on the explanation that he was unable, because of his state of health, to stand up to their insolence. They contrived to intercept his letters lest their evil deeds might become known, and the wretch who had stolen his stores began a campaign of slander that hampered him greatly.

7. *Towards the Lualaba River*

Health returned but slowly and it was not till July that he felt fit to resume his journeyings. Then poorly equipped as he was, he turned west, crossed the Lake, and plunged once more deeply into the unexplored. The Manyuema country in which he was to spend the next two and a quarter years, was then unknown, even to Arab traders. Stories were being circulated amongst them of great untapped treasures of ivory, and as a large caravan of Arabs and Swahili was about to set out, he felt justified in accepting an invitation to go with them, since he had noticed that his presence put a restraint on their violence.

With revived health, dormant ambitions awoke, and once more the Journal is full of plans. He will explore the Lualaba, that magnificent river he had seen flowing north from Lake Mweru; he will not spend much time on that this year—stores being scarce—only a short canoe trip; but next year, when supplies have come from Zanzibar, he will investigate it thoroughly. He will prove it to be the Nile.

He was full of the thought of the Nile at this time. "The discovery of its sources possesses an element of interest that the North-West Passage never had. The great men of antiquity have recorded their ardent desire to know the fountains that Homer called 'Egypt's heaven-descended spring.'" Moses, too, comes into the exciting picture. There is a fascinating legend that connected him with the Nile Sources, with the lost city of Meroe at the junction of the Lualaba rivers. "An eager desire to discover any evidence of the great Moses having visited these parts, found me spell bound." (Oct. 25th, 1870.)

It is difficult to understand why, since companying with them had many and serious disadvantages, Livingstone remained with the Arabs as long as he did. Their purpose being trade, their movements were slow, and they could not be expected to go where he, as an explorer wished to travel. Worse still, the natives naturally thought him one of them—indeed, he was believed to be the father of Dugumbé, an influential Arab trader of doubtful reputation. It was a very bad introduction. Later on, the Africans began to understand him, and would sometimes greet him with shouts of friendship. Indeed, he was inordinately pleased when, one day, he overheard one Manyuema say of him to another, "He is a good one." Most probably his reason was his uncertain health. He had already benefited by the Arabs' skill in medicine. His own fellows were much less competent.

There follows the customary record of soakings and fevers. He cannot walk uphill without panting. His teeth are decayed. He writes to his daughter Agnes: "If you expect a kiss from me you must take it through a speaking trumpet!" He cannot masticate properly and digestive trouble results. He is only 56 years of age but he is worn out.

In the end he separated from the Arabs and made Bambarre, the capital of the Manyuema country, his headquarters. From this point he made various excursions. Here he spent in his weakness, many weary months. The Manyuema country was fertile and beautiful, and the people handsome; but they were rude and deceitful, and their mannerless curiosity was often irritating. They seemed the most degraded tribes he had met. They had a reputation for cannibalism, though not as a general custom. The country was in disorder, and there was no strong chief to control. It was not till eighteen months had passed that he reached the Lualaba River. The Nazik boys had meanwhile deserted; not unnaturally, they had grown tired of the life. This left him with only his faithful three—Susi, Chuma, and Gardner. With these men he did some laborious exploration, and then his feet "failed him." He developed "irritable, eating ulcers that fastened on both feet." He "limped back to Bambarre in terrible pain," and remained a prisoner for eighty days in his hut. This brings the story up to July, 1870.

Not the least trying feature of this melancholy time was that, from a geographical point of view, there was so little to show for all his pains. So much time had been wasted in inactivity, waiting upon the convenience of the Arab traders; waiting for the return of health; waiting for the rains to pass; and now the long wait for the coming of the new porters whom Dr. John Kirk, now Political officer in Zanzibar, was sending.

It may be mentioned here that it was by Livingstone's influence that Kirk had been appointed and, to have his friend once more as colleague, gave him lively satisfaction. "It would be a great benefit to me to have you on the Coast," he had written. But the porters did not come.

About this time he ran short of writing materials and had to use as ink red colouring matter made from the seed of a plant called by the Arabs, "Zugifare," and any odd scraps of newspaper he could gather. He found some consolation during this weary time in the company of a small monkey -a Soko—that became comically attached to him.

8. Livingstone's Inner Life

With the exception of a very few letters which the Arabs failed to intercept, all that is known of Livingstone's movements from February, 1867, till Stanley's appearance in October, 1871, is told in his *Last Journals*. These, so rich in acute and accurate observation, are singularly unhelpful in another line of discovery—the exploration of the writer's inner life. In this respect, they are of less interest than the Diary of the first great journey. That was written with a certain freedom, because he did not expect that it would be read by eyes other than his own. Since he had become famous, however, he knew that such privacy was no longer likely. Hence no doubt his reticence.

Except for a number of beautiful little prayers that appear at regular intervals, on New Year days, and occasionally on birthdays, he reveals, directly, almost nothing of his religious experience.

He had lived for six years in an atmosphere of almost unrelieved barbarism and brutality. This was round him day and night—there was no escape. He was sensitive to it. He could not become accustomed to moral depravity. It never ceased to shock him. The downdrag was constant, and with it came the temptation to which so many Europeans in like circumstances succumb, the gradual relaxing of civilised habits and the conscious or unconscious accommodation to lower standards of morals.

He had nothing external to help him except his Bible. That, and *Smith's Bible Dictionary*,[1] were the only books he had with him before Stanley came.

---

[1] *Smith's Bible Dictionary*, published by John Murray in four large volumes, had wide popularity. A concise one-volume edition was published in 1865. It was probably this that D. L. carried.

Yet, in these years, he grew markedly in fineness of character, in meekness, humility, and charity.

It is true that in his letters there are occasional glimpses of the old brusqueness. He still had his grievances. For instance, he wrote (July 8th, 1868) to Oswell, harking back to the irritating directions the R. G. S. had given him. "I have suffered much needless annoyance from two blockheads, busybodies of the Council . . . I hope you are playing with your children instead of being bothered by idiots." That has quite the old ring.

It may be safely concluded that Livingstone protected himself from the moral contagion of paganism by the deliberate adoption of the defence mechanism he had advocated eighteen years before, when in the Barotze country, for all in similar positions. It was, he said, necessary "to cultivate a taste for the beautiful else there is danger of becoming either callous or melancholy."[1]

When on the march that was not difficult. There was always the world of nature amidst which to range his mind. But how did he withstand the almost inevitable deterioration of the months and months of weary inactivity that were forced on him.

H. M. Stanley throws a valuable light on this problem. He was struck with Livingstone's abstractedness. He wrote, "He had lived in a world which revolved inwardly, out of which he

[1] This beautiful passage is given in full in *Blaikie's Personal Life*, chap. VII.

326

seldom awoke except to attend to immediate practical necessities, then relapsed again into the same happy inner world, which he must have peopled with his own friends, familiar readings, ideas, so that by whatever he was surrounded, his own world always possessed more attraction to his cultured mind than that yielded by external circumstances."[1] It is good to be able to accept Stanley's feeling that this inner world was a pleasant one. That there were passing clouds, we know. The refrain of regret about his not having played with his children, makes it clear that Robert's tragedy was much in his thoughts. Then some of his latest letters show that the resentment caused by his differences with Edwards, Bedingfeld, and Baines,[2] still remained. It seems a strange incongruity in one grown so magnanimous that he should have been unable to let these old troubles, so long past, fade out of his mind. Was it the Celt in him, or was it only just a byproduct of that inflexible rigidity of mind that was one secret of his power? This at least is certain. Had any one of these men been in distress Livingstone would have helped him to the last ounce of his ability.

If we are to believe Stanley, however, and such glimpses as the *Journals* give, these were transient moods. The protective atmosphere that surrounded him was a placid one. But its main

[1] *How I Found Livingstone*, chap. XII., page 434.
[2] See Letters to Waller from Ujiji, 1871. Rhodes House, Oxford.

secret has not yet been touched upon. It lay, without question, in his religious faith.

It has already been emphasised more than once that Livingstone's fundamental belief was in the sovereignty of God and in himself as God's instrument. There is on record only one occasion when, for a moment, this certainty failed him (page 330). It was this axiomatic confidence that armed his courage and steeled his endurance and that explains the growth, in circumstances so unpropitious, of the gentleness, patience and charity that so impressed Stanley.

In the Journals, to the date, October 3rd, 1871, there stands alone this significant entry. "I read the whole Bible through four times whilst I was in Manyuema." The Bible was Livingstone's Shrine and his musings thereon the main secret of his spiritual growth.

Livingstone had all the reticence of his type on matters personal and religious. This, his diaries clearly show, and yet he has unwittingly left us another diary, this time an unwritten one, which is, within its limits, just because it is so completely unconscious, one of the most intimate spiritual autobiographies that exists.

It is a little pocket Testament (to be seen in the Blantyre Memorial), in which the marks of perspiring fingers and soiled thumbs show unmistakably his favourite passages. He had another bible for deliberate occasion. This worn little volume has all the appearance of having been carried in the pocket, and its condition makes it more than likely that it was his custom, when he needed encouragement, or when he felt his self-restraint slipping, to draw it out and read, not troubling whether, in the rain and the mud, his fingers were clean. And, so it comes about that because, as he would have said, "to the favourite waterholes the tracks are deepest," there are certain passages that are almost worn away by use. (Appendix II.)

Livingstone was not a mystic in the Church meaning of the term, as one who sought God through elevated religious feeling or ecstasy, but he was so in the sense that, in his long loneliness, God in Christ became real and near to him, and that this holy companionship grew into a constant or a rarely-interrupted experience.

9. The Massacre of the Manyuema

At last, after many months of tedious waiting, the porters whom he had asked John Kirk to send arrived but, from every point of view they had better not have come. They were a mutinous, disgruntled crowd—not the free men he expected, but slaves—"Banians," he calls them—slaves, that is, of Indians. They had been got at by his Arab enemies, who were anxious to force this unwelcome intruder out of the country. They declared, to Livingstone's annoyance, that they had Kirk's instructions to compel him to return and when they found him set on going on they struck for higher pay. This he was forced to give.

From Bambarre he, thereafter, moved once more to the Lualaba river and lived for a time in Nyangwe, a large market town on its banks. He built himself a house there. His intention was to go by canoe down the river—at this point 2000 yards broad. A letter to his brother John, in America, puts his plans plainly. "As soon as I ascertain where the western arm (of the Nile) joins the eastern I shall return and pray that the Almighty may lead me safely home. . . . Had I known all the toil, hunger and hardship and time involved in getting a clear idea of the drainage, I might have preferred a strait waistcoat and head shaven and a blister on it, to undertaking this task."

He found the Manyuema people very unhelpful. They had been abominably treated by the traders and were in consequence suspicious of him and all his efforts over a course of four months failed to secure the use of a canoe. Promises, many times given, were invariably broken. Even his life was schemed against. His Banian porters were overheard plotting to lead him into a Manyuema trap. This was the occasion referred to in the last chapter when he temporarily gave up hope and, for once in his life doubted "whether the divine will were on his side." All round him were evidences of cruelty and bloodshed. "The sights I have seen on this journey make my blood turn cold and I am not sentimental."

He had found some distraction and not a little pleasure in studying the, up till then, undisturbed life of the market town near which he had lived.

He sketches a few pleasant pictures of its colourful and peaceful scenes. Then suddenly, without the least warning, there happened a horror, a massacre, that upset him probably more than anything else in his life.

He had been strolling through the market at Nyangwe, admiring its happy activity, listening to the lively chaffering of the handsome women, and wondering at the variety of merchandise, when suddenly "Two guns discharged into the middle of the crowd told me that slaughter had begun: crowds dashed from the place, threw down their wares and ran. Volleys were discharged from a party near the creek on the panic stricken women who dashed at the canoes. These, some fifty or more, were jammed in the creek and the men forgot their paddles in the terror that seized all. The creek was too small for so many; men and women wounded by the balls poured into them, and leaped and scrambled into the water shrieking. A long line of heads showed that great numbers of them struck out for an island a full mile away." Most of these perished.

"Shot after shot continued to be fired on the helpless and perishing. Some heads disappeared quietly whilst other poor creatures threw their arms high, as if appealing to the great Father above, and sank. Three canoes, got out in haste, picked up sinking friends, till all went down together. By and by all heads disappeared. Some had turned down the stream to the bank and escaped.

331

"My first impulse was to pistol the murderers but Dugumbé protested against my getting into a blood-feud and I was thankful afterwards that I took his advice."[1]

Livingstone hoisted the Union Jack and thus saved some thirty people who crowded under its protection.

The slaves, now out of hand, began plundering and burning, and the air resounded with the wails of those who wept over the dead bodies of their relatives.

Dugumbé, though he had the power to bring the murderers to justice, refused to do so, and Livingstone, though greatly upset and indeed ill, as a result of the terrible scenes he had witnessed, decided to return at once to Ujiji. He was determined that there should be no delay in proclaiming to the world the full horror of the massacre. But to reach Tanganyika was no small task. He had only three trustworthy carriers and he was reduced to a shadow, a mere "ruckle of bones," he calls himself.

There was four hundred miles of weary foot-slogging ahead of him. The little party set out on the 20th July (1871), and by the beginning of August he was dead beat. Every step meant pain. At one village he was mistaken for Bogharib, an Arab of bad reputation, and an ambush was laid for them. They were surrounded in jungle so thick that they could see little. A dark shadow meant an "unfriendly savage," a faint rustle, a spear.

[1] *Last Journals*, Vol. II., pages 133-4.

One large assegai grazed his back: "I don't know how it missed me. The good hand of God was upon me." Another whizzed past within a foot. A gigantic tree, the roots of which had been previously burnt, crashed almost on the top of him. He sprang back and it missed him only by a yard, covering him with a cloud of dust.

For five hours they thus ran the gauntlet, creeping through the undergrowth, till, he says, he became so weary with constant danger that, not through courage, but because of sheer indifference, he ceased to care whether he were killed or not. By evening the villagers realised their mistake and became friendly, and the Chief offered to round up and punish the culprits. This Livingstone would not allow, though he was glad to accept a gift of goats in place of some he had lost. But his telescope, his umbrella, and other articles of value, had gone beyond recovery.

This exciting adventure passed, the company settled down to its weary plod towards Ujiji. "The road covered with angular fragments of quartz was very sore to my feet, which were crammed into ill-made French shoes." He speaks of himself as being reduced to a skeleton and of pining continually for good food. Gradually, however, strength returned somewhat, and buoyed up with the confidence that stores and medicines were awaiting him, he reached the Lake and was taken over to Ujiji. But once again he was to find that he had been plundered and that he, British Consul though he was, had been reduced almost to beggary. His goods had been placed in the care of a leading Arab called Shereef, a hypocritical rogue—a "moral idiot"—as Livingstone called him.

Here is Livingstone's immediate reaction. It is found written in an unsteady hand, on the back of an old envelope from Kirk and does not appear in the *Journal*.[1]

"23rd. (October 1871) Arrived at Ujiji and found that Shereef had sold all my goods for slaves and ivory, in spite of remonstrance by the chief men here. Came impudently and offered his hand.

"24th. Rest, dispirited and sore.

"25th. Call Shereef and demand my goods. Said Ludha (a Banian merchant) had ordered him to stay a month and then leave. Had divined Koran, found I was dead. Then sold all.

"26th. News from Garangenza. Many Arabs killed. Road shut up. One Englishman there." (This was, no doubt, H. M. Stanley.)

"Thursday 1st November—very hot, feverish—Rain soon."

His fortunes were at their lowest ebb.

10. *The Meeting with H. M. Stanley*

Livingstone's life abounded in dramatic moments but what follows must be regarded as the "high light" of his story. It has to be seen through Stanley's eyes. Beyond recording his

[1] Waller Papers. Rhodes House, Oxford.

extreme gratitude for a kindness that was "simply overwhelming," the tired man says little. It is a curious illustration of the way in which Livingstone had fallen out of touch with the outside world, that his calendar had dropped seventeen days behind—Stanley's date of the meeting is November 10th and Livingstone's October 24th (1871). It will be seen, moreover, from the extract given in the last chapter, that Livingstone's other dates were confused, reflecting, no doubt, the confusion of his mind.

Rumours were abroad of a white man at Tabora but the arrival was completely unexpected.

It is early afternoon. The old man is seated in the veranda of his mud house, weak and despondent. There are sounds of excitement in the town, of many volleys and much shouting, but Livingstone has not heard. Suddenly Susi appears, running at top speed and with a shout, "An Englishman. I have seen him," darts away again. Livingstone, bewildered, rises slowly and, looking across the square, sees with amazement a great crowd of porters, all the signs of luxurious equipment and in front, the Stars and Stripes; notices also a young white man with a semi-circle of Arabs behind him, who comes slowly forward. He is not unlike the Doctor in figure and even in feature, but tanned with travel and instinct with vigour.

Stanley, on his part, sees an old man who stoops, "pale and wearied, with a grey beard, wearing a bluish cap with a faded gold band round it, a red

335

sleeved waistcoat and pair of grey tweed trousers."

There is a moment of embarrassment. Neither finds speech easy. Stanley moves slowly forward and then, with a formality that, when known, made continents smile, says, "Dr. Livingstone, I presume?" "Yes," comes the reply, with pleased look and slight lift of the cap.

Livingstone then invites the visitor into his veranda and insists on his taking his own seat. The Arabs settle themselves in the square and watch for long this strange meeting. Then talk begins that lasts for hours.

Stanley has brought with him letters and would gladly sit still till these have been read but to this the old man does not agree. He searches for those from his children, "his face lighting up," and then puts the rest aside. "I have," he explains, "learnt patience. I have waited years for letters I can surely afford to wait a few hours longer. Tell me the general news." There is so much to tell. The tragedy of the Franco-Prussian war, the laying of the Atlantic cable, the death of Livingstone's constant friend, Lord Clarendon, and so much besides.

Thus began a happy time of great importance to both men. The invalid's health quickly improved. He seemed to drop ten years of his age. Conversation with a man of such quick intelligence was the best possible tonic. Also, instead of the meagre tasteless fare he had endured for years, Stanley provided him with an abundance of good food that his worn teeth could eat with comfort. In a week he began to grow stronger. His gratitude to Stanley was boundless. He kept repeating, "You have brought me new life. You have brought me new life."

Livingstone writes : "With characteristic American generosity he laid all he had at my service, divided his clothes into two heaps and pressed one heap on me; then his medicine chest, and to coax my appetite cooked dainty dishes with his own hand. The tears often started from my eyes at every fresh proof of his kindness."

A brief explanation of this remarkable meeting is called for. During the last three years no trustworthy news of Livingstone's movements had reached the outside world, and his friends began to have fears for his life. There was vague talk of another relief expedition but nothing had been done. Gordon Bennett, Jr. of the *New York Herald* —a newspaper magnate of genius, saw in the situation the opportunity of a "scoop" that would bring glory to his paper. So he gave H. M. Stanley, one of his war correspondents, carte blanche as to expenses, and ordered him to "find Livingstone."

Stanley landed at Zanzibar in January, 1871. He carefully concealed the purpose of his expedition and got together, with surprising quickness, a large and fully-equipped caravan, and set out with very little knowledge of Livingstone's whereabouts.

He was a practical campaigner, but none the less he found it a hard journey. His methods were very different from those of Livingstone. His party was heavily armed, and he never hesitated to use force. He indeed, rather foolishly, involved himself in a war between certain Arabs and a prominent Chief called Mirambo. He suffered severely from fever but with a tenacity worthy of Livingstone himself, held on his way. No one could tell him where Livingstone was, and the sudden meeting at Ujiji was almost as great a surprise to him as it was to the Doctor.

The four months that these men, so strangely brought together, spent in each other's company was of critical importance to both. The meeting probably saved Livingstone's life: it was the opening to Stanley of a brilliant career as explorer and administrator.

The contrast between the two men was striking. Stanley, a Welshman by birth (Rowlands was his real name), had had a most unhappy childhood and youth. Like Livingstone he had pushed his way forward by sheer grit and ability. He had fought on both sides in the American Civil War and had later taken to journalism. Life had been to him a hard battle in which every man must needs fight for his own hand.

Apparently when he started he knew and cared little about the person he was seeking. His philanthropy was accidental. All the greater was his surprise, and his admiration became deep and genuine. He was much struck by the elder man's gentleness and patience; by his big humanity; his general culture; his sense of humour and his laugh, which was " a laugh of the whole man from head to heel." But perhaps he was impressed most by his

338

religion, "his deep belief in the goodness of Providence," "his confidence that all will come out right at last"; a religion that made him "the most companionable of men and the most indulgent of masters."

The popular idea that Stanley was there and then converted to Livingstone's way of life is, however, not borne out by the facts.[1] None the less, the impression made was deep and lasting, and to this Knight-errant of Journalism all Livingstone admirers must remain eternally grateful.

11. The Parting with Stanley

When Livingstone's health was sufficiently restored the friends engaged in a simple, but at the same time, important piece of exploration.

Livingstone's inquiries, amongst Arabs and others, had given him reason to believe that Lake Tanganyika's outlet was towards the north, and that its waters joined the Nile. Suggestions from the R. G. S. that this matter should be investigated gave an opportunity that Stanley was eager to embrace. Livingstone gives little space to the story probably because he knew Stanley was recording it in detail.

The tribes were unusually unfriendly, even on occasion dangerous. Stanley, time and again, was amazed at the unruffled calmness with which

[1] See Coupland. *The Exploitation of East Africa*, page 324.

Livingstone dealt by mildness and patience with situations that, to him, were so threatening, that the use of firearms seemed the only possible solution.

The exploration proved that reports had been wrong. They discovered only a quite unimportant little river and that flowed into, instead of out of the Lake. The trip was short, carried out in comfort, in canoes, but Stanley suffered severely from fever, and greatly appreciated Livingstone's experienced aid.

Soon after Christmas (1871) they decided to travel together to Unyanyembe (Tabora) where Livingstone's goods were still detained. To Stanley's surprise the elder man stood up amazingly to the hardships of the road. On one occasion the American, fearing that his friend would become overtired, sent back a litter for his use, but the old traveller scorned the help and tramped the whole eighteen miles and was as cheery at the end as if it had been only one. Again it was found that goods had been plundered, but this time not so completely, and with that Livingstone had to be content.

At Unyanyembe Stanley was already a fourth of the way back to Zanzibar. Eager to have his priceless "copy" with the least possible delay in the hands of the New York Herald he had to hurry on. Would Livingstone go with him? Stanley had used all his powers of persuasion but to no purpose. The temptation must have been great. His family needed him. His labours and sufferings in the last six years had been so stupendous that, though the

Nile problem was still unsolved, he could have returned with honour and left the completion of his task to Stanley or some other younger man.

But Livingstone felt that he had not fulfilled his promise and, when it came to a question of duty, nothing could ever shake his decision, and so they parted on March 14th, 1872, with the keenest regret on both sides. Stanley had completed his task brilliantly and could do no more. Livingstone was convinced that with the help of the few good porters that Stanley promised to send him, six months would see the glorious completion of his work, "Then Home and rest." He gave into Stanley's care his Diary and other papers, with instructions to deliver these to the Royal Geographical Society.[1]

The American's return was no easier than the inward journey and at Bagomoyo, the town opposite Zanzibar, a surprise awaited him. He found there a British Search Party containing, among others, Oswell Livingstone. Stanley had kept his secret too well. Not even Kirk, the Consul, had had any inkling of his purpose. Much chagrin was naturally felt by the newcomers and as there seemed no reason for their continuing, the Expedition was disbanded.

Livingstone's journal-entry on the news of his son's turning back is characteristic in its extreme brevity. What scope it leaves to a sympathetic

[1] An obelisk marks the site of the Arab house where Livingstone and Stanley stayed. It is about four miles from Tabora.

imagination! "June 27, 1872. Received a letter from Oswell yesterday, dated Bagamoio which awakened thankfulness, anxiety and deep sorrow."

Stanley's heroic journey had two unfortunate sequels. When he reached London, where he expected appreciation, he found his word doubted and, indeed, the whole story treated, in some newspapers, as a complete myth. This feeling was due to jealousy. It was galling to many that the rescue of their national hero should have been accomplished by a "foreigner," and a newspaper correspondent at that. The only mitigation of this discreditable incident lies in the fact that when the truth was known, when, that is, the Livingstone papers were found to be genuine, prompt and full reparation was made. None the less, the whole affair left Stanley, whom early hardships had made sensitive to slights, soured and disappointed.

The other matter concerned a temporary rift in the warm friendship between Livingstone and John Kirk. The comradeship on the Zambezi had continued. It had been one of Livingstone's constant consolations that Kirk was doing for the slave at the coastal ending of the long line, what he himself was trying to do in the interior.

The trouble arose through resentment on Livingstone's part of the type of carrier that had been sent him; at the plundering of his goods, and at the slowness with which his letters reached him. So he forsook his usual friendly, "My dear Kirk," and sent the Consul a stiff official letter of complaint beginning, "Dear Sir." Livingstone had ample cause for grievance but whether it was fair to blame Kirk is another matter.

Kirk resented the tone of the letter. The situation was made the more unpleasant to him, as he believed the Journalist to have hatched the trouble, and Stanley loved Kirk as little as Kirk loved Stanley.

On arrival in London the American made charges against the consul that were vindictive and unfair, charges which, later, he withdrew. It is questionable whether, at a distance of 1500 miles, Livingstone understood the situation that had arisen. His resentment against his friend, such as it was, was a passing thing. His next letter reverted to his usual friendly mode of address. There is a note dated 1st July, 1872, from Unyanyembe, that runs, "I regret much that Dr. Kirk viewed my formal complaint as a covert attack on himself. If I had foreseen this I should have borne all my losses in silence. I never had any difference with him though we were together for years and I had no intention of giving offence now."

By the Kirk family it is affirmed, based on the authority of Sir John himself, that no reconciliation was needed, because there had been no breach of friendship.

12. Alone

Livingstone had received at Unyanyembe much needed replenishment of his wardrobe. "Four flannel shirts from Agnes." "Two pairs of fine

English boots from Waller." There were also books and many letters.

On March 19th in the Journal stands this prayer: "My birthday—My Jesus, my King, my Life, my All, I again dedicate my whole self to Thee. Accept me and grant O gracious Father that ere this year is gone, I may finish my work. In Jesus name I ask it. Amen."

There was nothing to be done but wait for the arrival of the new porters. Through no fault of Stanley they were very long in coming. The favourable season for travel was all too quickly passing. Rain would greatly complicate his task— "Weary, weary," is his only entry on the 5th of July, and that was the dominant note in this monotonous five months.

He filled his time as best he could with natural history notes and correspondence. He wrote a letter of thanks to Gordon Bennet in which there occurs the sentence that is quoted on his grave in Westminster Abbey:

"All I can add in my loneliness is, may Heaven's rich blessing come down on every one—American, English or Turk, who will help to heal the Open Sore of the World."

The hope of a quiet old age was at times, too, in his thought. He wrote to Waller, "I beg your aid to secure lodgings for me, say anywhere near Regent's Park, comfortable, decent and not expensive." Lodgings and artificial teeth.

But he had other and different thoughts. He would like to be buried "in the still still forest, and no hand ever to disturb my bones, but I have nothing to do but wait till He who is over all decides where I have to lay me down and die. Poor Mary lies on Shupanga brae 'an' beeks fornent the sun.'"

His mail brought him news of the death of Sir Roderick Murchison—a heavy blow. "The best friend I ever had, true, warm, abiding."

Some time during these months he had made a momentous change in his plans. He had after long thought—with necessarily some pangs of doubt, decided to give up further exploration of the Lualaba and complete, instead, his examination of the country around Lake Bangweulu, which he had become confident was the true source of the Nile waters.

It was not till the middle of August that his state of wretched suspense ended. The new band of carriers arrived, a good lot as it turned out. Among them was Jacob Wainwright, a Nazik boy, who knew some English and on whose account we rely for what happened during the last days. He had still with him, the faithfuls, Chuma and Susi.

After a few days' rest they started. The caravan was well fitted out. There were donkeys for the Leader to ride. The route was back to Tanganyika And so begins a journey of incredible toil and suffering that lasted eight and a half months.

After less than four weeks' travel there appears this ominous entry: "I am ill, having eaten nothing for eight days." It was apparently a recurrence, with complications, of the old trouble against which Dr. Syme, the surgeon, had warned him, in 1864, and which he had neglected. It is hardly too much to say that Livingstone was now a dying man and rarely free from pain.

The Lake reached, there followed tiresome travel down the east side and round the south end. It was a mountainous route, painfully up and down. They passed Zombe and over the river Lofu and there struck South-west. The donkeys were a great help but one of them contradicted his theory that asses were immune to the bite of the tsetse fly, by succumbing to the disease. The other carried him to the end.

South of the Lake the weather broke and there were incessant drenchings in all the months that followed. It was the worst time of the year but Livingstone felt that he could afford no delay and pushed on unwaveringly. In spite of his strength-sapping illness he continued to show a wonderful physical stamina.

He could not entirely rid himself of the old fear that, after all, he might be on the wrong track—as indeed he was. What if it should be the Congo after all? Well! thank God, he never knew.

At last they reached the northern end of Lake Bangweulu—instead of the east side, as he had intended. Travel from now on became terribly difficult. The whole country was practically under water. He speaks of the amount of water they met as being "prodigious." Wherever possible canoes were used but the natives were hostile, and deceitful, and canoes were very difficult to hire. "Rain, Rain, Rain, as if it would never tire." "Carrying me

346

across one of the deep sedgy rivers is really very difficult," he writes. "One was more than three hundred yards. The first part of the main stream came up to Susi's mouth and wetted my seat and legs. One held up my pistol behind and one after another took turn." It was often impossible to know where bank ended and the Lake began. It was hardship that only the strongest could face—and his strength was ebbing daily, but he bore up and had even in this most desolate country an eye for flowers. He noted gladioli, jonquils, orchids and clematis—and many more. But always, "drip, drip, drip, and drizzling from the North-west."

When they crossed the Chambezi River it turned cold. A wind tore the tent and all the loads were soaked. Though they had attractive barter goods, food was often hard to procure. Could physical discomfort go further? Yet this amazing man writes: "Nothing earthly will make me give up my work. I encourage myself in the Lord my God and go forward." The undaunted spirit was still willing but the flesh was growing dangerously feeble. "I am pale and bloodless and weak. Oh, how I long to be permitted by the Overpower to finish my work."

At one point he speaks of himself as being so feeble that he can hardly hold a pencil, and to carry a stick is a burden. But even then his sense of humour did not quite fail him. "It is not all pleasure this exploration," he remarked, and the wry smile can be imagined.

The fortitude and faithfulness of the men was wonderful. They reminded him of his Makololo and than that he could pay no higher compliment. They suffered from torn feet and sore shoulders; they were hungry frequently, and always damp, and there is nothing depresses Africans more than constant rain with little chance of the comfort of a fire. But they held on steadfastly.

13. Ebb Tide

Though conscious of failing strength there is no sign that he realised that his condition was rapidly becoming critical.

He was very slow to relinquish the habitual routine—services were held and observations made in the old conscientious fashion. But from March onward he was no longer able to sit upon his donkey, and he had to submit to being carried in a machila. His handwriting grew so shaky that the effort involved is clear. Dysentery had now gripped him and he suffered agonies. The slightest movement caused intense pain. A mile or a mile and a half a day was all, towards the end, they could cover, and that with frequent rests. Still they marched on. His "boys" treated him with much gentleness.

On April 25th they had reached the Lulimala river (which in his weakness he called the Moli-lamo). Here, in a shaky uncertain hand, he made the final entry in his note-book. "Knocked up

348

quite and remain—recover—sent to buy milch goats. We are on the bank of the Molilamo."

Goat's milk was now his only diet, but it was not forthcoming. So they prepared to cross the river. The Chief was helpful. As the patient could not walk, part of the wall of the hut in which he had passed the night had to be pulled down. He was then carried to the bank and laid gently in the bottom of the canoe. Over the river was the village of Chief Chitambo. But so excruciating was the agony movement caused that before they reached it he had to ask to be put down several times. To the faithful Africans it was plain that death was near. A grass hut was built for him; a rough bed made, and on this the sufferer was laid. Rain was falling, and curious villagers gathered round to see this great White Chief now grown so weak.

The night passed quietly. In the morning Chief Chitambo called but, Livingstone, feeling unable to talk with him, asked him to return next day.

In the afternoon he summoned Susi to come and help him to wind up his watch. Later, he asked whether they were on the Luapula river and, learning that they were still three days distant, he sighed, "Oh dear, Oh dear." A little later he asked for his medicine chest and, though apparently half blind, helped himself with great difficulty to a dose of calomel, and then dismissed the man with a gentle "All right. You can go now."

That was his last word.

A lad was placed at the hut door to be at call during the night. Towards evening he peeped in through the doorway and saw his Master kneeling as in prayer. He withdrew. It was not till cock crow that, looking in again, he was alarmed to find him in the same attitude. Susi was at once called. Quietly and afraid they stepped inside. There was no sign of life in the still figure and when they touched him he was cold. Gently they lifted him on to the bed and went out to tell the others that the Bwana beloved had died.

Strange as it may seem, Livingstone had not realised that death was nearing. Had he done so he would, without question, have given instructions as to the disposal of his precious papers. He gave none.

When, in the peroration to his great speech in Cambridge, he had said that he knew that he would be "cut off" in Africa, he was not speaking rhetorically. At many times in his life this presentiment was heavy upon him but as the conviction of a happy consummation to his mission grew, the feeling passed. He wrote, "I had a strong presentiment during the first three years that I would never live through the enterprise, but it weakened as I came near the end of my journey."[1] And at the Journey's End there was none.

14. Why?

Why did Livingstone resist Stanley's invitation to go home with him? This question has been dis-

[1] *Last Journals*, Vol. II., page 72.

cussed at great length and from many angles. He had, in all sane judgment, more than fulfilled his promise to the Royal Geographical Society. They had contracted for two years of his life. He had given them seven. He stood now higher than ever in the esteem of his countrymen.

There is no evidence that he even considered the matter, any more than he had done a similar temptation at Loanda twenty years before.

There were, indeed, many reasons that made it impossible for him to relinquish his quest and of the strongest of these he was himself, probably, only dimly conscious.

First, he felt that his honour was deeply involved. He had promised to explore to the utmost of his strength the sources of the Nile and to have returned with an unfinished task would have appeared to him almost a disgrace. Devotion to duty was always the dominant note of his character, and that he set a supreme value on the integrity of his promised word, has been made abundantly plain many times in this story. It is not exaggeration to say that his life seemed to him a light thing in comparison.

There is no question, further, that in spite of occasional doubts, he sincerely believed that he was on the verge of one of the greatest geographical discoveries in history. In six months he would prove to the world that the spongy quagmires of Lake Bangweulu held a secret that, since the days of Ptolemy, men had tried in vain to solve. All the eagerness of his passion for exploration had been focused on this aim. But that was not all; not the greatest ambition. His life purpose was still the destruction of the loathsome slave traffic. Could he but solve the problem of the Nile it would, he devoutly believed, give him such a status in the civilised world, that the clarion call he was preparing to sound would ring round the globe, and raise such a storm of moral indignation that it would sweep the Evil Thing into Hell.

In a letter to his brother John, written four months before the end, he made this aspect clear.

"If the good Lord above gives me strength and influence to complete the task in spite of everything, I shall not grudge my hunger and toils. Above all, if He permits me to put a stop to the enormous evils of this inland Slave Trade, I shall bless His name with all my heart. The Nile sources are valuable to me only as a means of opening my mouth with power."[1]

Perhaps a yet more powerful motive was something that had grown out of his lifelong habit of concentration of purpose; an adamant determination, "a defiant force of will" that, once a duty was clear to him, would flinch before nothing, but would disregard suffering, sacrifice, and even at times reasonableness itself. The footsore Makololo at the Kebrabasa Rapids, Kirk on the Rovuma, had thought him on such occasions mad, and Stanley in his heart probably agreed.

To those, however, who believe in the Divine ordering of the world, there appears a still more

[1] Quoted in Campbell's *Livingstone*, page 327.

ENDURANCE

THE LAST DAYS. SUSI PROTESTS

(Gift of the Baptist Union of Scotland)

THE LAST JOURNEY
CARRYING THE BODY TO THE COAST
*(Gift of the Bamangwata tribe—Chief Khama's
People—through Chief Tshekedi)*

powerful reason; one before which Livingstone, had he been able to survey his life from its conclusion, with all its consequences, would have bowed in glad humility. It would have supplied him with the final confirmation of what had been from early manhood his underlying confidence. He had, as has already been said many times, thought of himself merely as an instrument, and when it became clear that his life purpose was to be a fight for the overthrow of the slave traffic, he accepted this high mandate without question and dedicated to its execution, without reserve, every power that he possessed. Yet when he died, had he been able to think about it, it must have seemed that he had failed absolutely. It was not given to him to perceive that, as with the Master, whom he so humbly followed, the supremely triumphant moments of his life were those of the most complete, apparent failure.

The first half of this last journey had been geographically most successful. The discoveries of the Lakes Bangweulu and Mweru were feats of the highest order, but in contrast the remaining time was from the point of view of exploration, ineffective. A great part of the two and a quarter years in the Manyuema country was spent in wandering about, apparently without definite plan, under the protection of his opponents, or sitting in his hut in enforced idleness, thwarted, helpless, and frequently ill. And the last year of his life was spent in following a will-o'-the-wisp and, grand as the fight was and without reserve its sacrifice, geographically its results were almost nothing. Looking back, however, it is unquestionable that the supreme crises of his life, when he was most obviously used to achieve a great social victory, were just the two, when from a personal point of view he most markedly failed. When, during the massacre at Nyangwe, overwhelmed with horror he struggles helpless in frenzied but futile rage; and when, at Chitambo's village, a pathetic wanderer on a wrong track, utterly worn out and beaten, he relinquished a hopeless quest. Yet, can it be doubted that it was exactly these two moments of failure that became the source of final victory? It was the realisation of the horror of the one and the heroism of the other, that did more than anything else to rouse the torpid conscience of the Nations, and that led, before many years had passed, to the eradication of that "Open Sore," to remove which it had been Livingstone's glorious privilege—a Willing Martyr —to be set apart.

EPILOGUE

THE LAST JOURNEY

1871

CHITAMBO'S VILLAGE, ILALA, BAGAMOYO,
WESTMINSTER ABBEY

" *Open the Abbey door and bear him in*
  To sleep with king and statesman, chief and sage,
The missionary come of weaver kin,
  But great by work that brooks no lower wage.

" *He needs no epitaph to guard his name,*
  Which men will prize while worthy work is
    known.
He lived and died for good, be that his fame ;
  Let marble crumble: this is Living-stone.
        "PUNCH," April 25th, 1874.

355

1. Like Master, Like Followers

He is truly great who makes others great.

The world-famed story of how Livingstone's African "boys" carried the body of their Leader, through many dangers, to the Coast, to the safe custody of the people of his own country, is one fit to be placed alongside his own great achievements. It is a testimony alike to his deep influence and to their loyal heroism.

The news of the death was made known about four o'clock, and at dawn his men gathered in council. All his boxes were opened, and a scrupulously careful inventory entered by Jacob Wainwright, the Nazik "boy," in one of the little notebooks. Next, Susi and Chuma as the most experienced of Livingstone's followers, were appointed leaders. All promised to obey, and all kept their word.

It was decided to conceal the news from Chief Chitambo, lest he should impose a heavy fine—but the story soon leaked out, and it was found that they had misjudged the man. So far from penalising, he gave them all the help in his power. He led his people to where the body lay and, with loud wailing and lamentation, paid his respects to the Dead.

Outside the village, a temporary encampment was built, and a stockade in which the body was placed. One of the party had been servant to a doctor in Zanzibar, and knew something of the simpler methods of post-mortem examination. The heart and viscera were removed, put into one of Livingstone's tin boxes and buried under a large Mulva tree,[1] near the place where a monument now stands.

Jacob Wainwright then read the burial service from the English Church prayer book. Guns were fired and it is added with simple pathos, "we sat down and cried a great deal."[2]

The remains of the body, so emaciated as to be little more than skin and bone, were afterwards dried in the sun, and roughly embalmed with salt and brandy. In fear lest the tribes, who dread the bad luck that a dead body is believed to bring, should bar the way, the limbs were drawn up to shorten the package and make it look like a bale. It was then wrapped round in calico and the whole encased in sailcloth and bark and lashed to a pole. Wainwright cut in deep letters an inscription on the tree, and this Chitambo was charged to protect.

The route chosen was round the south-west of Lake Bangweulu and over the Luapula river and thence to Unyanyembe (Tabora). The caravan was well supplied with goods for barter, but at times the going was very difficult. In a very few days half the party was down with fever and Susi became critically ill. There was a full month of

[1] Some authorities call the tree an "Mupundu."
[2] There is conflict of evidence as to the actual dates. The *Journal* gives it as 1st of May. On the inscription in Westminster Abbey it is given as the fourth. Wainwright, actually, had no record of the dates.

delay. The wonder is that, with such a start, they persisted.

After the Luapula was crossed the way became easier but at Chawende, unfortunately, they came into conflict with the chief and fighting resulted. They were determined that no one should interfere with their trust. After this point, the journey was peaceful, and they turned towards Lake Tanganyika and there struck straight for Unyanyembe. As they neared this place they learned that a Relief Party, of which it was rumoured that Oswell Livingstone was a member, was waiting—the news of the death had gone before them.

Wainwright thereupon wrote out the story, and Chuma, on the 20th October, 1873, hurried ahead and handed the paper to Lieutenant Cameron, who was in charge. Cameron used all his influence to persuade the Africans to allow the body to be buried there. He told them of the dangerous state of the country that lay farther on. But they were adamant. "No! no! very big man, cannot bury here," was their answer. They would surrender their sacred charge only to those who would undertake to see that it was buried in his native soil. Cameron took from them, unfortunately, since they were never returned, Livingstone's instruments, and let them go.

Farther on—near Kasera—they met dangerous opposition—caused, they believed, by the fear of the dead body, but by a clever ruse, carefully planned, and most skilfully carried out, they got through unharmed.

In February, 1874, they reached Bagamoyo, where they handed their sacred trust over to the Acting British Consul. They had traversed 1500 miles, and had been on the march nine months. Surely there had been few more remarkable journeys and never more remarkable loyalty.

What was the motive that made this gallant band face without flinching so long and dangerous a road. Not hope of reward: they received none, hardly even thanks! Not mainly, as Professor Gregory has suggested, the wish to protect themselves from the suspicion of having killed their Master. That idea was probably present, but that it was no main motive is made clear, surely, by their stubborn resistance to Lieutenant Cameron's pressure. It may have been, in some degree, an expression of the primitive African superstition that makes burial in the ancestral lands imperative, lest the spirits of the tribe become disappointed and enraged. They may well have felt dimly that what was so important to them must be equally so to him. Who can tell all that was in their minds? But whatever other motives were present it is clear that the dominant thought was loyalty and devotion to one whom they realised to have been a great lover of their people. And it was, as Horace Waller aptly puts it, "a testimony to the good will and kindness that exists in the heart of the African."

The body was taken by a cruiser to Aden and thence by the P. and O. Steamer, *Malwa*, to

Southampton, which was reached on April 15th, 1874. From there it was removed, amidst signs of universal respect, to the rooms of the R. G. S., in Savile Row, London.

There still lingered a doubt as to the identity of the body. There were those who thought the story too romantic to be true, and it was only when a medical examination (conducted, among others, by Dr. Loudon of Hamilton—the family physician), showed the fractured joint, the damage that, thirty years before, the lion had caused, that uncertainty was removed.

Saturday, April 18th, 1874, was a day of national mourning. The cortege passed through thronged streets to Westminster Abbey. The pall-bearers bore names all familiar in the story—Mr. Oswell, Mr. Webb, and Sir Thomas Steele, associates of his earliest explorations; Dr. Kirk, his comrade in the Anti-Slavery Campaign; the Rev. Horace Waller, of the Universities' Mission, Editor of the *Last Journal*, H. M. Stanley, and E. D. Young, who led expeditions to find him; and, not least, as the centre of interest—Jacob Wainwright, a squat little Negro, only five feet high, but stepping proudly, as representing a noble band. He, Chuma, and Susi, had been brought over by the generous thoughtfulness of James Young.

The Abbey was crowded. The most illustrious of the land were there. Dean Stanley officiated. The service was as simple as Livingstone would have wished, but there were those present who, to the end of their days, recalled the emotion that swept the vast congregation when his favourite hymn—best-known in Scotland as the "Second Paraphrase," was sung:

"Oh God of Bethel, by whose hand,
Thy people still are fed.
Who through this weary pilgrimage
Hast all our fathers led."

In the great assembly there was no figure more striking or impressive than that of Livingstone's father-in-law, Dr. Robert Moffat, who outlived him by ten years.

2. *The Livingstone Legacy*

It is sixty years since Livingstone died, and it may, with confidence, be claimed that his influence is as great, and perhaps greater, than ever. In life he towered high but it is only in retrospect that his true prominence is clear.

Since then Africa has greatly changed. Much that he did has taken its place in the pattern of Africa's history and has ceased to have immediate interest. The stockades against which, with apparent fruitlessness, he hurled himself, have capitulated. The source of the Nile is no longer a mystery; the problem of healthy sites for missionary and other homes is no longer acute—thanks to Sir Ronald Ross and his colleagues, malaria is no longer the deadly scourge that it was; the partitioning of the Continent by the Powers of Europe had put an end to tribal feuds and massacres; names like Chaka and Mosilikatsi no longer terrify, and the dreaded Angoni and Matebele have learned the arts of peace. The brutal slave trade is so long dead that its chains and shackles are now known only as museum exhibits; while, in recent days, a Governor of Rhodesia had to apply to Blantyre, Scotland, for an authentic slave stick!

None the less the great problem of Africa—still fundamental as in his day, remains unsettled and acute. A solution can be looked for only through harmonious co-operation and on the principles that Livingstone himself applied with so outstanding a success.

It has been well said that Livingstone's greatest work was not the exploration of Africa but the discovery of the African. Before his day the Negro was, in general, regarded as a creature of a lower order of being, useful, docile—though sometimes unaccountably ferocious, but still almost sub-human. This opinion was one of the reasons for, as it was also one of the results of, the abominations of the slave traffic.

Livingstone wrought a revolution. He proved by his life of unremitting self-sacrifice that he rated the African highly and thought him worthy of all he had to give. Then these same men, by an act of splendid loyalty that compelled the admiration of the world, showed that he was right.

Together they lifted the African peoples to a higher place in the estimation of the world. Livingstone thus led the way to those who strive to prove that Africans can no longer be looked upon merely as "hewers of wood and drawers of water," but are worthy of a place with the White as fellow helpers in the development of their country and their people.

Not less valuable is the reputation that still lingers in the territories through which he travelled, of Livingstone as the example of a gracious Christian Gentleman; of one who could be infinitely patient, yet resolutely firm; whose method was persuasion and not force. "Whose words were gentle and whose manners were always kind. . . . A leader whom it was a privilege to follow." Yet one like steel in the championship of the weak, and as a flaming fire against oppression.

There can now be few if any, Africans, who met and remember him, but those who have come to know him through books and an ever-widening education are a growing multitude. To them he has become the type of man who can win his way into the confidence of their race and become a trusted Leader.

What place there may remain for Imperialism in the uncertain world that lies ahead none can predict, but this can, with confidence, be said, that the only type that deserves to continue is that of David Livingstone—an Imperialism that is prepared to accept responsibility for undeveloped

363

races, and do so in a spirit of unselfishness that steadily keeps their interests in view.

But the greatest Livingstone Legacy of all is the inspiration of the story that this book has tried to tell.

APPENDIX I

The Livingstone Memorial, Blantyre

This Memorial, to which many references have been made in this book, was opened in October, 1929, by Her Majesty Queen Elizabeth, then Duchess of York.

The birthplace has been restored and made a centre of pilgrimage, which aims at stabilising the Livingstone Tradition.

The old house, which after the liquidation of the Monteith firm early in this century, had been allowed to become dilapidated, was ordered to be demolished. To prevent this a Committee, of which the writer of this book was Chairman, was formed in 1926, and an appeal made for funds. The response, especially in Scotland, was most generous. The task of restoration was put into the hands of Mr. F. C. Mears, R.S.A., F.R.I.B.A. The result is a memorial that is unique.

The general plan is as follows. The twenty-four small rooms that make up the large tenement building have been transformed into what may be called a profusely illustrated biography, each room taking its share in the story.

It begins with the "Ancestry Room," where wall panels in tempera by Mr. A. E. Haswell Miller,

R.S.W., tell the romantic story of Livingstone's ancestry. Next comes the little birth room (10 feet by 14 feet), Nannie Hunter's cosy "single kitchen," where may be seen several articles of the original furniture. There follows the "Youth Room." Here eight more of Mr. Miller's panels tell the well-known tales of the boyhood. Adjoining is the "Blantyre Room," which is rich in reminders of Livingstone's youth; the arithmetic book scribbled over with his signature; the little collection of poems that hints at a love story, and much more of interest. Close by is the library and then the "Adventure Room," where more pictures depict the "lion," and other dramatic stories.

From here the visitor descends to the "Livingstone Gallery" This is the work of the well-known sculptor, Mr. C. d'O. Pilkington Jackson—an experiment in art that is supremely successful. Four of the little rooms have been thrown into one—to form a long dark chamber. In the old bed recesses there have been placed eight "Tableaux"—groups of coloured statuary in bas relief. These are shown under modern lighting conditions. The colour is partly on the figures, and in part comes from lights hidden above. They are themselves unlit. A switch operated by the spectator causes them to glow up slowly out of the darkness, into which they again as gradually disappear.

The visitor thereafter passes on to the "Relic Rooms" where, under the headings in which this book is arranged, are shown a wonderfully complete collection of personal relics: the manuscript of the *Missionary Travels*, the *Consular Cap*; the little bible, the old coat, the surgical instruments and much else, including a statuette, a replica in bronze of the Memorial at the Victoria Falls.

On the ground floor there are shown a variety of maps, working models, and African curios, and the beautiful group, "The Last Journey." The whole ends with the "Shrine," on the wall of which hangs a rough cross made from the wood of the tree under which Livingstone's heart was buried. The great story is told by means of short inscriptions at appropriate intervals.

The Memorial became at once popular. More than half a million people have since then passed the turnstile. There are wide playing-fields with up-to-date play apparatus. The place is now the great children's centre of the West of Scotland.

Blantyre is nine miles from Glasgow and is easily reached by rail or bus. From Edinburgh the approach is via Holytown and Hamilton.

Appendix II

Livingstone's Pocket Testament

This little volume is a Cambridge University publication, printed by J. Archdeacon and J. Burges in 1795. It contains all the books up to and including Proverbs and, bound up with them, is the metrical version of the Psalms. It is leather-covered and has flaps like a pocket note-book. There are marks of damp throughout, but certain parts are so soiled by use that the Reader's favourite passages are made thereby more plain than if they had been specially underlined.

The Book of Proverbs was obviously frequently read, as also the Song of Solomon, to which Livingstone evidently gave the mystical interpretation usual in his day. Curiously, the Book of Job does not seem to have interested him, and the reading of the historical sections was done, it would appear, in the other bible he carried. If the interpretation of the book's use given in the text be correct, what may be called his "emergency reading" was mainly in the Psalms—and the proof of this is unmistakable. Favourite chapters are deeply soiled by thumb marks and certain much-used pages are worn away almost past deciphering. Of those the outstanding only can be mentioned.

The page that contains the four psalms, the 40th

to 43rd, is marked top and bottom. They suited his state of mind intimately. Then, the 46th is in parts too grimy to be read. Another section, obviously a solace, is that which begins with the 95th, while the 90th and 113th psalms are especially heavily thumbed.

It is known from the story that among the Psalms Livingstone's particular favourites were the 23rd and the 121st—the two used on the last night at home. It is surprising to note that they are almost clean, apparently hardly used. The reason is quickly seen, however, if the metrical version be opened. There these passages are covered all over with thumb and finger prints. The old association had been with the words as sung, rather than read, and that the homely familiarity carried its comfort cannot be doubted.

A sympathetic reader can penetrate further "ben" to this great soul's inner life through this shabby little book than in any other way.

Appendix III

The "Consular" Cap

It is generally accepted that Livingstone wore this unusual headgear because it gave him prestige among Arabs and others and marked him off as British Consul. That is, no doubt, true, as far as he was concerned, but the cap itself had no connection with the Service, and there is proof that he wore it many years before he was appointed consul.

In a letter (preserved in the Blantyre Memorial) written to his tailor, Henry Drummond of Glasgow, dated 19th June, 1848, from Kolobeng, he orders "Two blue caps similar to those worn by officers of the Navy. The upper part having plenty of wadding, the best protection against the sun I know." Further, in the entry in his private Diary which records the various articles he undertook to procure for Sekeletu (1856) occurs this phrase, "two blue naval caps." There is little doubt that he got the pattern from the Captain of the *George* on the way out. Dr. Moffat wore one somewhat similar.

The cap was worn, in the first case, obviously for convenience, but why one who shunned publicity, as he clearly did, should have persisted in wearing it everywhere in Britain is a most curious little problem. Nothing could have made him more conspicuous. Of four people whom the author has met who remember seeing the Explorer, three mentioned spontaneously his wearing the famous cap. In the Blantyre Museum there may be seen a quaint old photo of the British Association meeting in 1864—the ladies are shown in light summer dresses, the men in morning-coats and tall top hats, and in the middle Livingstone in his cap!

There is record of only one occasion when he wore any other head covering. From Poona (India), in September, 1865, he wrote to John Kirk: "I walk about here as much as in Africa. All are so afraid of their heads that I adopt a big hat, not to be singular." "Not to be singular."!! Why was there no photographer near?

Appendix IV

Livingstone's Letters

Livingstone's correspondence was enormous. It was in his first years in Africa the main outlet for his love of friendship, and in his early letters are many grumbles that friends at home were slow to answer.

His letters were small pamphlets in size—never less that 1500 words, and often multiples of that. They were, most of them, sent before the days of adhesive stamps and were written on thin paper, eighteen by twelve inches in size, folded into three, and again into three, so that the middle section of the second folding could carry the address. Every inch, except that reserved for the address, is covered with writing.

The writing is characteristic and that of a very rapid penman, distinct, but with letters imperfectly formed. The letters contain much repetition. Either he, in the case of his less intimate correspondents, made extracts from his Diary, or else his memory was such that he repeated himself automatically.

The number of his letters that still exists in public or private hands is very large. A partial collection, edited by Mr. David Chamberlin, formerly Editorial Secretary of the L.M.S. is in process of publication. But the present location of many letters to which Dr. Blaikie, in his *Personal Life* refers, is not known.

It is most desirable that a record as full and accurate as possible of all Livingstone's manuscripts and relics should be made. The Scottish National Memorial is prepared to undertake the task. The author of this book would be glad to receive (addressed to the Livingstone Memorial, Blantyre) all information on the subject.

Appendix V

" Livingstone," or " Livingston"

The longer is the older form of the name, as may be seen in the "Ulva certificate" (page 27). Apparently after the arrival of the family in Blantyre the shorter form was adopted, and the Explorer followed that spelling till his return home in 1857. There is, however, in the archives of the L.M.S., one letter, dated 1852, in which he writes, "Mrs. Livingstone and the children," but concludes with his signature without the "e."

A tradition which may well be correct says that Neil, the father, objected to "Livingston," because local pronunciation turned the "stone" into "stun," and that David fell in with the old man's wish and changed the spelling. The change "dates" all manuscripts, 1857 being the dividing line.

Appendix VI

Date and Place of Arrival in Africa

UNTIL recently nothing has been known with certainty as to the actual place of Livingstone's landing or within a fortnight, the date. Dr. Blaikie passes the matter over with the phrase, "Arriving at Cape Town." Livingstone himself (*Missionary Travels*, page 8), says the voyage took three months and most of his biographers are content with this general statement.

W. E. Elliot, however, in his valuable little book called *Nyaka* states that the passage took eighty-two days and names February 28th, 1841, as the date of arrival. The data for this calculation can only be guessed at but it looks as if the remaining twenty-three days of December (Livingstone sailed on the 8th) had been taken and the number of the days of January and February added. Dr. R. J. Campbell, on page 72 of his *Livingstone*, adopts this figure, having failed to notice that the letter he prints (on page 77) by Dr. Philip contradicts that date. Dr. Philip, he shows, wrote to the L.M.S., on April 16th, as follows: "The brethren Ross and Livingstone after having been four weeks waiting for their ship, have left us for Algoa Bay." This points to the middle of March as the date of arrival.

This date is put beyond question by a letter

to his friend Drummond, of the L.M.S. Tahiti, received by the Memorial Trust, which runs:

> "On the Barque George,
> "10th March 1841

"We are within fifty miles of land and hope to anchor tomorrow morning in Simon's Bay where our vessel discharges her cargo. My Colleague and I go by land to Cape Town and remain there till she comes round to Table Bay for us."

Then, later in the same letter:

> "18th March, Cape Town. We arrived here on the 15th currt and are now living in Dr. Phillip's (sic) house."

The boat did not actually reach port till the 15th March 1841. This was doubtless because of wild weather, since Livingstone in the first part of this letter describes the *George* as "staggering before a furious North Wester."

It is clear, therefore, that the party landed in Simon's Bay on the morning of the 15th March and pushed on to Cape Town—a distance of 28 miles—arriving the same evening.

THE END

INDEX

INDEX

Fever. *See* Malaria.
Finney's *Revivals of religion*, 63.
Fleming, George, 146.
Food problem, 162-4.
Fort Jameson, 307.
Free Church of Scotland in Livingstonia, 276.
Frere, Sir Bartle, 279, 295.
Gabriel, Edmund, 168-9, 172, 179.
Gardner, 323.
Gladstone, W. E., L. visits, 286.
Glasgow, L. as student in, 42-5; passes medical examination, 51; made Freeman, 202.
Golungo Alto, 168.
Goodwin. *Memoir of Bishop MacKenzie*, 264 (n).
Graham, Dr. Thomas, 44.
"Great Trek," 18.
Gregory, Prof. J. W., 192.
Grey, Sir George, 198, 215.
Habib, Ben, 182.
Hamilton, L. builds cottage for family, 201; family in, 282; last visit, 291-2.
Hankey, S. Africa, 69.
Helmore, 239.
Hottentots, 19-20, 69, 132-3.
Hunter family, L.'s mother's family, 28-30.
Ilala, 276.
Inveraray, L. visits Duke of Argyll, 286-7.
Jackson, C. d'O. Pilkington, 366.
Johanna Island, 248.
Johanna men carriers, 304-5, 306.
Johnstone, Sir Harry, 180.
— *Livingstone*, 20 (n).
— *Lugard at Lake Ngami*, 297 (n).

José, Amaro, 191.
Kabwabwata, 314, 316, 317.
Kalihari Desert, 76, 100, 114, 120, 239.
Kariba Rapids, Zambesi River, 241.
Kasera, 358.
Katema, Chief of Lobale, 162, 176.
Kebrabasa Rapids, 223, 238, 241-3, 247, 352.
Khama, Christian Chief, 76.
Kilimanjaro region, 234.
Kirk, Dr. John, 210, 213-4, 223-4, 227-8, 234-6, 238, 246, 248, 263, 265, 270, 272, 276, 324, 329, 342-3, 352, 360.
Kirk Range, 273.
Kolobeng, 100-6, 108, 129-30; station wrecked, 139-41.
— River, 99.
Kongone, 228, 237.
Kota, Kota, Lake Nyasa, 272.
Kuruman, 50-1, 68-71, 77, 86, 121-2, 139; L. married, 86-8.
Kwango valley, 166.
Lacerda, Senor, 287-8.
Lady Nyasa, 268-9, 271; second, 276-9, 292.
Laws, Dr. Robert, 276.
Lechulathebe, Chief, 116, 120.
Leeba River, 159-60.
Lees, John A., 7.
Lepelole, 74, 80.
Lesseps, M. de, 292.
Limavi, 129.
Linyanti, 143, 145-7, 150, 176, 179, 181-2, 240.
Lions, L. mauled by, 82-5.
Lisunga, 308.
Livingstone, Agnes, 282, 288, 292, 310.
Livingstone, Anna Mary, 232, 282.

377

INDEX